SETTLERS

SETTLERS

NEW ZEALAND IMMIGRANTS

FROM

ENGLAND, IRELAND & SCOTLAND 1800-1945

Jock Phillips & Terry Hearn

AUCKLAND
UNIVERSITY PRESS

First published 2008

Auckland University Press
University of Auckland
Private Bag 92019
Auckland
New Zealand
www.auckland.ac.nz/aup

ISBN 978 1 86940 401 7

Published in association with the Ministry for Culture and Heritage

National Library of New Zealand Cataloguing-in-Publication Data
Phillips, Jock.
Settlers : New Zealand immigrants from England, Ireland and
Scotland 1800-1945 / Jock Phillips and Terry Hearn.
Includes bibliographical references and index.
ISBN 978-1-86940-401-7
1. Immigrants—New Zealand—History. 2. New Zealand—
Emigration and immigration—History. 3. England—Emigration
and immigration—History. 4. Scotland—Emigration and
immigration—History. 5. Ireland—Emigration and immigration—
History. I. Hearn, T. J. (Terrence John) II. Title.
304.8930941—dc 22

Front cover: Alexander Turnbull Library, EP1046-1/2
Back cover: Lithograph by E. Noyce, Alexander Turnbull Library, E-079-005

Cover design: Spencer Levine, Base Two

Printed by Printlink Ltd, Wellington

Contents

Foreword

Who were New Zealanders' Pakeha ancestors? Who were the thousands of people – perhaps as many as 500,000 – who left Britain and Ireland in the century and a half after 1800 to journey 12,000 miles to a new land, the people who became for two-thirds of New Zealanders their 'first generation' here? Where on those islands did they come from? Where did they settle when they reached the new land? And do the origins of the country's British and Irish settlers tell us anything significant about the society which emerged in New Zealand? These are the central questions which this book sets out to answer.

The answers are largely based upon a systematic and statistical analysis of sources such as passenger lists, provincial and central government immigration records, and, most importantly, death registers. The findings revealed by these sources are laid out fully in chapter 3. The first chapter provides the historiographical context. It explores the interesting story of why it has taken so long for New Zealanders to examine their United Kingdom ancestry, and then examines the methods we have used to come up with answers. Readers not concerned with historiography may wish to start at chapter 2, which provides an overview of the history of migration from the British Isles and is essential for understanding the later findings. In chapter 4 we leave the statistics behind and try to speculate on the larger meaning of the patterns we have uncovered.

Necessarily this book presents a large body of tables and figures, which can be intimidating to some readers. We have tried to give life to those findings by leavening the analysis with a considerable number of personal stories. We have drawn these almost exclusively from two sources: family histories collected by the New Zealand Society of Genealogists, and the more than 3000 biographies now available in the *Dictionary of New Zealand Biography*. We are very grateful for the use of these sources and hope this book gives a new meaning to their accounts of individual lives.

This preparation of this book has been a cooperative enterprise. It began in 1996 as a multi-year project funded by the Foundation for

Research, Science and Technology and administered by the Historical Branch of the Department of Internal Affairs. The project was supervised by the Department's Chief Historian, Jock Phillips, with the assistance of John Martin. Those who were employed to collect and analyse the statistics were Nicholas Bayley, Paul Hudson and Terry Hearn. Kerry Taylor also worked for a short time collecting material on the pre-1840 period. Sue Upton compiled statistics of arrivals by sea up to 1852. Once the material had been collected, Terry Hearn prepared a major draft which presented the findings chronologically. This draft with its detailed figures is now available on the world wide web at http://www.nzhistory.net.nz/node/370 and it is the basis for the story to be found here. The data collected has already attracted considerable interest from other historians of immigration and from genealogists, but the draft was too long for publication in book form, so this overview was written by Jock Phillips with the help of Terry Hearn. It is intended to provide a succinct overview of the statistics and includes some informed speculation on the larger meaning of the figures.

We are very grateful to the many people and institutions who made this publication possible. The History Group of the Ministry for Culture and Heritage has been remarkably patient while the book has inched towards completion, and we are especially grateful to the Chief Historian, Bronwyn Dalley, for her advice. Brian Clarke, of Births, Deaths and Marriages, was generous in giving us access to the death registers. Librarians and archivists, especially those at Archives New Zealand, the Alexander Turnbull Library and the Hocken Library, were unfailingly cooperative. The drafts were read helpfully by Michael Campbell, Caroline Daley, Deborah Montgomerie, Chris Maclean and Susan Harper. Susan Brierley with David Green did a fine job tidying the text. Without their support and advice the book would be very much poorer. For the integrity of the figures, and the interpretations and speculations to which they give rise, we alone are responsible.

Jock Phillips
Terry Hearn
11 November 2007

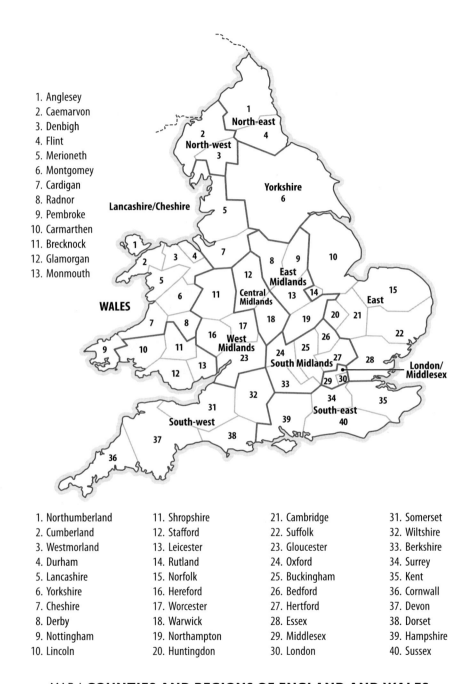

1. Anglesey
2. Caemarvon
3. Denbigh
4. Flint
5. Merioneth
6. Montgomey
7. Cardigan
8. Radnor
9. Pembroke
10. Carmarthen
11. Brecknock
12. Glamorgan
13. Monmouth

North-east
North-west
Yorkshire
Lancashire/Cheshire
WALES
East Midlands
Central Midlands
West Midlands
South Midlands
East
London/Middlesex
South-east
South-west

1. Northumberland	11. Shropshire	21. Cambridge	31. Somerset
2. Cumberland	12. Stafford	22. Suffolk	32. Wiltshire
3. Westmorland	13. Leicester	23. Gloucester	33. Berkshire
4. Durham	14. Rutland	24. Oxford	34. Surrey
5. Lancashire	15. Norfolk	25. Buckingham	35. Kent
6. Yorkshire	16. Hereford	26. Bedford	36. Cornwall
7. Cheshire	17. Worcester	27. Hertford	37. Devon
8. Derby	18. Warwick	28. Essex	38. Dorset
9. Nottingham	19. Northampton	29. Middlesex	39. Hampshire
10. Lincoln	20. Huntingdon	30. London	40. Sussex

MAP I **COUNTIES AND REGIONS OF ENGLAND AND WALES**

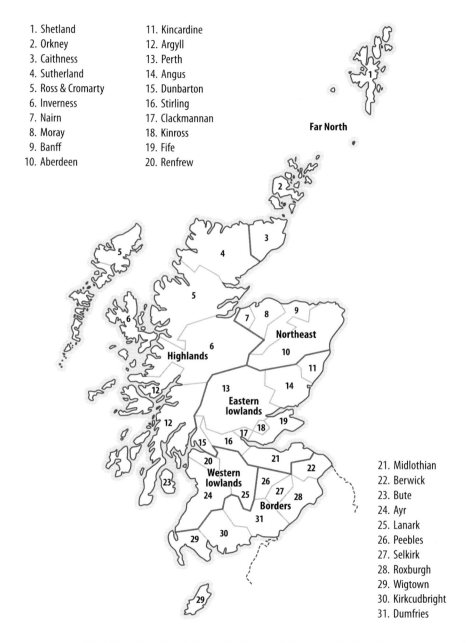

1. Shetland
2. Orkney
3. Caithness
4. Sutherland
5. Ross & Cromarty
6. Inverness
7. Nairn
8. Moray
9. Banff
10. Aberdeen

11. Kincardine
12. Argyll
13. Perth
14. Angus
15. Dunbarton
16. Stirling
17. Clackmannan
18. Kinross
19. Fife
20. Renfrew

Far North

Northeast

Highlands

Eastern lowlands

Western lowlands

Borders

21. Midlothian
22. Berwick
23. Bute
24. Ayr
25. Lanark
26. Peebles
27. Selkirk
28. Roxburgh
29. Wigtown
30. Kirkcudbright
31. Dumfries

MAP 2 **COUNTIES AND REGIONS OF SCOTLAND**

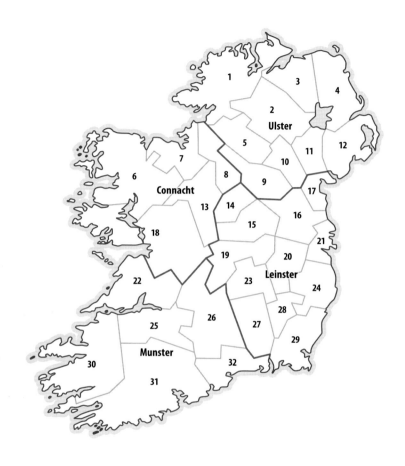

1. Donegal	9. Cavan	17. Louth	25. Limerick
2. Tyrone	10. Monaghan	18. Galway	26. Tipperary
3. Londonderry	11. Armagh	19. Kings	27. Kilkenny
4. Antrim	12. Down	20. Kildare	28. Carlow
5. Fermanagh	13. Roscommon	21. Dublin	29. Wexford
6. Mayo	14. Longford	22. Clare	30. Kerry
7. Sligo	15. West Meath	23. Queens	31. Cork
8. Leitrim	16. Meath	24. Wicklow	32. Waterford

MAP 3 **COUNTIES AND PROVINCES OF IRELAND**

1 *Setting Off*

HOW WE FORGOT OUR ANCESTORS

IT WAS MID-SUMMER, 9 JUNE 1842. There were cheers from well-wishers onshore as the *Duchess of Argyle* was towed by the paddle-steamer *Samson* down the Firth of Clyde to begin its journey south towards New Zealand. On board were 178 adults and 128 children, nearly all inhabitants of the town of Paisley, close to Glasgow. The cheers temporarily hid the pain that accompanied the ship's departure. Paisley was a weaving town that had attained some fame as the home of the Paisley shawl. But the early 1840s were not a good time for weavers, or trade in general. In the ten months leading up to March 1842 a quarter of the population of Paisley, some 12,000 people, had been 'kept from actual starvation by means of soup kitchens' or charity. In consequence, a meeting of unemployed workers had resolved to ask the British government to support migration to Canada, Australia, the Cape of Good Hope or New Zealand.[1]

In fact, a Paisley New Zealand Emigration Society had already been formed in the town. Originally it had been a Canadian society, in the belief that everybody who went to New Zealand 'was liable to be eaten up by cannibals'. But when no support for a Canadian venture was forthcoming New Zealand became the alternative, and there was a positive response. In April the *Paisley Advertiser* reported that the Colonial Land and Emigration Commission had decided to send two ships to 'that prosperous colony' of New Zealand, specifically to

Auckland, 'the future seat of Government'. The commissioners called for tradesmen 'accustomed to prepare the materials for building' and people 'accustomed to field work'.[2] Within two weeks 350 applications had been lodged, and in all 514 persons left aboard the *Duchess of Argyle* and her sister ship, the *Jane Gifford*. Among those on board the *Duchess* were Daniel Munro and his wife Elizabeth. For them, as for the other 500 souls, it cannot have been easy to set sail. Daniel came from a clan with some 700 years of history. He had been a soldier and a weaver. Paisley was his home-town. It must have been hard saying goodbye to friends and family. Elizabeth, the daughter of a shoemaker, and probably a Protestant, had already left her home, Cork in Ireland. For her, moving a second time may have been easier. But she had the anxiety of taking their four children, aged from two to thirteen, across tumultuous seas to a land where perhaps there would be cannibals to greet her.[3]

Four months later, on 8 October, the *Duchess of Argyle* stranded on a sandbank near Auckland, and the next day the family disembarked. They waded ashore through mud and water, carrying their children and their boxes of precious possessions. They received a friendly welcome from Maori on the beach.

Today we would love to be able to look inside their boxes to see what the Munros brought with them. What did Daniel wish to carry to the new land from his Paisley background? What were the physical mementos, and what were the cultural traditions he brought? We know that when his eldest daughter, Ellen, gave birth to her first New Zealand child nine years later she followed Scottish naming patterns and called her son after his paternal grandfather. And Elizabeth? What did she bring from Cork?

Daniel and Elizabeth and their four children were among the first of the thousands of people, over half a million, who came out from Britain and Ireland to a new land on the other side of the globe between 1800 and 1945. They were a varied lot. In Auckland the Munros would soon be joined by Irish peasants who had come via Australia, and later by non-Conformists from the Midlands. There were miners from Cornwall, domestic servants from Belfast, hop-pickers from Kent, knitters and fisher folk from the Shetlands in the far north of Britain, even seamen from Jersey in the English Channel. Each came with a distinct accent, language and customs. Their habits, beliefs and prejudices were not erased the moment they stepped on board ship. Such people helped build the Pakeha culture that emerged in New Zealand and eventually came to dominate the Maori culture already established here. To get to know these people better we need to find out exactly where they came from, in what numbers, and what their backgrounds were. Providing a solid statistical basis for this understanding is an essential first step in explaining the origins of New Zealand's Pakeha culture.

It may seem strange that only in the last two decades have New Zealanders begun to explore this question systematically. The Munros' story was one of over a hundred such family histories that were collected in a 1990 competition held by the New Zealand Society of Genealogists to commemorate the 150th anniversary of the Treaty of Waitangi. It is striking how often the authors of these essays commented on their prior ignorance about their ancestors. Val Wood, wondering at the significance of her father's name, Charles Heaphy, asked, 'Who were we? Where did we come from? Where had the family lived before I was born and before my dad was born?' All she knew was, 'at the back of my mind I can hear someone saying he had jumped ship and covered up his tracks'.[4] It turned out that her ancestor had nothing to do with the famous painter Charles Heaphy, nor had he jumped ship. He had been a labourer in County Galway, Ireland. He had joined the army, and eventually came out in 1847 with his wife Catherine as one of a group of ex-soldiers, the so-called Fencibles, who were given land in return for helping to guard Auckland.

Val Wood's ignorance of her family history is not unusual. Many New Zealanders remain surprisingly ignorant of their own particular immigrant ancestors. Maori, most of whom have Pakeha forebears, have stories of their founding waka, but rarely of their European ancestry. There are some intriguing possibilities as to why this collective amnesia exists. For some of the immigrants themselves there was little incentive to remember the family back home. There were those who had left to escape embarrassing or difficult personal situations, and for whom the new country offered a fresh start and a clean slate. Some may have been thrown out of their families after a youthful misdemeanour, others may have wished to escape an unfortunate marriage, while a few were born out of wedlock and wanted to escape the stigma of illegitimacy.

Mary Ann Müller had reason to forget her English background. Born in London, she had married James Griffith there in 1841. When she arrived in Nelson with her two children in 1850 she was described as a widow, but it seems likely that she had come to New Zealand to escape a cruel marriage. She later married a doctor, Stephen Müller, and in contradiction of her second husband's views she began writing New Zealand's first articles on women's rights under the pen name 'Fémmina'. 1/2-021456; F, ALEXANDER TURNBULL LIBRARY

Marianne Dockery, the daughter of a Kent gardener, fled to Nelson in 1842 with her new husband when her parents opposed her marriage.[5] Another daughter of a Kent gardener, Mary Small, came across from Australia under an assumed name to escape her husband, who mistreated her and her three children.[6] Such people did not want to remember their families. A few would have been like the great West Coast explorer Charlie Douglas, who presumably hid the fact that he came from a middle-class Edinburgh accountant's family because it would have been a hindrance, not a help, among mates in the bush. On the other hand, Thomas Porter, a prominent soldier in the New Zealand Wars and the South African War, falsified his past to give himself airs. He claimed to be the son of John William Porter, a military officer serving in India, when in fact his father was a Surrey labourer called John Potter.[7]

More common were those, like the Munros, who came to New Zealand because they were driven from home by declining financial circumstances and the fear of imminent poverty and hunger. Once they arrived in New Zealand such migrants often exaggerated the negative qualities of the Old World, and they had no great incentive to recall with affectionate longing the details of home life. Practicalities also made regular contact with the folks at home difficult. Although many, perhaps up to a third of nineteenth-century migrants, left New Zealand disillusioned, few except the rich went home just for a temporary visit to catch up. Quite a number of the first-generation migrants were not literate, and it was clearly difficult to sustain a correspondence when there was six months between writing a letter and receiving a reply.

There were countervailing factors. Most migrants had left behind friends, if not family, and many diaries recall the tears and the anguish, particularly from women migrants, as they boarded the ship for the 100-day journey to New Zealand.[8] Once settled here, many new arrivals sent letters flowing back across the seas, often intended to encourage other members of the family or local community to make the journey. In 1885, to take one year, almost 1.1 million letters left New Zealand for Britain and Ireland from a UK-born population of about 230,000 – some five letters for every person born in the United Kingdom, or about one letter a month for each household.[9] The continued importance of British family connections for second- and third-generation New Zealanders may be judged by the numbers of New Zealand-born soldiers who visited their relatives when they were on leave in Britain during the First World War. There is hardly a soldier's diary that does not record his efforts to find Mum's cousin or Dad's aunt.

But when those soldiers returned to New Zealand and travel back 'Home' declined, and as increasing numbers of Pakeha New Zealanders became the third or fourth generation to live in the new country, there was a diminishing incentive to recall family origins. As individuals moved around New Zealand the boxes of letters were lost. In popular writing, especially the autobiographies that flowed out in the years between the wars, there was an emphasis on the 'pioneering' experience in the new country rather than on the authors' particular Old World origins.

A First World War soldier on leave with his English relations. This photograph was taken by a New Zealand soldier, Percy Simmons, who later was killed in action on the Western Front. He described the photo as 'Ted and his sisters'. It seems likely that Ted was one of the many English immigrants in the years before the war who then joined the New Zealand Expeditionary Force. Like other Kiwi soldiers, he would have taken the opportunity of leave in England to catch up on his English relations.
PAI-0-1211, ALEXANDER TURNBULL LIBRARY

There was of course a general sense of New Zealand's 'British' heritage – Britain was still 'Home' until after the Second World War, and New Zealand went to war in 1939 on the principle 'Where Britain goes, we go'. But this was more an identification, drummed in at school, with Britain's cultural and military heritage rather than with any personal knowledge of an individual family's origins. The Old World heritage came increasingly to be redefined in terms of upper-class traditions, not the regional traditions from which a majority of New Zealanders had descended. Some members of the elite did recall their Old World origins because they had the resources to keep hold of their family heirlooms – such as portraits and diaries – and on occasion could afford to travel back to Britain. But even they tended to elevate the New World pioneers over their Old World ancestors – so in Dunedin there

Armistice Day celebrations in Levin, 13 November 1918. The fancy dress group, which includes 'John Bull' with accompanying bulldog, pays tribute to the British heritage of New Zealand. 1/4-023268-G, ALEXANDER TURNBULL LIBRARY

were the walls of portraits of 'early settlers', in Canterbury there were those who emphasised their lineage from 'the first four ships', and in Wellington there were proud members of the 'Founders' Society'.

Nor did the historians piece together New Zealand's Pakeha lineage. The first great New Zealand historian, William Pember Reeves, in his 1898 classic *The Long White Cloud*, was primarily interested in showing the New Zealanders as a 'British race' numerically dominated by 'whites' as distinct from 'browns' and 'yellows'. Pember Reeves stressed the transforming effect of the environment, which produced a bronzed 'island race' who lived close to 'trees, flower gardens and grass'. However, he did observe the comparatively large Celtic element, and noted the 'Scotch' in the south and the Irish in the mining districts. He argued that the 'Scotch' were prominent in politics, commerce,

This wall of grim Scots ancestors graces the Otago Settlers Museum in Dunedin. There was a considerable veneration of the first generation of Scots migrants in Otago, but little knowledge of the background of the settlers before their arrival. OTAGO SETTLERS MUSEUM

finance, sheepfarming and the work of education. He also suggested incisively – and this is a point to which we will return – that the New Zealanders were 'a British race in a sense in which the inhabitants of the British Isles scarcely are' because they lived together, met daily and intermarried.[10]

These promising insights were not followed up. For the first half of the twentieth century, the view to be found in such texts as *Maori and Pakeha*, by A. W. Shrimpton and Alan Mulgan, was that New Zealand's immigrants were essentially 'better British'. Influenced by G. H. Scholefield, they argued that the superior character of New Zealand's immigrants followed from the selective process of immigration itself. Those who came by themselves had to pass the test of individual courage and enterprise, while those who came out with the New Zealand Company or in later schemes of assistance had been deliberately selected for their capacity and character. Even the goldminers were praised as 'a virile, energetic, warm-hearted body of men'.[11] Their moral superiority was the important point about the cultural baggage of New Zealand's immigrants.

When serious academic historians interested in New Zealand emerged after the Second World War they tended to be driven by a nationalist vision that emphasised developments and influences in the New World. They were more interested in the transforming impact of the frontier, whether in the form of the bush or the frontier's indigenous inhabitants, than in the background of the immigrant groups from Britain and Ireland. The doyen of the Auckland historians, Keith Sinclair, positively relished describing the way frontier reality undermined Old World visions, and in *A History of New Zealand* he gave no more than a couple of lines to the great migrations of the 1870s.[12]

There were other factors that led to a downplaying of emphasis on immigrants and their contribution. The Second World War itself had encouraged a perspective that looked to explanations based on environment over genetic inheritance – perhaps influenced by the reaction against Nazism and racism. Migration studies of a large enough scope to say something about New Zealand as a whole were difficult to pursue in a pre-computer age, and the absence of census schedules in New Zealand made detailed analysis more difficult than in other migrant societies such as the United States. The secularism of the nationalist agenda also deflected attention away from the range of religious traditions brought by settlers from the United Kingdom.[13] The result was that for almost 40 years after the war studies of New Zealand's British and Irish immigrants were surprisingly thin – little more than a few theses on topics that were highly restricted in time and place, such as immigration into Canterbury in the provincial period, or to Hawke's Bay in the 1860s and 1870s.[14]

Even historians (such as W. H. Oliver) who were interested in the cultural baggage brought from the Old World focused not on the migrants themselves but on the institutions and ideals established by the elite.[15] There was discussion of democracy and economic individualism, and even Puritanism,[16] but much less of the particular food habits or rituals that might have arrived here in the bags of people from particular places in the British Isles.[17] In historical writing, as in the popular culture, the term 'British' became a catch-all, a term that was superimposed on a number of national and regional cultures and obscured the distinct traditions and aspirations brought by migrants to New Zealand. It also hid the very distinctive contribution of the Irish. Patrick O'Farrell wrote: 'The image and reputation of New Zealand is English: narrower even than the circumscribed British. Ireland and the Irish do not enter Keith Sinclair's Pelican *History of New Zealand....*' New Zealand, he concluded, 'was the only British colony where it was both possible and conceptually necessary to completely purge the Irish from national and historical consciousness'.[18]

By 1990, in both popular culture and historical writing, knowledge about New Zealanders' 'British' and 'Irish' origins was surprisingly weak. In a survey of New Zealand historiography in that year, Jock Phillips noted the lack of attention that had been paid to the range of cultural influences in New Zealand and called for 'a cultural history, a history which can recover in loving detail the diversity of cultures that once settled here'.[19] Two years later Erik Olssen also observed that the ethnic diversity of those who migrated to New Zealand had been the victim of a 'curious lack of interest'.[20]

Interestingly, both among families and in the written history, it was within the smaller minority immigrant groups that knowledge of origins survived. Books were published about such peoples as the Chinese, Indian, Dalmatian, German and Dutch settlers,[21] and even among those from the United Kingdom, the smaller and more suspect the group the more likely we were to find some sense of a distinctive tradition. There were good books about the Shetland settlers, and the Highlanders who settled in Waipu, but not about the far greater numbers from the Scottish Lowlands.[22] Irish families were more likely than English families to recall their Old World origins. In general there was a widespread amnesia about our British and Irish heritage – and even for those descended from the Irish the ignorance was greater among the large numbers descended from the Protestant Irish than among the Catholics.

Over the last two decades the situation has begun to change. One reason has been the greying of the population. As increasing numbers of educated New Zealanders reach retirement age, there has been a surge of interest in family history. In June 2007 the New Zealand Society of Genealogists – whose work has been greatly facilitated by the spread of the Internet – had 83 branches and about 9000 members. This is a phenomenon of the western world. More particular to New Zealand has been the example of Maori people. The revival of Maori culture within New Zealand and the increasing exposure of Pakeha to Maori ways of thinking have pointed up the centrality of whakapapa to Maori society. Inevitably this led some Pakeha New Zealanders to ask questions about their own whakapapa.[23]

The historians began to respond. Internationally there was an explosion of migrant studies, and slowly New Zealand historians became aware of the work being done overseas. By far the most notable early contribution was Rollo Arnold's *The Farthest Promised Land: English Villagers, New Zealand Immigrants of the 1870s*, which appeared in 1981. Arnold's book examined in impressive detail the English origins of some of the assisted migrants of the 1870s, and drew on the shipping lists of assisted immigrants for 1873–76 to prepare a map of their English origins.[24] We are hugely indebted to that pioneering work. Apart from two fascinating articles by Raewyn Dalziel on the Plymouth Company immigrants who settled in New Plymouth in 1841–43, Arnold's book remains the substantial work on the English.[25]

In 1990 the pace quickened. Charlotte Macdonald published a significant monograph on single women, drawing on a database of over 4000 individuals who came out as assisted migrants to Canterbury in the 1850s and 1860s.[26] The same year, in *Half the World from Home*, Donald Akenson threw down a generic challenge to New Zealand historians about the lack of good work on New Zealand's immigrants and then explored the Irish migration with considerable insight. Akenson used the shipping records of assisted immigrants for 1876 to make some statistical claims about the character of Irish migration, and he challenged the only previous work using a statistical framework, a 1973 thesis by John Morris.[27]

Although Akenson's statistical analysis was also suspect (he generalised about Irish migrants from one year's arrivals), his path-breaking book helped stimulate some interesting publications on the Irish, especially by Lyndon Fraser and Alasdair Galbreath.[28] Fraser drew on shipping lists and probate records to establish the nature of the Irish flow to Christchurch in the 1860s, and he has now followed this up with a study of the Irish on the West Coast.[29] It took a bit longer for publications on the Scots to appear. There was an important 1991 thesis by Rosalind McClean on Scots migrants from 1840 to 1880, which used Otago shipping records and provincial gazettes to draw up a list of 6000 individuals, a third of whom McClean traced back into the Scottish census. Tom Brooking's biography of John McKenzie also raised questions about Scots migrants, but the first scholarly book devoted to the Scots, *The Heather and the Fern*, did not appear until 2003.[30]

Study of the Irish and Scots also benefited from the establishment of the Irish–Scottish studies programme at the Stout Research Centre in Wellington. The centre sponsored a series of conferences on the Irish and Scots and produced a number of publications.[31] Alongside these studies of national flows there were several attempts to examine the immigrants from all nations. In a 1995 article Margaret Galt set out to ask 'Who came to New Zealand 1840–1889?' She drew on two large samples, one of 5920 people listed in the turn-of-the-twentieth-century regional volumes of the *Cyclopedia of New Zealand* which were essentially self-promotional exercises, the second of 4276 people whose estates were valued for probate purposes. She conceded that these sources were biased toward males, the rich and the successful.[32] In his general history of New Zealand, James Belich noted the importance of understanding the founding fragment of Pakeha New Zealand and acknowledged the complexity of the migration flows. He picked up on the key fact that 'willingness to migrate to New Zealand from the British Isles was not evenly distributed'.[33] Tony Simpson also published a work, promisingly entitled *The Immigrants*, in which he insisted that 'It is important for us to know . . . who these immigrants were'; that was the one question he failed to answer.[34]

Significant progress has been made, and this book has drawn heavily upon the work of earlier historians. But our understanding of the immigrant flows from Britain and Ireland remains at best patchy. Most studies focus on the 1870s; the character of the flows before and after that decade has been much less explored. Of particular importance are the very large flows in the ten years before the First World War, and then again in the 1920s. There are also major difficulties with respect to the representativeness and reliability of much of the statistical data used. The extensive use of the shipping records of assisted immigrants leaves unexplored the very considerable numbers of people who were not assisted, and it ignores the large numbers who came across the ditch from Australia rather than on the long voyage direct from the United Kingdom. Often, findings cannot be easily related to the work of other migration scholars. Coverage of groups beneath the national level – regional or occupational subgroups – has been especially lacking, so that the richness and distinctiveness of the migration to New Zealand has not been fully revealed. *Settlers* provides for the first time a comprehensive, soundly based survey of New Zealand's immigrants from England, Scotland and Ireland from 1800 to 1945, a survey that aims to highlight some of the peculiarities of New Zealand's Pakeha population.

The effort of gathering together this information is worth making. Pakeha New Zealand was profoundly affected by the particular experience and background of those who migrated to this country. Most of the 500,000 people who made the long journey here had spent their formative years as children and young adults in a particular part of Britain and Ireland, where they had developed a host of habits and ways of living – patterns of speech, a taste for certain foods and drinks, religious practices, ways of relating to family and friends, forms of leisure and recreation, and different styles of expressing feelings from humour through to stoicism and even anger. Such cultural practices were not stripped off the moment the migrant got on the boat. They were

Pakeha New Zealanders at the 1950 Wellington–British Lions rugby game at Athletic Park, Wellington. At this time, before the large-scale arrival of Dutch, Pacific Islanders, Asians and Africans, non-Maori New Zealand was far more exclusively descended from people of the British Isles than in the half-century that followed. 114/162/10-G, ALEXANDER TURNBULL LIBRARY

carried to the New World where they helped determine the way the newcomer faced a different environment and a new mix of neighbours and institutions. If we are to understand the evolving culture that was Pakeha New Zealand then we must have a solid understanding of who our Pakeha settlers were. This does not mean, of course, that all these ways of living flowed into the evolving culture of Pakeha New Zealand, but it is one essential starting point.

Finally, we have already noted how much popular understanding of New Zealand's Pakeha founders was obscured under the idea of being 'British'. Many New Zealanders believed that until the last 40 years Pakeha New Zealand was essentially a monocultural 'British' society. This has made more visible, and for many people more uncomfortable, the diversification of New Zealand since the Second World War. As European groups, especially Dutch, arrived in the 1950s, then Pacific Islanders in the 1960s and 1970s, and people from Asia in the 1980s, 1990s and 2000s, some New Zealanders looked back with nostalgia to more simple days when there was a dominant British culture alongside the exotic and relatively quiescent Maori culture. 'Multiculturalism', as it came to be called, has been a difficult adjustment. Any study which fragments that British inheritance and begins to unpick the regional and occupational groups who settled New Zealand will suggest that Pakeha New Zealand has been considerably more multicultural in its origin than popular opinion has it.

In emphasising some of the regional and local cultures of Britain and Ireland, in breaking down the monolithic 'Great Britain' into its parts, we have clearly been influenced by that disaggregation of the United Kingdom that has been such a significant development in British and Irish historiography – a development which, ironically, was first sparked off by a New Zealander, John Pocock, in the J. C. Beaglehole lecture he presented to the New Zealand Historical Association in 1973.[35] This British historiography implies that nineteenth-century Pakeha New Zealand, which until the 1890s was almost 50 per cent UK-born, was a world in which different accents would have been heard and British and Irish regional traditions would still have been visible. It is under-standings such as these that have driven this study and underline its importance.

HOW WE FOUND OUR ANCESTORS

It is not easy to establish the characteristics of these migrants from the British Isles who formed so determinative an influence on New Zealand life. There are major problems of evidence. Much of the available official information is fragmentary and inconsistent. The British and Irish data are limited. Before their abolition in 1873, the (British) Colonial Land and Emigration Commissioners produced annual reports with the numbers and nationalities of persons leaving the United Kingdom, and this was useful for the 1840–52 period. A separate British return identified by nationality the numbers emigrating to New Zealand in the years 1860–63. The emigration data collected by the Registrar-General of Ireland from 1876 did identify the numbers and county origins of those emigrating directly from Ireland to New Zealand, but the returns appear to understate the numbers involved, and do not include the substantial numbers of those of Irish birth who left for New Zealand from England, Scotland or Australia.

New Zealand sources also have grave limitations. Until 1921 the immigration statistics did not distinguish between short-term visitors and long-term arrivals. As the number of tourists and trans-Tasman workers grew from the 1890s the statistics of gross migration became increasingly unreliable. Nor until 1897 do the statistics give any information relating to place of birth in the United Kingdom, with the exception of the assisted immigrants who arrived in the period 1871–92. The published census data is helpful with regards to the country of birth of those living in New Zealand at the time of the census, but because all the original returns have been destroyed the stories of individual lives have vanished.

In the absence of census returns, the core source for this study is a sample of death registers. These are valuable from 1876 when the information collected became relatively comprehensive. From that year the registers provided information which included, among other things, a person's gender, place of birth, father's occupation, years in New Zealand, age and place of death, marital status at death, occupation, and age and place of marriage. While the person's religion is not given, the denomination of the officiating minister at the funeral is stated.

There are obviously problems in interpreting and using the death registers. The information on the death certificate was provided by friends or relatives of the deceased, so details of those who died unmarried, widowed or without children are likely to be shaky. Such matters as the occupation of the person's father, or even the number of years in New Zealand, must often have been roughly estimated. The use of the term 'farmer', for instance, with respect to father's occupation suggests a high degree of imprecision, since in many cases the father was more likely to have been a labourer on a farm than a farmer.

Further, using death certificates to make judgements about all UK immigrants presupposes that those who remained and died in New Zealand had similar characteristics to the substantial numbers who

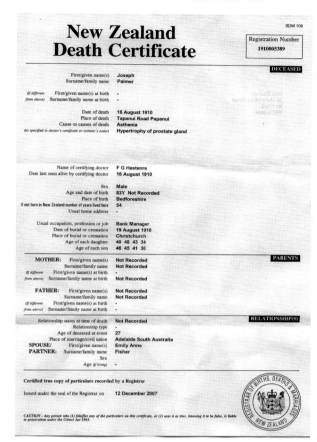

The death certificate of Joseph Palmer, a Christchurch banker, who arrived in Lyttelton in 1856 and died in 1910. COLLECTION OF JOCK PHILLIPS

migrated and then left. This may not be a major problem for our purposes, since arguably the ones who stayed and died in New Zealand were the migrants of long-term significance. They were the settlers. For those who arrived before 1876 we are forced to draw on the certificates of those who died in 1876 or after. Thus, to provide evidence of the earlier migrations, we must assume that those dying before 1876 were no different in their characteristics from those who died later. This creates a greater likelihood of distortions, and there is obviously a major distortion with respect to the age of arrival since older migrants were more likely to have died before 1876 and so leave no trace in our sample.

There is also the major problem that the person officiating at a funeral may not necessarily have shared the religious beliefs of the person who died, but rather those of the spouse, child or friend who organised the funeral. Some questions on the forms, such as place of birth, did not request specifics such as town or even county, and the certificates show considerable variation in detail. Place of birth is also a poor substitute for the equally interesting question of a person's place of last residence before migration.

Despite all these issues, the death register is an invaluable source of information. It is comprehensive, including virtually everyone who died in New Zealand except for Maori. Maori were not required to register deaths until 1913. While this is a tragedy for New Zealanders' knowledge of their past, it is of no concern to this study since Maori, of course, were not immigrants. The death register includes women and children, groups that are often hard to trace. It makes no distinction between those who arrived as assisted immigrants and those who paid their own way, so it overcomes a major problem that arises in studies that rely on shipping records. The death registers also do not distinguish between those who came direct from the United Kingdom and those who migrated to New Zealand by more circuitous routes, such as via the Victorian goldfields. So long as a person was born in the United Kingdom and died in New Zealand they qualify for the sample. Finally, the death registers are consistent in their form after 1876, so they allow for accurate comparison over time.

Moreover, the information may be more accurate than one at first suspects. For a start, the fact that so many informants in responding to the question of birthplace did specify county and town of birth suggests that many were confident enough to offer such details. Second, where the cumulative statistical findings from the death certificates can be compared with the census figures there is a remarkable and comforting level of consistency. Third, where the details of individuals' lives as derived from the death certificates have been checked against other sources, their reliability has been fully validated. This exercise was done for those who arrived on the Otago goldfields between 1861 and 1870, using such sources as electoral rolls, street directories, marriage records and probate records. A recent analysis of over 6000 Scots immigrants using data provided by genealogists reveals a quite remarkable consistency with our findings, even down to the ranking of county of origin by decade.[36]

So the death registers remain a highly useful source, and the information they provide forms the core of this book. For each period of major migration to New Zealand a sample of over 1000 people who were born in the United Kingdom was taken, a total of 11,651 people.[37] Their details (but not their names) were recorded. From these were derived figures on such matters as country and county of birth, year of arrival, age and marital status on arrival, occupational background, religion, and place of death. Place of marriage was also recorded since it provided interesting clues about migratory pathways. In addition the death registers were used to provide large samples of particular migrant groups, among them the Auckland immigrants of the 1840s, '50s and '60s, and the miners of the Otago and West Coast gold rushes.[38]

A second major source of information was ships' passenger lists, particularly for those who came to New Zealand on assisted passages. These are the lists used extensively by earlier scholars looking at the assisted immigrants of the 1870s: John Morris in his 1973 thesis, Don Akenson in his study of the Irish, who used one year's sample (1876), and Rollo Arnold who used those for 1873–76. Similarly, Charlotte Macdonald and R. H. Silcock drew on the lists of those assisted by the Canterbury provincial government. These lists do provide valuable information with respect to age, gender, marital status, occupation and county of origin.

Once again there are problems: in the 1870s, for instance, some ships' registers did not survive and it is impossible to know how this might affect any sample. There has always been some doubt as to the reliability of answers with respect to occupation, since prospective immigrants may well have been encouraged to adjust the occupation they gave to suit the recruiter's needs. The meaning of 'county of origin' is always difficult to interpret – was it the county of birth or the county of last residence (although the fact that separate counties were sometimes listed for husband and wife suggests that it was normally county of birth)? These lists offer details only of people who were assisted, so they exclude those who paid their own way, and they only include those migrating direct from the United Kingdom, although as we know Australia was consistently a major stopping-off point for many British and Irish migrants on the way to New Zealand. For those coming from Australia the *Passenger Lists, Victoria, Australia Outwards to New Zealand* are useful, but only for the period 1852–70. Finally, from the introduction of the old age pension in 1898, the New Zealand government began to keep shipping lists in order to determine whether people qualified for the pension. Such lists were supposed to provide details of country of birth, age, marital status, gender and occupation. They also had the great advantage of including both paying and assisted migrants. Sadly, the details were frequently poorly completed, but despite their limitations passenger lists are a useful source, and they have been extensively used in this book.

A range of other sources also provided samples of varying reliability. The analysis of the English immigrants assisted by the New Zealand Company between 1839 and 1850 is based on the Register of Emigrant Labourers held at the Public Record Office in London and originally compiled by clerks of the company.[39] Registers of immigrants assisted under the Waikato Immigration Scheme, the Waikato Militia rolls and lists of returning Great War servicemen applying for assistance for wives and fiancées were also used. Publications treating the Auckland Fencibles and soldiers of Imperial regiments provided further valuable information.

In sum, the sample from the death registers remains the core, but around this core are clustered a range of other sample groups and subpopulations to give as complete a sense of New Zealand's British and Irish immigrants as possible.

2 *The Ebbs and Flows of Migration*

THE BRITISH AND IRISH IMMIGRANTS WHO arrived in New
Zealand from about the turn of the nineteenth century formed
a tiny part of one of the great migrations in human history.
Some 11 million people left the United Kingdom between 1821 and
1914 – just under a quarter of the 50 million who left Europe during
that period in what was one of the world's major reshufflings.[1] There
were strong incentives to leave Britain and Ireland. The population of
the United Kingdom increased from about 16 million in 1800 to 37
million in 1910, and although over the long term the average real wage
rose, the social changes that occurred in the nineteenth century – the
rise of industry and the growth of the cities – brought considerable dis-
ruption. In large parts of the British Isles rural labourers lost rights to
land as the spread of pastoral farming led to commons being enclosed,
and in Scotland crofters were cleared off their lands. Industrialisation
destroyed the livelihoods of many who had earned a living from domestic crafts like spinning and weaving. In Ireland the potato famine
brought death to hundreds of thousands. In the cities conditions were
often dirty and disease-ridden, and work was monotonous and dangerous. Throughout the United Kingdom many people looked across the
seas to new and, they hoped, better worlds.

Only a very small proportion of the emigrant flood ended up in New
Zealand. The first 'new worlds' to which any British Isles emigrant aspired were the United States or British North America (later Canada).

The *Cospatrick* on fire off the coast of the Cape of Good Hope, November 1874. The ship
was carrying migrants to New Zealand, a number of them recruited from Oxfordshire. It is
thought the fire started when a crew member or passenger pilfering cargo set fire to straw.
The ship burnt for 40 hours before sinking, but only two lifeboats were launched successfully,
carrying just 62 of the 473 people on board. One boat was never seen again. When the second
boat was found ten days later only five people were still alive, and two of them died soon after
being rescued. The news of the disaster halted immigration efforts in Oxfordshire, and the
people of Shipton-under-Wychwood put up a memorial to those from the village who died.
WOOD ENGRAVING BY SAMUEL CLAVERT, PUBL-0047-1875-09, ALEXANDER TURNBULL LBRARY

By the nineteenth century there were 200 years of movement across
the Atlantic, and routes to the ports, especially Liverpool, were well-
trodden. New Zealand, by contrast, was the most distant new world of
all, and therefore the most expensive and difficult to reach. Because it
was the last to be discovered by Europeans, there was no established
tradition of going there.

The average cost of a fare to New Zealand in the nineteenth century
was over four times that of the fare across the Atlantic and, until the
coming of steam power, the voyage usually took about 100 days 'in a
leaky boat'. The journey across the great southern circle was often cold
and rough, and conditions were cramped. Three months or more of
seasickness and poor food was hardly an alluring prospect. On occasion
major disasters on the journey were reported in Britain, such as the fire

By order of the Board,
JOHN WARD, Secretary.
New Zealand Land Company's Office,
1 Adam street, Adelphi,
14th August, 1839.

FREE PASSAGE.

EMIGRATION to NEW ZEALAND.
The Directors of the New Zealand Land
Company hereby give notice that they are ready to
receive applications for a Free Passage to their
FIRST and PRINCIPAL SETTLEMENT, from Mechanics,
Gardeners, and Agricultural Labourers, being
married, and not exceeding 30 years of age.
Strict inquiry will be made as to qualifications and
character. The Company's Emigrant Ships will
sail from England early in September next.
Further particulars and printed forms of appli-
cation may be obtained at the Company's Offices.
By order of the Directors,
JOHN WARD, Secretary.
No. 1 Adam street, Adelphi,
June 15, 1839.

NEW ZEALAND COMPANY, EMIGRATION.

THE COURT OF DIRECTORS
NEW ZEALAND COMPANY
Are prepared to assist in Emigrating to their Settlements in New Zealand,
AGRICULTURAL
MECHANICS,
FARM LABORERS,
Domestic Servants
Of good character, who will assist themselves by defraying a portion of their own expenses.
The Directors will receive Applications accordingly, until
WEDNESDAY, the 9th AUGUST,
From persons of the above description desirous of proceeding on these terms by the Ship

AJAX

Appointed to Sail from the London Docks on
Monday, the 4th September next.
Further Particulars and Forms of Application may be obtained at New Zealand House,
By Order of the Court,
Thomas Cudbert Harington.
New Zealand House, 9, Broad Street Buildings, London.
24th July, 1848.

Advertisements offering passages to New Zealand became steadily more alluring over the years. To the left is a simple newspaper notice lodged by the New Zealand Company in 1839. By 1848 (middle) a poster with bold calligraphy was being produced and the offers had extended to domestic servants, although only assisted, not free, passages were promised. By 1912 (right) images of a rural paradise and domestic comfort were being used to attract domestic servants alone. 12523-A, AUCKLAND CITY LIBRARIES; HOCKEN LIBRARY, UNIVERSITY OF OTAGO; EPH-A-IMMIGRATION-1912-COVER, ALEXANDER TURNBULL LIBRARY

on the *Cospatrick* in 1874 in which 470 passengers and crew died. There was always the danger of epidemics sweeping through the passengers, bringing death especially to the young.[2] Further, for at least the first 30 years after organised settlement began in 1840 the reputation of New Zealand was distinctly mixed. Settlers were thought to be in danger of being killed in earthquakes or eaten by cannibals. There was strong competition from attractive destinations – the United States, with its image of prosperity and opportunity; the British North American colonies such as Newfoundland and upper and lower Canada, which were perceived as a 'British' version of Uncle Sam; and Australia, the 'workingman's paradise'. As the *Dublin University Magazine* noted in 1845, New Zealand was 'the most recent, remotest, and least civilised of our colonies'.[3]

In these circumstances there had to be special incentives to attract people to New Zealand, and it is these incentives that largely explain the story of British migration to this country. The most important was the offer of assisted migration, sometimes extending to a free passage, which was first used by the New Zealand Company in 1840. Then after

1852 a number of provincial governments provided assisted migration, and finally between 1871 and 1890, and from 1904 until the Second World War, the New Zealand government provided assistance.

From the beginning these schemes depended on a network of recruiting agents, who often travelled to likely destinations in Britain and Ireland selling the idea of a promised land in the South Pacific. Sometimes they took on the role part-time and were responsible for a small area. The agents usually offered the carrot of either a free passage or one that was considerably cheaper than the norm. Occasionally, as happened with Auckland's scheme in the 1850s and 1860s, migrants were bribed with the offer of free land, a mechanism that had been widely used in the peopling of North America.

On quite a number of occasions the job of selling these schemes was taken on by an individual or a small group who had a vision of establishing an arcadia in the New World and would effectively negotiate a bulk purchase of land and assisted passages. In the early 1860s, for example, a group of non-Conformists from the Midlands sent out some 3000 people who were intended to settle on land they had been granted at Albertland, on the Kaipara Harbour (although in the end only about half made it that far). In the next decade George Vesey Stewart, a gentleman entrepreneur from County Tyrone in Ireland, hoped to repair his fortune by land speculation in New Zealand; he is said to have been responsible for bringing about 4000 people to New Zealand in the ten years after 1875. The exact proportion of immigrants who came to New Zealand under assistance schemes is not easy to quantify, since we do not have exact figures for the provincial schemes. In addition, the gross immigration statistics include many short-term arrivals and departures, while the net migration figures would have excluded some of the assisted who subsequently left. The indications are that at least a third of those people who came from the United Kingdom as long-term migrants were assisted.[4]

A second form of 'assisted' migration came as a result of the New Zealand Wars, which brought regiments of soldiers to the South Pacific in the 1840s and again in the 1860s. Some of these soldiers took their discharge here. Others were brought here deliberately as 'soldier settlers' to assist in the defence of areas of white settlement, especially Auckland, against possible Maori attack.

A third incentive was the promise of quick wealth, in particular the lure of gold. Men – and there were far more men than women who came for this reason – were prepared to travel long distances and endure considerable privations when they got the glint of gold in their eyes. Another special case comprised those who had already travelled five-sixths of the journey from the British Isles by migrating to Australia. If you were in New South Wales or Victoria, it was not such an obstacle or too expensive to get on a boat and cross the Tasman – especially since at least until the Great War the southeast of Australia and 'Maoriland', as New Zealand was known, were part of one world with frequent travel and communications. When economic fortunes favoured this side of the Tasman over the other, numbers would cross the ditch. Equally, of course, when fortunes favoured those in Australia the outflow from New Zealand was considerable.

Finally, even when these special circumstances applied, there were obviously personal incentives that might explain an individual's decision to choose New Zealand as a 'new country' – a woman might follow a husband, a sister or a brother, a friend follow a friend. Certain communities established patterns of migrating to New Zealand over other destinations. Shetlanders, for example, began to follow other members of their community to New Zealand from the 1870s. Health was a relatively common factor. Tuberculosis sufferers came in the hope of relief in New Zealand's clear air. Ann Alabaster came out in 1859 because her husband Charles had been told that only a long sea voyage would allow him to recover from TB. Sadly he did not recover, and after his death in 1865 Ann supported herself by running a school which became recognised as the leading preparatory institution in Canterbury.[5]

Many professional people, such as ministers, university teachers or scientists, were happy to travel round the globe when offered the chance of furthering their careers. New Zealand, like other new societies, also attracted individuals who believed that in a new country they could fulfil their political or religious dreams. Ernest Allen, to take one example, was the son of a butcher who became a staunch socialist.[6] In 1912, as the 'red federation' emerged in New Zealand, he set off for this country in the belief that it was the world's best hope for revolutionary unionism.

The importance of these special incentives in attracting immigrants

Mary Pulling came to New Zealand purely for professional reasons. A distinguished teacher at English high schools, she was invited by the Anglican Bishop of Auckland to come out and start a church school for girls. Diocesan High School for Girls began soon after her arrival in 1904, and by the time she retired 22 years later it was recognised as a fine institution with a high academic reputation.
DIOCESAN SCHOOL FOR GIRLS

helps to explain the fact that migration to New Zealand from Britain and Ireland was not a microcosm of the general outflow to new worlds during the nineteenth and early twentieth centuries. People came to New Zealand from particular places, affected by the presence of agents selling assisted passages or by family and community traditions. Certain areas came to be 'New Zealand-prone'. Furthermore, the flows to New Zealand were not even; migration occurred in fits and starts as particular incentives came into play.

The uneven tempo of the migration from Britain and Ireland is vividly illustrated in the graph opposite,[7] which charts migration from all countries to New Zealand between 1840 and 1945. Since 90 per cent of the immigrants were from Britain and Ireland, the graph provides a good chronology of the course of migration of people from the United Kingdom (bearing in mind, of course, that at certain periods many of

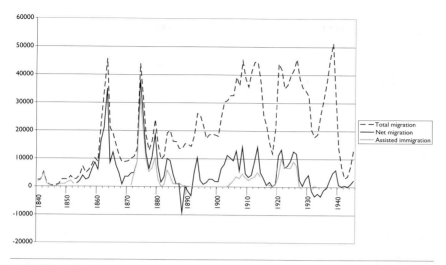

ANNUAL MIGRATION TO NEW ZEALAND, 1840–1945

those people would have come from Australia rather than direct from the Old World). The graph shows distinct highs and lows, particularly when we look at net migration (that is, the numbers who arrived minus those who left New Zealand in any one year). One of the striking facts about migration to New Zealand through this period is that residence was often temporary. A high proportion of migrants came, saw and did not conquer. For many who endured the long voyage here, New Zealand was not the promised land.

The graph reveals a series of distinct inward flows that document the exceptional situations bringing people to New Zealand. To better understand the ebbs and flows of the migratory tide, we have divided the whole period into six shorter units – the years up to 1840; the years of Crown Colony government (1840 to 1852); the years of provincial migration (1853 to 1870); the years of central government assistance (1871 to 1890); the prewar period (1891 to 1915); and finally the inter-war years (1916 to 1945).

1769–1839
In the years before the 1840s the numbers arriving were very small. For 70 years after Cook's 'rediscovery' of New Zealand, the distance and

expense of the journey remained an obstacle to settlement from Britain and Ireland. The small number who did migrate to New Zealand were exceptional people, either those – James Belich's 'Tasmen'[8] – who were already in Sydney, or the few who came to the Pacific in the single-minded pursuit of their trade.

Most of the initial migration came from across the Tasman. The earliest group were the sealers, who were the first non-Maori to live for any length of time in this country – at Dusky Sound in 1792. Few sealers stayed very long. Practically the only settlement they established, in about 1825, was on Codfish Island, off the northwest coast of Stewart Island, although within a few years most had moved onto Stewart Island itself or to mainland Southland.[9]

The early whalers had often travelled far to follow their prey and they too did not often stay, but when shore-based whaling began in the late 1820s there was a greater incentive to settle. Shore-based whaling stations were established along the coasts from Foveaux Strait to East Cape, and some acquired substantial populations of between 40 and 80 men.[10] Quite a number of these early shore-whalers came from Sydney; many were ex-convicts who had been taken to New South Wales against their will and either escaped or sought a new life across the Tasman after serving their sentence. Such a man was the Englishman Jacky Guard, who had been arrested in St Marylebone, London, for stealing a quilt in 1813, and was subsequently sent out to Sydney. After serving his time Guard became a sealer and ship's captain. He set up his shore station in the Marlborough Sounds some time between 1827 and 1829, but retained contact with Sydney. Certainly 15-year-old Elizabeth, whom he married in 1830, had been born there to another ex-convict family.[11]

Another group with strong Sydney origins were those who were interested in trading in flax for rope or timber for naval spars. James Busby's census of 1836 indicated that almost a third of the European adult males in New Zealand were involved in the timber trade.[12] Some eventually settled as Pakeha Maori, acting as intermediaries between their Maori suppliers and their Australian customers.[13] These early sealers, whalers and traders were largely males, and they included a rich assortment of men. There seems little doubt that a considerable number of them did have convict backgrounds, and therefore they

John Howell, seated right, was born in Sussex. He stowed away on a ship bound for Australia, where he joined a whaling ship, and arrived at Kapiti Island as a whaler in about 1828. He served with the prominent whaler and trader Johnny Jones, and then established a whaling station at Jacob's River (later Riverton) in the mid-1830s. At first he refused to follow the whalers' convention and take a Maori wife, but eventually he agreed and in fact did so twice. He had nineteen children. The man seated at left is another well-known whaler, the American Lewis Acker. WALLACE EARLY SETTLERS MUSEUM

tended to be either English or Irish, since very few Scots or Welsh were transported.[14]

People of a very different stripe were the missionaries, sent out by church organisations to convert the heathen. In a sense they too had come a long way in pursuit of their trade. Samuel Marsden initiated their settlement in the Bay of Islands in 1814. Some of the mission stations acquired substantial European populations: Rangihoua had reached 45 by 1819, and by 1830 over 60.[15] They included quite a number of women, such as Marianne and Jane Williams, the wives of the missionary brothers Henry and William Williams. Marianne, who was from Yorkshire, came out with Henry in 1823. Jane was the daughter of a dissenting family from Nottingham, England; she arrived in the Bay of Islands with William in 1825. The two women developed a close working partnership which later led to a rich correspondence. When Jane finally died at the age of 95 she was the last of the pre-annexation missionary band which, including families, numbered 206 by 1839.[16]

Finally, in the late 1830s, a few free settlers came across from Australia in the expectation of British annexation and to escape difficulties across the sea caused by drought and increased prices for Crown land.[17] It is difficult to find reliable evidence of the numbers of these early immigrants. Arrivals seem to have been few and sporadic until about 1830, and they began to increase from 1833. But it was never a flood. Most estimates give the European population of New Zealand at the end of 1839 as about 2000. Those who settled in New Zealand before 1840 were a small and select bunch.

Crown Colony, 1840–1852

In 1840 the first major wave of settlement in New Zealand began. British annexation, with the signing of the Treaty of Waitangi, and the emergence of the New Zealand Company, which had big ambitions for British settlement, changed the situation markedly. In the United Kingdom the 1840s saw a dramatic rise in outward migration to all places as agricultural and industrial distress hit hard.[18] The ebb and flow of out-migration to the New World followed cyclical fluctuations in the British economy. There was a marked depression in the years 1837–42, a period of improving prosperity during the mid-1840s, and finally another period of economic depression and social distress with major crop failures, notably in Ireland, but also in the Highlands and islands of Scotland, and in Cornwall.[19] The fluctuations in migration to New Zealand during these years were clearly affected by these broad trends, although the famine-hit Irish overwhelmingly travelled across the Atlantic rather than to the south.

Between 1840 and 1852 (the Crown Colony period) about 27,500 people arrived in New Zealand, of whom about two-thirds came direct from the United Kingdom.[20] The numbers were not great, but they were significant in establishing future patterns. The major explanation for this migration is the recruiting efforts of the New Zealand Company and its offshoots, the Canterbury Association and the Otago

Association. Though inspired by Edward Gibbon Wakefield's vision for an ordered community, the company was a business proposition. It purchased land from Maori for on-sale to investors who were expected to come out as 'colonists'. Many of them chose not to do so, especially those who bought land in Nelson, but a few did and became significant figures in the new communities. One such was Samuel Revans, the son of a London surgeon who trained as a printer. After setting up as a merchant he suffered a financial reverse, and he decided to invest his remaining assets in New Zealand Company land orders. Before leaving on the *Adelaide* in September 1839 Revans purchased printing equipment, and he produced an edition of the *New Zealand Gazette* only a month after landing on Petone beach. For a time he was a great promoter of the Wellington settlement, before leaving printing to invest in Wairarapa land and enter politics. Ironically, in the first general assembly of 1854 he became a bitter opponent of Edward Gibbon Wakefield.[21]

Although the New Zealand Company attracted some investors such as Revans, its success depended on recruiting a sufficient number of labourers. They could provide a workforce and a market to ensure there was a steady demand for land. Of the 27,500 people who came to New Zealand in these years, about 14,000 – over half – came as assisted immigrants, their passage paid for by the Company or its successors. Among those who came to Wellington on the second New Zealand Company ship, the *Aurora*, were Andrew Brown and his sons. This was in part because Samuel Revans had recommended Andrew to the company. Andrew himself was the son of a tenant farmer near Dundee in Scotland, but he had moved to Camberwell in London where reportedly he was a retailer. His wife had died, and perhaps to make a new start he came to New Zealand with his two sons, all three applying to the company as carpenters. Andrew set himself up as a storekeeper on an island (which came to be known as Brown's Island) at the southern end of Kapiti, catering to whalers. His two daughters eventually migrated to join the family in 1855.[22]

Immigrants like the Browns came in two distinct waves. Some 10,000 arrived in the first few years of settlement at the company towns of Wellington, Nelson, New Plymouth and Wanganui. The year 1842, with some 5000 newcomers, saw the largest number of immigrants for

Samuel Parnell, June 1890. Parnell was a London carpenter who came out on one of the first New Zealand Company ships, *Duke of Roxborough*, and landed at Petone beach in February 1840. On board ship he agreed to build a fellow passenger's store, but only on the condition that he worked for eight hours a day. Subsequently, it is said, he met incoming ships and enlisted the support of the new arrivals in his cause. The photograph was taken on the jubilee of Wellington's settlement, when Parnell was fêted as 'the father of the eight-hour day'. He died soon after. 1/1-020462; G, ALEXANDER TURNBULL LIBRARY

the next fifteen years. Because of the English leadership of the company, most of the assisted settlers were English. Many of those who came out to New Plymouth had been recruited around Cornwall and Devon by the Plymouth Company, an auxiliary of the New Zealand Company. They included, for example, 33 families, largely agricultural labouring people travelling in steerage, who came from the Devon–Cornwall border around Holsworthy.[23]

In the mid-1840s the number of such immigrants fell to a trickle as the company faced legal and financial difficulties, the Northern War broke out and there was growing pessimism about the colony's future. Then came a second wave of assisted migrants. There was an organised group from Scotland led by Free Church Presbyterians, who arrived with boatloads of Scots in Otago in 1848. Two years later the Church of England Canterbury Association brought the first four ships of English settlers to Lyttelton.

Most of those arriving in company settlements had come direct from the United Kingdom. This was much less true of those who peopled the non-company areas in and around Auckland. Here different factors had an influence. One important group comprised those who arrived in response to the outbreak of war with Maori in the north. The 58th Regiment, for example, was in Australia when it was summoned in 1845, bringing such men as Alexander Whisker from County Armagh. Whisker kept a memorandum book in which he recorded his episodes of drinking and fighting among the grog shops of Auckland. He also recorded his involvement in the battle of Ruapekapeka, where his fellow soldiers included our Paisley migrant Daniel Munro, who had joined the Auckland militia. Some 700 of these soldiers were given their discharge in New Zealand and some, like Whisker, brought wives and children across the Tasman to settle. Despite a series of arrests associated with strong liquor, Whisker became a dairyman and eventually fathered six sons and two daughters.[24]

Another 2500 people, including women and children, were brought to New Zealand as the so-called Royal New Zealand Fencibles in 1847–48. These were settlers who were granted land in the area south of Auckland on the understanding that they would be prepared to undertake military service and help provide protection to the young capital.[25] Like many British soldiers, a good proportion of these were Irish. One such was Walter Murphy, originally from County Galway in Ireland, who had served in the British Army for sixteen years before being declared medically unfit. He became a Chelsea pensioner receiving a small allowance, but he jumped at the chance of land in return for military readiness in New Zealand. In 1847 he arrived in Auckland with his wife Catherine O'Shaughnessy, and the family were given a wooden cottage and some land at Howick, where his two children were baptised into the Catholic church.[26]

Auckland also attracted a few smaller organised groups. In 1842, amid claims that the British government had breached an understanding not to send convicts to New Zealand, 98 young boys from Parkhurst Reformatory arrived. Another 31 followed a year later, but such was the outcry that the experiment was not repeated. Also in 1842, as we have already seen, 514 people from Paisley, near Glasgow, came out to Auckland as a response to the depression in the local shawl-making industry. There were also over 400 assisted under the Poor Law Amendment Act, administered by the Colonial Land and Emigration Commissioners.

Although the numbers involved in these groups were not large, the impulse behind their migration needs to be seen within the context of the reform of the Poor Law in Britain at this time. Traditionally, local communities would support the poor and underemployed in their district, but during the 1830s and 1840s this tradition came under attack. Instead, relief would only be given 'indoors', in newly built workhouses. Migration overseas was seen as a ready alternative to charity by offering the unemployed the possibility of an independent living on the new lands across the sea. Although the numbers sent to New Zealand directly by the new Poor Law were not large, its punitive provisions were a significant factor in encouraging many to apply for assisted passages.[27]

Finally, the 1840s saw some free settlers arriving in the colony as individuals. There were some government officials, merchants and aspiring younger sons of the respectable class who came out to make a mark in the colony. Auckland attracted a number of independent immigrants from across the Tasman, including quite a few people with an Irish background. One interesting story is that of some Cornish miners who came across from South Australia as individuals, although presumably following their mates, when they heard about the discovery of copper on Kawau Island in 1844. They had originally come out to South Australia as a result of distress in the Cornish mining towns, and about 300, including women and children, followed their hopes to Kawau. When mining was abandoned, some of these families took up farming.[28] In such ways, whether through the dreams ignited by New Zealand Company promotion or in the hopes of individual wealth, the obstacles of migration to New Zealand were overcome and the country began to be settled by British and Irish.

1853–1870

Between 1853 and 1870 the Pakeha population rose from about 30,000 to over 250,000. Much of this increase was the result of immigration. During these years almost 250,000 people migrated to New Zealand and about 100,000 left, resulting in a net gain of almost 150,000. Probably two-thirds of the long-term migrants came direct from the

United Kingdom (with the rest largely from Australia), but this was just a small portion of the over 150,000 people each year who poured out of the British Isles to New World destinations during the early 1850s and the 1860s. The graph of net immigration to New Zealand (page 27) shows a steady rise during the 1850s, a dramatic rise in the early 1860s, then an equally dramatic falling away in the late 1860s. This was a period of energy and growth, characterised by three significant factors – the importance of the provincial administrations, the impact of the gold rushes, and the effect of the New Zealand Wars. Each of these factors had a crucial effect on the course of immigration, and together they largely explain these figures.

The provincial governments took responsibility for immigration under the New Zealand Constitution Act 1852. For the next eighteen years, until the central government began to take over immigration, most of the provinces had schemes for encouraging migrants. Usually provinces hired agents in Britain and Ireland to go out and recruit immigrants with the offer of cheap (that is, 'assisted') or free passages to New Zealand. Immigrants were seen as the key to growth and prosperity. Hawke's Bay, Wellington, Nelson and Southland all had small schemes for bringing in immigrants. Otago province was more active, but unfortunately most of its records have been lost.

Most of these provinces were looking for the same kinds of people as the New Zealand Company had tried to attract – farm labourers, builders and domestic servants. They gave priority to families and unmarried women, and a number of provinces accepted nominations from relatives. The most energetically promoted scheme was that of Canterbury, which brought in about 18 per cent of New Zealand's gross immigration between 1858 and 1870; almost two-thirds of these migrants were assisted. There was a significant flow of assisted immigrants to Canterbury in 1858 and 1859, then larger flows again in 1862 and 1863.

One large family who came out in 1863 as assisted passengers was that of Henry and Grace Penberthy, from the Cornish mining town of Helston. Henry was a builder, a preferred occupation for assistance, and their local community was suffering overcrowding and disease. Perhaps Henry and Grace were also influenced by New Zealand's reputation as a place where single women were in demand. Three unmarried

Margaret McKinlay, a dairymaid from Lanarkshire in Scotland, came out to Canterbury as an assisted passenger in 1863 after a quarrel with her father's third wife. As was expected she initially worked as a domestic servant, but within three years she had married George Gardner who had been an officer on the immigration boat. The couple established a farm and flour-mill at Cust, and when George killed himself while handling a loaded gun Margaret Gardner took over managing the farm, the expanding mill company and her ten children. A woman of some physical strength, she is said to have beaten her sons well into their teens. ½-197504; F, ALEXANDER TURNBULL LIBRARY

daughters came out, along with two sons. The older son also brought his wife, her sister and her niece. So the total group was ten people, for whom Henry paid £89 5s, while the province paid £47 5s. Perhaps the choice was also influenced by the presence in Christchurch of a Helston friend, a preacher at the Wesley Chapel. But for this family, as for many migrants, the New World was not entirely a paradise reborn. The eldest son, Henry, was declared bankrupt in 1870, and by 1990 only one descendant still carried the family name.[29]

Auckland province used a different system to attract migrants – the lure of land. Under a scheme introduced in 1858, agents in the United Kingdom had authority to grant land orders to prospective emigrants at the rate of 40 acres for every person aged eighteen or over, and 20 acres for those between five and seventeen. In the ten years of the scheme 15,516 land orders were issued, and these were probably responsible

Some of the non-Conformist settlers who came out from the English Midlands in the early 1860s stand in front of their new post office at Albertland on the Kaipara Harbour.

for bringing in over 40 per cent of Auckland's immigrants during these years. Given that Auckland attracted over 20 per cent of New Zealand's net immigration gain, the land scheme was a significant contributor to the country's increasing population.

Auckland also saw two special schemes of settlement. First, there was the famous Highland Scots migration of Norman McLeod's followers, some 800 strong. Norman McLeod was a lay preacher who was unhappy at the liberalism of the Church of Scotland and hoped to restore the fierce Calvinism of John Knox. A charismatic preacher, he first led his intrepid followers across the Atlantic to Cape Breton Island in Nova Scotia in 1820. Later, when failing crops threatened the community, 300 followed the prophet first to Australia, then on to Auckland, where they arrived in 1853. A year later they settled at Waipu in Northland, and over the next six years they were joined by four more shiploads of Highlanders from Nova Scotia.[30]

The second special scheme involved a group of some 3000 English non-Conformists who came out between 1862 and 1865. The Albertland scheme was initiated by William Brame, a journalist and the son of a Baptist minister, to mark the bicentenary of the expulsion of non-Conformists from the Church of England in 1660. Brame hoped to establish a 'model' agricultural community. The association obtained 70,000 acres on the Kaipara Harbour under Auckland's '40 acre' scheme. Farm labourers and craftsmen were recruited from the Midlands, Yorkshire and Lancashire, and eight shiploads landed in Auckland in 1862–63. Only about half of the new arrivals finally settled at Albertland itself, on the Kaipara Harbour.[31] Among those who never made it to the Kaipara were the journalist Henry Brett, who was the group's historian, and the famous late-nineteenth-century landscape painter Charles Blomfield.

If free land or cheap fares enticed some immigrants, gold was an even more powerful magnet. Although there had been a small rush to the Coromandel in 1852, and a larger flow to Golden Bay and the Aorere Valley between 1857 and 1859, it was Gabriel Read's discovery in Otago in May 1861 that triggered real interest across the seas. The steep climb in the immigration graph over the subsequent two years was largely (although not wholly) a testimony to the migrants' hopes of a golden fortune. Figures peaked at a gross inflow of over 45,000 people in 1863, which would remain the largest annual inflow for the next 100 years. Then in 1864, just as returns started to decline in Otago, there were discoveries in the Wakamarina in Marlborough and on the West Coast. The following year the West Coast rushes were in full swing, and they continued to attract immigrants in significant numbers until 1867.

On the surface these migrants were rather different from those who had come before. The gross migration figures suggest that a clear majority came from across the Tasman where the Victorian rushes of the previous decade had attracted thousands from England, Scotland and Ireland. Considerably fewer, probably half the number of those from Australia, heard the news in far-off Britain and Ireland and travelled to catch a boat south. The Irish were least likely to have come direct.

The miners came unassisted, and very often came alone rather than in families. They were overwhelmingly male, usually men in their twenties and thirties. Of those arriving from Victoria who reached Otago or the West Coast fields about 87 per cent were men, and the women who did come often followed a year so later, about half of them following their husbands. Despite the image of the goldminers as a horde who chased the gold from California to Victoria and on to the South Island, there were very few 'forty-niners' or even Americans among them. All but about 10 per cent came from the British Isles, and there was a relatively even spread of English, Scots and Irish – the Scots better represented in the Otago rushes, the Irish the largest single country of birth among the West Coast miners.

Those from Australia tended to be a transient lot, much more likely to go back across the Tasman when the pickings became thin than were those who had come direct.[32] A few examples illustrate some of the pathways taken by the miners. Take John Shannon, born in Belfast in 1836. At the age of 21 he sailed to Melbourne, after which he spent several years on the goldfields of both Victoria and New South Wales. In 1861 he joined the rush to Gabriel's Gully, then went on to the Dunstan and Arrow rushes before finally heading for Hokitika in 1865. George and Tryphena Beer represent a slightly different but not unusual pattern. George was the son of a Wiltshire flourmiller. In 1859, aged 21, he married Tryphena and they immediately left for Australia, where they eventually headed for the Victorian goldfields. In 1863 George decided to cross the Tasman to the Otago fields with his brother Henry, leaving his wife and two sons behind. When the brothers struck gold Tryphena and the children were summoned, and they settled at One Mile Creek near Queenstown. Over the next decade a sister and two other brothers came out to the district. The last brother, John, ended his days alone at Te Anau, having earned the nickname 'Jack the hermit'.[33]

The third important factor that brought people to New Zealand during the 1860s was the New Zealand Wars. The number of soldier-migrants was not huge, but they were a significant group. Some were men who had been brought to New Zealand with Imperial foot regiments and received their discharge here – many of them at the end of conflicts in Taranaki and the Waikato between 1865 and 1867. There were some 2000 such men, and there must also have been a number who were deserters during the wars. Some of the ex-soldiers, such as William Russell, later had distinguished careers. A trained officer who first came to New Zealand temporarily in 1855 with the 58th Regiment, to duties that were little more than roadmaking, Russell returned when conflict broke out in 1861. Evidently he preferred the life of a landowner to that of a soldier, as he resigned his commission and acquired 31,000 acres of Hawke's Bay land. He eventually entered national politics, becoming a cabinet minister and the acknowledged leader of the opposition during Richard Seddon's long reign as premier.[34]

Edward Lofley was one of the more unusual people brought to New Zealand by the New Zealand Wars. He arrived in February 1863 on the naval vessel *Orpheus*, which was bringing troops to the wars. When the ship was wrecked on the Manukau Harbour bar it resulted in the greatest loss of life of any New Zealand shipwreck. Lofley fought in the Waikato War, joined the Armed Constabulary, and then set up a spa and bath-house at Taupo, where he became a favourite guide of tourists on account of his eccentric manner and amusing anecdotes. As in this photo, he usually wore the Armed Constabulary's bush shirt and kilt. ½-044655; F, ALEXANDER TURNBULL LIBRARY

Another group who came to New Zealand as a result of the wars were the so-called Waikato Militia and their families. These men were recruited to serve as militia and settle on land between Auckland and the frontier, to provide both protection for the colonists and a base for further land acquisition. Some were recruited in Otago, rather more in Australia, especially on the goldfields of Victoria, in late 1863 and 1864. If we include over a thousand who settled in Taranaki, the census of 1864 reported over 6000 military settlers (although well over a thousand of these came from Otago rather than from overseas). The Waikato Militia included some interesting characters, such as the Londoner 'Garrulous Garrard', who came from Sydney in 1864 with the 4th Regiment. He used to orate on street corners on behalf of the unemployed, claiming that he had served in war 'to protect the capitalist' and received nothing but 'starvation'. In fact, he was later appointed Auckland's first dog ranger.[35]

At the same time as the Waikato Militia were being recruited there was an associated scheme to settle migrants a bit further north on confiscated land to provide a defensive barrier for Auckland. Originally 20,000 people were to be brought in, but in the end under 5000 arrived between November 1864 and June 1865. This scheme brought settlers from Cape Town, London, Glasgow and two ports in Ireland (Queenstown and Kingstown), many of whom settled around Pukekohe.

Provincial immigrants, goldminers and soldiers therefore formed the bulk of New Zealand's new settlers during these years. Since all three of these groups came in especially large numbers in the years 1862–65, it is hardly surprising that those years represented a torrent that would not be equalled until the mid-1870s.

1871–1890

That next flood largely resulted from two factors: in Britain the early and later 1870s saw over 200,000 people pack their trunks each year and head overseas as the economic dislocations in the rural areas began to hit; and in New Zealand Julius Vogel unveiled an ambitious scheme to develop the country. Vogel, a Londoner with a Jewish background, had come out to the Victorian goldfields but soon discovered that mining stories was more to his taste than mining gold. When news of the Otago strikes reached him he decided to ply his trade in the newest gold centre, and in 1861 he migrated to Dunedin. By 1870 Vogel was colonial treasurer. Realising that the gold boom was fading, he believed the central government had to encourage and organise the economic growth of the country. Foreign loans and investment in infrastructure, especially the railways, were part of his vision. The other part was organised immigration which would provide the labour to exploit the new opportunities. It was also hoped that immigrant settlement and public works like roads and railways would help settle down the North Island frontier following the New Zealand Wars. The migrants might become established on land confiscated from Maori.

The Immigration and Public Works Bill, introduced into Parliament in 1870, gave the central government power to enter into contracts to

The carpentry plane of Thomas Dewson, an Englishman who joined many other builders and carpenters as assisted migrants to New Zealand in the 1870s. Dewson worked in New Zealand making furniture and carving the coats of arms on government buildings. PRIVATE COLLECTION

bring to New Zealand the number and type of immigrants requested by the provincial superintendents. Over the next few years government involvement became more extensive. Eventually the central government's responsibilities included providing for subsidised and free passages, a scheme that allowed friends, relatives and employers to nominate people for assisted passages, the centralisation of recruitment in the hands of the London-based office of the agent-general, and extensive efforts using recruitment agents and lecturers to attract people to New Zealand. The groups who were particularly targeted in these campaigns were agricultural labourers, builders and craftsmen, young married couples and single women who were expected to come out as domestic servants.

Over the next 20 years 115,578 assisted immigrants came to New Zealand, about a third of the gross immigration in the years 1871–90. In fact this figure slightly underplays the importance of the schemes, for in the years of really large assisted flows (1871–79), when almost 100,000 assisted migrants arrived, they represented 54 per cent of all immigrants. Further, for the whole period the assisted made up almost six in every ten of those who came direct from the United Kingdom. Of course the less visible immigrants were the 40 per cent of incomers during these years who came from Australia, but many of these were short-term migrants who flitted back across the ditch when times got tough.

So government assistance made a major contribution to New Zealand's settlement, especially if we consider how often the promotion of New Zealand by immigration agents and the letters back home from those assisted encouraged paying migrants to get on a ship south. The work of attracting the migrants was in the hands of an army of agents scattered around the British Isles. By 1872 there were 53 in England and Wales, 78 in Scotland and 46 in Ireland.[36] The year 1874 saw a flood-tide as 32,000 assisted migrants entered the country. Thereafter the overall numbers fell, while the proportions from Scotland and especially Ireland rose.

Among those who came from England married couples with or without children predominated, whereas among the Scots, and especially the Irish, single men and women were more common. A good example of an English assisted family were the Fissendens. They came from Birling on the Medway in Kent, where several generations had been farm labourers and dissenters. As rural populations rose and commons in the area were enclosed, times became tough. At one stage five members of the family were in the Birling Poor House. One of the family, Frederick, had twelve children, and five of them came out to New Zealand on assisted passages. First Ellen and John came together on the *Avalanche* in October 1874, and both settled in Nelson. Then the wife of a third sibling, Phillip, died in November of that year leaving three young sons. Phillip wanted to follow his brother and sister but the immigration regulations did not provide assistance to widowers. So when he boarded the *Hannibal* for New Zealand in March 1875 he came as a single man and a farm labourer, while one son went as a child to his sister Emily, and the other two to a second sister, Eliza.

It was not all happiness in New Zealand. Ellen, who had come out as a domestic servant, married in 1877 but died two years later. Her brother John died in January 1893 in what the *New Zealand Herald* described as 'a lonely death' as a result of too much drink and too little food. Phillip, however, remarried, had eleven children, bought a farm in Marlborough and died as the family patriarch aged 75.[37]

One of the many single Irish women who came out was Annie Dowd. Born in County Kerry, she came out on an assisted passage in 1878 as a 16-year-old general servant. Her arrival was unusual as the ship, *City of Auckland*, was grounded on Otaki Beach and she walked to

Waikanae and on to Wellington. But her troubles were not over. She married Louis Chemis, an Italian labourer, who was then convicted of stabbing and shooting to death a landlord. Annie fought to prove his innocence, and got a job as a charwoman in Parliament Buildings. Louis was finally released, but sixteen months later blew himself up with dynamite. Annie became the longest serving charwoman in the public service and eventually retired after 32 years of cleaning.[38]

The 1870s also saw several special settlements. The assisted immigration drive was kicked off by an agreement with the railway contractor John Brogden and Son, who was responsible for bringing out over 2000 people in 1872–73 to work as navvies on New Zealand railways. Despite this, many of the men recruited were agricultural labourers, not navvies, and nearly all were from southern England.[39] Then in 1871 Colonel H. W. A. Feilding obtained the Manchester block of 106,000 acres in Manawatu from Wellington province on behalf of the Emigrant and Colonists' Aid Corporation, a philanthropic group that assisted people who were out of work. Over a thousand people, again overwhelmingly English, came out to settle in the Halcombe area in 1874–77. The third scheme was that of Colonel Vesey Stewart, which brought out two shiploads of Protestants from northern Ireland to Katikati in the Bay of Plenty in 1875–78. Then in 1880–83 Stewart recruited settlers from throughout the British Isles for a settlement at Te Puke.

In the 1880s, despite continuing migration from Britain generally, the numbers of assisted immigrants and total British immigrants to New Zealand were small, except for a brief revival of assistance in 1883–84. Economic depression began to bite, and there was public opposition to immigration. In December 1887 nominated immigration was stopped and immigration offices were disestablished.[40] Large numbers of people who had come to New Zealand in the boom times of the 1860s and mid-1870s began to move across the Tasman where, especially in Victoria, wages were higher and jobs more plentiful. One who had already moved back by 1880 was Patrick Hannan, an Irish emigrant who had initially gone to the Victorian goldfields then come out to the New Zealand fields in the 1860s. His decision to return to Australia was obviously a wise one since he subsequently achieved fame and temporary fortune as the discoverer of the richest goldfield in Australia, at Kalgoorlie in 1893.[41] From 1885 to 1890 the numbers who departed New Zealand's shores exceeded those who arrived by over 4000 people. In 1888 alone over 9000 people said goodbye to New Zealand. The last 44 assisted migrants arrived in 1891.

1891–1915

The 1890s was also a decade of slow immigration. From 1891 to 1903 there were no schemes for assisting immigration and the continued sluggishness of the economy was a disincentive to come to New Zealand. In every year of the 1890s apart from 1893, net immigration was well under 5000 people. The turn of the century brought better times as the returns from refrigerated meat and butter fuelled a growing national self-confidence. The first fifteen years of the century brought one of the most important, but least acknowledged, migrations in New Zealand history. Almost 300,000 people born in the United Kingdom landed on New Zealand's shores. In 1904 assisted immigration was again introduced, and for the next eleven years assisted migrants comprised about a third of the people arriving direct from the United Kingdom. Those years saw over a quarter of a million people leave the United Kingdom each year, and New Zealand was able to capture a small part of this massive outflow.

However, by this time direct migration from the other side of the globe was no longer the dominant source of immigrants to New Zealand. Throughout the last decade of the nineteenth century and the first decade of the twentieth, Australia was very important as a point of departure. Over twice as many of the arrivals had spent time in Australia as came direct from Britain or Ireland (although the numbers are distorted by the inclusion of short-term visitors in the official figures). Some of those who arrived from Australia were people who had migrated from the British Isles to New South Wales or Victoria, then moved across the Tasman as economic depression and drought led to tough times. Others were Australian-born children of British and Irish immigrants – people like Michael Joseph Savage, the son of an Irish immigrant to Victoria, who came across in 1907 to join fellow Victorian Paddy Webb, who had arrived two years earlier. Thirty years later the two would be members of the same Labour cabinet along with three other Australian arrivals in these years – Mark Fagan, Robert Semple and William Parry.

Walter and Lotty Nash on board ship on the way to New Zealand in 1909. Although born in Worcestershire, Walter had spent most of his early life in Birmingham, where he sold tobacco and sweets. When economic depression hit the area and the family suffered illness and the death of a daughter, the couple decided to make a fresh start in New Zealand. 1/2-035215, ALEXANDER TURNBULL LIBRARY

The migrants who arrived from Australia were especially important in 1892 and 1893, and again in the first few years of the new century. In general they included more men than women, while those coming direct from the British Isles included many family groups including children. Since domestic servants (along with farm labourers) remained an occupation of preference for assistance, quite a number of single women also came out. Nomination by relatives was again used as a basis for assistance, and indeed about half the assisted came out on this basis, quite a number being the wives and children of men who had migrated earlier.

It is also clear from the passenger lists that four in every five coming direct from the old country in these years were English and very few (about 3 per cent) were from Ireland. By contrast the Australian incomers did include considerable numbers of people of Irish or Scots birth. The English included a growing number from the north of England, such as the Dickinson brothers who had worked in the cotton mills of Preston, in Lancashire, and who came to join their mates in Sydenham, Christchurch.[42] There were also some middle-class migrants, such as Cecil Brooke and his two teenage sons. Cecil was a lawyer in Surrey, and 'a fine upstanding English gentleman, devoted to his maker, to his Monarch, to his country and to his family'. The three came out in 1910 to purchase land at Kaikoura.[43]

Migrants of a rather different stripe were the 'Clarionettes'. Their migration was the brainchild of William Ranstead, the son of a Cheshire fitter, who became a Fabian socialist. Following a visit to New Zealand in 1899 during which he met Richard Seddon and was impressed by the labour laws, Ranstead wrote glowing articles about this 'socialist Canaan' in his newspaper the *Clarion*. He then organised a migration of working people to come out in four ships. In all about a thousand of them reached New Zealand, where they were among the founders of the New Zealand Socialist Party.[44]

1916–1945

Not surprisingly the Great War brought a halt to large-scale immigration, but with the coming of peace the pace increased. Between 1919 and 1927 trans-Tasman movements were not large, but there was a new and substantial movement of people direct from Britain, and to a very much lesser extent Ireland, to New Zealand. Once more schemes of assistance played a significant role in the movement of people: indeed, of the 120,000 who arrived direct from the United Kingdom between 1919 and 1930 almost 60 per cent (over 70,000) came with some form of assistance. In 1921 the right to nominate people for assisted passages was extended from relatives to any New Zealand resident who could promise the applicant employment. This was a recognition that new immigrants 'would not all be farm immigrants'.[45] Nevertheless, domestic servants and farm labourers could still apply for passages, and some 4000 domestic servants did so.[46] However, 90 per cent of those who came as assisted migrants were nominated rather than applying independently.[47]

There was a variety of schemes of assistance. Up to and including 1920, most of the assisted were the British wives, children or fiancées of New Zealand servicemen. These liaisons were often hurried. May

Four English fiancées of New Zealand soldiers on board the train to London to catch the 'brides' ship', the *Mahana*, which headed for Wellington in 1920. *WEEKLY NEWS/ NEW ZEALAND HERALD*

Beare was a munitions worker who during a strike in 1918 travelled home to Torquay in the train. On the journey she started talking to two soldiers in 'funny hats'. The next morning she was walking down the street when she heard wolf-whistles. It was one of the soldiers off the train. May and Les Pruden had a hurried courtship of six weeks before Les left for New Zealand. They wrote to each other for two years, and in 1920 May arrived in New Zealand on the 'brides' ship' *Mahana*. They were married in Te Puke and had nine children.[48]

Between 1921 and 1924 over 12,000 British ex-servicemen and their families came out, largely at the expense of the British government. In 1922 the British initiative expanded with the introduction of the Empire Settlement Act, under which the New Zealand and British governments jointly supported family emigration. Over 44,000 people

48

Young men on board ship to New Zealand in 1929, on a scheme established by the Salvation Army to bring youth from Britain's overcrowded cities to the healthy colonies. EP1046-1/2, ALEXANDER TURNBULL LIBRARY

came out to New Zealand under this scheme. There was a very large migration from Scotland during these years, reflecting the long-term decline in Scottish industry, which led to an outward flow to many countries; like the flow from England, there were very even numbers of men and women.[49]

There was one other interesting scheme during these years – the migration of juvenile boys. The impulse here was a fear that young boys of British stock were ending up on city streets and in what were called 'blind alley occupations'. It was hoped that in the healthy atmosphere of the dominions they might be able to improve morally and contribute to the strength of the Anglo-Saxon race. The number who came to New Zealand under these schemes was only about 1400, significantly fewer than to the other dominions. They included, for example, 266 boys and 26 girls who came out to Flock House, which was set up by New Zealand sheepfarmers to train as farmers the sons and daughters of British seamen killed or wounded in the Great War.[50]

From 1927, as economic conditions in New Zealand worsened, immigration began to falter. Thereafter, through the lean years to the Second World War, the number of British people arriving in New Zealand for long-term residence was not great.

On the surface this overview of immigration to New Zealand from the British Isles suggests a picture of diversity and complexity. Sudden influxes alternate with periods of substantial outflow; highly publicised schemes attracting groups from particular areas of Britain were followed by flows of nameless and barely visible individuals from across the Tasman. Yet there were certain continuities – the crucial importance of assisted passages which for a long time gave preference to agricultural workers, builders and domestic servants; the encouragement given to families by their ability to nominate immigrants, and the importance of those 'hidden' migrants, often of an Irish or Scots background, who came across from Sydney or Melbourne. The question to which we now turn is whether these continuities produced a distinctive character in New Zealand's founding settlers.

3. *The Settlers*

HOMELANDS

THE MOMENT IMMIGRANTS BOARDED THE ship to come to New Zealand, there was a subtle change in their identity. At home they had thought of themselves as inhabitants of Paisley, or Belfast, or from the counties of York or Kent. But on the boat larger groupings became more significant, and shipboard journals talk about the 'rowdy Irish' or the 'careful Scots' in steerage, or the 'English gentleman' in cabin class. National groupings and identities rose to the surface. So the first question to explore is the largest unit of analysis – country of origin. To what extent were those who settled New Zealand from the British Isles a fair representation of the national groupings at home? Was New Zealand's self-perception as 'more English than the English' an accurate description of the settlers?

Some answers can be found in Tables 1 and 2, which summarise our major findings – Table 1 from the sample derived from the death registers, and Table 2 including information from all sources. The figures should be compared with Tables 3 and 4, which give the relevant census information for the United Kingdom and New Zealand. The graph shows the distribution of country of origin for each year of arrival, again based on the death register database. Not unexpectedly, the figures for each period hide the considerable variation of flows within those periods.

TABLE I. NATIONAL COMPOSITION OF UNITED KINGDOM IMMIGRANTS TO NEW ZEALAND (PERCENTAGES)

	1800–39	1840–52	1853–70	1871–90	1891–1915	1916–45
England	62.1	64.3	46.6	54.6	65.0	60.1
Wales	1.6	1.1	1.1	0.8	1.1	2.1
Scotland	20.4	20.6	30.2	21.5	22.2	28.7
Ireland	15.6	13.5	21.4	21.7	10.9	8.6
Isles	0.3	0.5	0.7	1.3	0.9	0.5
	100.0	100.0	100.0	100.0	100.0	100.0
Number	314	1061	2464	3446	2109	2571

Source: Death registers

TABLE 2. NATIONAL COMPOSITION OF UNITED KINGDOM IMMIGRANTS TO NEW ZEALAND (PERCENTAGES)[1]

	England	Wales	Scotland	Ireland
1800–39	62.1	1.6	20.4	15.6
1840–52	64.3	1.1	20.6	13.5
Auckland	45.3	0.8	17.6	35.9
NZ Company	80.3	1.1	15.0	1.7
Discharged soldiers	42.8	0.2	2.6	54.4
1851 New Ulster census	58.8	0.4	13.0	27.8
1853–70	46.6	1.1	30.2	21.4
Discharged soldiers	40.2	0.4	2.6	56.8
Auckland	52.9	0.4	17.8	27.8
Canterbury assisted	56.6	1.4	19.9	22.1
Otago miners	36.6	1.7	30.1	31.6
Westland miners	28.0	3.8	19.3	47.9
1871–90	54.6	0.8	21.5	21.7
Assisted	53.7 (incl. Welsh)		18.4	27.9
1891–1915	65.0	1.1	22.2	10.9
1916–45	60.1	2.1	28.7	8.6

Sources: Death registers, Register of Emigrant Labourers, passenger lists

TABLE 3. DISTRIBUTION OF THE UNITED KINGDOM POPULATION WITHIN THE UK (PERCENTAGES)

Living in	1841	1851	1861	1871	1901	1921
England	55.4	61.0	62.7	65.3	72.2	74.5
Wales	3.9	4.2	4.0	4.5	4.8	5.6
Scotland	9.8	10.5	10.3	10.5	10.8	10.3
Ireland	30.4	23.8	22.6	19.2	12.1	9.2
Isles	0.5	0.4	0.4	0.4	0.2	0.3

Source: UK census

TABLE 4. DISTRIBUTION OF UNITED KINGDOM-BORN MIGRANTS IN NEW ZEALAND (PERCENTAGES OF ALL UK-BORN IMMIGRANTS)

Born in	1861	1871	1891	1911	1945
England	59.3	49.7	53.5	58.5	63.3
Wales	0.7	1.0	1.0	1.0	2.2
Scotland	25.5	27.3	23.7	22.6	24.2
Northern Ireland					5.0
Ireland	14.5	22.0	21.8	17.9	5.3

Source: New Zealand census

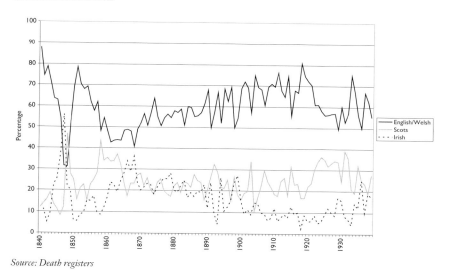

Source: Death registers

COUNTRY OF ORIGIN OF IMMIGRANTS TO NEW ZEALAND FROM THE UNITED KINGDOM, 1840–1939, BY YEAR

The first significant point to note is that New Zealand received very few immigrants who had been born in Wales. From the mid-nineteenth century the Welsh comprised at least 4 per cent of the population of the United Kingdom, rising to over 5.5 per cent by 1921. Yet not until the twentieth century did the Welsh comprise 2 per cent of New Zealand's immigrants from the UK, and during the great period of migration to New Zealand from 1853 to the Great War, the number of Welsh migrants equated to less than a quarter of their representation in the British Isles. The Welsh did include an interesting range of people who often brought traditions from home. At the end of the nineteenth century there was Henry Pheloung, who brought his musical prowess to Oamaru as a bandsman, and was known as the cornet player with the 'rubber lip'. George Manning, for ten years (1958–68) the popular mayor of Christchurch, brought his non-Conformist Christianity and his commitment to the labour movement.

Yet at no time did the Welsh ever come in any numbers or in any organised groups. We can only speculate about why this was so. The small numbers were certainly not because the Welsh were averse to migration in general. They moved in considerable numbers to other places, such as the United States and Canada.[2] Perhaps it was because the more industrial nature of south Wales, the origin of many Welsh emigrants generally, did not attract recruiters from the New Zealand Company, the provinces or the New Zealand government, all of whom consistently looked for people with a farming or craft background and all of whom ignored Wales. Perhaps it was because the tradition of moving across the Atlantic was so strong that it was difficult for the New Zealand option to become established. The numbers of Welsh who went to Australia were also low, so we received few Welsh from that source.[3]

Perhaps it was because the ports from which New Zealand boats departed were very rarely Liverpool or Bristol, the ports closest to Wales. For a Welsh person to catch a boat to New Zealand would probably have required them to make the long journey to London. Yet, as we shall see, this did not stop other groups from the far corners of the United Kingdom, especially if they came as assisted migrants, which meant their internal journey was also paid for. For whatever reason, despite the close links New Zealanders have had with Wales through their shared national game of rugby, New Zealanders do not have a great deal of Welsh blood in their veins.

The Scots' story is very different. Throughout the nineteenth century people living in Scotland consistently comprised only about one in ten of the UK population. Yet from 1840 on, the Scots represented more than one in five UK immigrants to New Zealand, and in both the 1860s and the 1920s the proportion was close to one in three. By 1891 about a quarter of the UK-born population of New Zealand was from Scotland. In other words, New Zealand was well over twice as Scottish as the homeland.

Of course the Scots migration to Otago is well-known and highly mythologised in the names of the capital (Dunedin) and the local

Mary Jane Lewis came to New Zealand from Monmouthshire in Wales with her brother in 1870. She met and married a Scotsman, Charles Innes, who was a brewer but not good with money. In fact he became bankrupt twice. Mary, however, had business skills. In 1888 she took over management of the Te Awamutu Brewery, followed soon after by the Waikato Brewery. From 1900 the company she had created, C. L. Innes and Company, traded successfully in the brewery business for over 60 years. 8975, WAIKATO MUSEUM OF ART AND HISTORY

rugby team (the Highlanders), for example, yet Scots were to be found throughout New Zealand. Nor did their large representation simply reflect a Scottish propensity to leave home. Certainly Scots moved in their thousands to other places such as Canada, Australia and the United States. Yet they moved to New Zealand in unusually large numbers. For example, while the Scots consistently made up over 20 per cent of New Zealand's UK-born settlers, in Australia the figure was never more than about 15 per cent.[4] In certain periods such as 1860–63 (years for which we have emigrant figures) New Zealand was the chosen destination for about a third of those leaving Scotland, which made it the most popular destination of all for Scots emigrants at that time.

Why did New Zealand have such appeal for Scots? It started early. Even before annexation in 1840 a fifth of those in our sample were Scots, with seamen well represented. Particular flows set up patterns.

We began our story with the 500 migrants who came from Paisley, near Glasgow, to Auckland in 1842. Once the Otago Association had been formed in Edinburgh there was a major recruiting of Scots for the Edinburgh of the South in the late 1840s. From that time on Otago and Southland were particular magnets for Scots. But even before the Otago settlement began, those from north of the border were considered desirable. The New Zealand Company had agents in Scotland who recruited successfully there. As early as February 1840, only weeks after the first arrivals, the *Bengal Merchant* arrived in Wellington from the Clyde with 160 passengers, mostly drawn from Glasgow. They included the Reverend John Macfarlane, who was the first in New Zealand to proclaim the gospel in Gaelic.[5] A year later Wellington received a 'Scots ship', as the *Blenheim* was known, when it brought 197 passengers under the leadership of laird Donald McDonald. Many of these people came from his own or neighbouring clans in Inverness, while the Lowlanders were also from Paisley. The party settled in what was known as 'the Scotch settlement' at Kaiwharawhara.[6] Of those recruited by the New Zealand Company to the Wellington, Nelson, Taranaki and Wanganui settlements, some 15 per cent were Scots. In the 1848 census of New Munster (Wellington and the South Island), 16.8 per cent of Wellington's British-born were Scots.

The New Zealand Company helped establish the view among the largely Protestant and English elite who initially controlled New Zealand politics that the Scots were the kind of immigrants this country wanted. Despite the occasional jokes from Englishmen such as Alexander Majoribanks that Scotsmen hastened to New Zealand principally out of a sense of duty, to relieve the first settlers of every sixpence they legitimately could, most opinion-makers in New Zealand regarded the Scots as highly desirable.[7] They were Protestant, considered hard-working and moral, and despite Scotland's industrialisation many of those available were from an agricultural background, often quite close to Glasgow or Edinburgh. The Highland clearances had encouraged Scots with agricultural origins to move to the Lowlands. So as New Zealand provincial governments, and later the central government, established schemes of migration assistance, they were happy to see their agents going north to Scotland and recruiting, especially in the periphery of the cities.

Of those who were given assisted passages by Canterbury province in the 1850s and 1860s almost 20 per cent were from Scotland. Even in Auckland more than one in six of those who came in during those years were Scots, numbers boosted by the special settlement of Highlanders at Waipu in Northland. By the time the New Zealand government set out to attract immigrants in 1871 the Scots were clearly seen to be a desirable group, more so than the Irish, and agents were sent in numbers to the north. By October 1872 no fewer than 73 of the 116 agents appointed were in Scotland.[8] In all, 18.4 per cent of those given assisted passages by the New Zealand government were from Scotland, and the Scots were even better represented among the later schemes of assistance, probably making up well over a quarter of those assisted in the 1920s.

So the Scots came in large numbers partly because they were wanted, and once they had arrived traditions of migration became established. Many others came as paying migrants. In particular the Scots were exceptionally well-represented among those who were drawn to New Zealand by the lure of gold. Almost one in three of Otago's immigrant goldminers had been born in Scotland. Many of these miners had migrated via the Victorian goldfields – some 19 per cent of those who were recorded as arriving either in Otago or on the West Coast from Victoria during the gold rushes had been born in Scotland.[9] They included Charles McQueen, son of a Renfrew fender-maker who followed a fairly typical path, emigrating from Scotland to Victoria in about 1859, then on to Dunedin in 1862 or 1863. McQueen became one of the pioneers of gold-dredging on the Clutha before eventually returning to Victoria when the dredging boom collapsed.[10] Numbers of Scots also came direct from the old country during the gold years, presumably attracted by news from compatriots on the other side of the globe. One of these was 'Big John Ewing', who arrived direct in 1863 and established a highly successful mining operation at St Bathans, and a fine reputation, despite occasional hiccups such as his imprisonment for four months for shooting a Chinese miner and a period of bankruptcy.[11]

The one form of migration in which the Scots were poorly represented was that associated with the military. Only 2.6 per cent of the soldiers discharged from Imperial forces in the 1840s and again in the

George Fairweather Moonlight originally came from Glenbervie in northeast Scotland. He left there in 1848 to join the Californian gold rush, before heading to Australia and on to Otago in 1861. As a miner he had the distinction of giving his name to two creeks, both sites of successful strikes, one on a tributary of the Shotover in Otago and one on a tributary of the Grey River on the West Coast. For a time he was a publican, but he died in 1884 while out prospecting. 1/2-008604, ALEXANDER TURNBULL LIBRARY

1860s came from Scotland, and few fiancées or wives from Scotland arrived after the Great War. However, as unemployment hit Scottish industry in the 1920s the numbers coming to New Zealand, as to Australia, rose. How many of these were following relatives who had come out in the 50 years before it is difficult to know.

Circumstances of war apart, the Scots were consistent and hugely significant immigrants. And it is the combination of an early and sustained reputation as desirable Protestant types, together with patterns of chain migration, that probably explains why they make up such a disproportionate number of New Zealand's founding British.

The factors that made the Scots so desirable in New Zealand also help to explain why the Irish were not favoured migrants. Apart from those in the north the Irish were predominantly Catholic, and vestiges of anti-Catholicism remained in colonial New Zealand. True, the Irish were overwhelmingly of a rural background, which is what promoters of migration to New Zealand wanted. But both among the respectable organisers of the Wakefield settlements and among the largely English-born community that dominated New Zealand provincial governments, the Irish were considered to be poor unlettered peasants likely to be unreliable workers, with few skills and a propensity to drink.

H. F. Alston, the New Zealand Company's superintendent of emigration, wrote to an agent in Dundee that a number of the people he had recruited had been turned down because 'Irishmen are not considered desirable emigrants'.[12] Later, Canterbury province's emigration agent John Marshman was advised that 'Irish emigrants should be refused altogether'.[13] So in the early years of migration antagonism towards the Irish was clearly present. At first few came on assisted passages. It was also true that there were few boats that came direct to New Zealand from Ireland, which meant the added expense of a trip to London or Glasgow was required before setting out. Indeed, before 1864 not a single ship (with the exception of a couple carrying soldiers) began its voyage to New Zealand from an Irish port.[14] In 1874, when four ships left from Ireland and free passages were available, the numbers of Irish rose significantly.

The Irish, like the Scots, were quite willing to move overseas. In the 70 years after the devastating famine of the late 1840s over five million people (equal to those remaining in Ireland) streamed away from their native land, with about four million going to the new worlds of America and Australasia. But compared with those going to Canada or Australia the numbers coming to New Zealand were small. In Australia some 30 per cent of the nineteenth-century migrants from the UK came from Ireland, and they made up a quarter of all overseas-born;[15] in New Zealand only in the 1870s and 1880s did the proportion of UK immigrants from Ireland reach 22 per cent.

In 1861, in the immediate aftermath of the Great Famine, only 14.5 per cent of New Zealand's UK-born were from Ireland, despite the fact that the Irish had been almost one-third of the UK population in 1841, and were still over one-fifth in 1861. The number of Irish was especially low among those assisted by the New Zealand Company in the 1840s, when the famine emigration was at its height. Only 1.7 per cent of company-assisted passengers came from Ireland. Admittedly there were a few people of Irish origins among the leaders of organised settlement in those years, such as Edward Stafford in Nelson and John Robert Godley in Canterbury, but these were men from a Protestant Anglo-Irish background. As members of the Protestant Ascendancy they may have seen their situation weakened at home by Catholic emancipation and the emergence of Irish nationalism. Few of their compatriots joined them. In 1848 the province of New Munster had a mere 175 Irish-born inhabitants.

Despite this lack of assistance the Irish did make it to New Zealand. They came, at least until the 1860s, largely under their own steam, and they came to Auckland. In 1851, in contrast to the situation in New Munster, 2871 (almost a third) of Auckland's population of 8840 were of Irish background, and of British Isles immigrants into Auckland during these years almost 36 per cent were of Irish birth. Few had come direct from the homeland. Most had come via Australia. Men of an Irish background, many coming out of the convict community of Sydney, were to be found among the early gangs of traders, whalers and sealers. They included such settlers as Jacky Marmon, a Pakeha Maori who was the son of an Irish convict, and Dublin-born Frederick Maning, who later became a trader and author.

Almost 16 per cent of those in our sample before 1840 were of Irish birth. In the 1840s the numbers of Irish coming across the Tasman to Auckland grew. Some, like Patrick Donovan, had come as far as Australia and then seen opportunities in the Auckland area. Donovan had been born in County Cork, married, and come out to Van Diemen's Land in 1837 before moving to Port Phillip (Melbourne) as a harness-maker. Realising that the Treaty of Waitangi and the activities of the New Zealand Company would increase the value of New Zealand land, he came to Auckland and bought land in Shortland Street in 1840. There he built an inn with a large taproom to which he gave the ecumenical name 'Shamrock, Rose and Thistle'. By the time he died in 1898 Patrick Donovan owned 780 acres of land and a number of racehorses, and was known for his parties, his generosity, his support of the Catholic church and his gambling.[16]

The 1840s also saw significant numbers of Irish ex-soldiers settling in Auckland. Some of these were men who were discharged from British regiments brought to New Zealand in 1845–46. Over half of the soldiers given release in New Zealand during these years were Irish. Others came with the Royal New Zealand Fencibles, the majority of whom were Irish, who were settled with their wives and children to provide protection for the area south of Auckland town in 1847. In the graph showing the country of origin of UK immigrants (page 53) there is a striking spike in Irish representation in the mid-1840s. Over a third of those from our sample of Auckland death registers in that decade were Irish-born.

In the 1860s dreams of gold once again brought the Irish to New Zealand without assistance, first to Otago, where they comprised almost a third of the miners born in the UK, and then more dramatically to the West Coast. Some 48 per cent of the Coast's miners in our sample had been born in the Emerald Isle. A large number were Catholic, an equally high number were male, and many had moved on from the Victorian goldfields across the Tasman. Martin Kennedy was a typical example. Born in County Tipperary in about 1840, he migrated to Victoria in 1860 to try his luck on the diggings. Hearing of the gold discoveries in Otago, he sailed to Bluff, then set himself up as a merchant in Queenstown. In 1868 he followed the miners to the West Coast, where he became a leading owner of coal mines and shipping interests. Later he moved on to Wellington, becoming a director of the Bank of New Zealand and a leading member of the settlement's Catholic community.[17]

Auckland province also attracted the Irish in the 1860s, and once more they included discharged soldiers from regiments that had been brought out to fight in the New Zealand Wars (56.8 per cent of the discharged soldiers were Irish by birth). Some 1500, mainly Ulster Protestants, were brought to the area around Pukekohe as part of the Waikato Immigration Scheme to provide a buffer between Auckland and the Kingite Maori further south. They were joined by about 500 Irish who came after a sojourn in South Africa.[18]

Even in Anglican Canterbury the Irish began to appear. Despite Canterbury's emigration agent, John Marshman, being instructed to avoid the Irish, some 22 per cent of the immigrants assisted by the province were from Ireland. This was in part because the Canterbury

Ann Gleeson, the daughter of a reasonably well-off farmer in County Limerick, came to Melbourne in 1858 with her cousin Johanna Shanahan and friend Mary Maloney. She married a stonemason from Belfast, Patrick Diamond, who brought the family across the Tasman and joined the Gabriel's Gully gold rush. In 1865 they followed the gold once more to the West Coast, and still with Johanna and Mary's help, Ann set up Diamond's Hotel at Red Jacks. With a concert hall and billiard room, the hotel became the social centre of this isolated mining community.
F-190586-1/2, ALEXANDER TURNBULL LIBRARY, EDWARD MATTHEWS COLLECTION (PACOLL-7098)

agents decided to seek domestic servants and married couples among the Protestant population of Ulster;[19] about 60 per cent of Canterbury's assisted Irish immigrants came from Ulster. Even more significantly, the Irish came out because they were nominated for assisted passages by family members already in Canterbury. Indeed, of those assisted to Canterbury in the years 1863–67, 59 per cent had been nominated rather than recruited by agents (as compared with 23 per cent of all assisted migrants).[20] One of these was Ellen Silke, the daughter of small landholders in County Galway. At the age of twelve she was seen by John Crowe, who managed to persuade her father to promise her hand in marriage. John migrated to New Zealand, and about eight years later he presumably nominated Ellen, who received a free passage from Canterbury province as a domestic servant. The pair later married and moved to join the Irish Catholic community in Southland.[21] In all, for the period 1853–70 Irish people comprised 21.4 per cent of New Zealand immigrants from the UK, which was not very different from the percentage of Irish in the UK population as a whole – 22.6 per cent in the census of 1861. The numbers of Irish coming to New Zealand continued to rise during the great migration of the 1870s. In fact, between 1871 and 1890 the Irish outnumbered the previously preferred Scots, comprising 21.7 per cent of immigrants from the British Isles. They were especially well-represented among those given assisted passages (27.9 per cent). This was not because they had suddenly become a favoured group – indeed, there was considerable controversy in the early 1870s about the government's alleged bias against the Irish. Certainly in October 1872 only eight (of 116) recruiting sub-agents were based in Ireland. Of 124 advertisements for immigrants, only 15 had been placed in Irish newspapers, and then only around Belfast and Londonderry in the more Protestant area of Ulster.[22]

There were two reasons for the numbers of assisted Irish. First, those who had come in the 1860s, many of them attracted by gold, now nominated their relatives for assisted passages. Ellen Crowe, for example, nominated her young sister Mary in 1871, followed by her widowed mother and her three brothers in 1874, and a fourth brother in 1876. The second reason was that New Zealand immigration agents, following the lead of those who had worked for Canterbury province, appear to have begun to target the Protestants of the north as distinct from the Catholics of the south. They saw Ulster as a source of the hard-working Protestants it was believed New Zealand needed, and the area continued to be regarded as an especially good place in which to recruit reliable domestic servants. During the 1870s more Irish women than men came to New Zealand, a distinct reversal from the previous period.

But the Irish newcomers during these years were not just domestics. Families, especially Protestants, were also given assistance. John Chambers and his wife Ellen were living in County Armagh, not far from Portadown, on just over an acre of land. Their earnings were supplemented by weaving, but as factory production developed, this became an unreliable source of income. They decided to come out to

New Zealand with their five children as assisted migrants. After landing in Wellington they followed friends to the Ellesmere district outside Christchurch. John, who was illiterate, bought land, farmed and
worked on the roads. But life was not easy. Two daughters died of diph-
theria, and in 1908 John hanged himself in his stable. Ellen, a stalwart
member of the Leeston Methodist Church, lived on until 1919.[23]

The majority of Irish immigrants during the 1870s and early 1880s
who came to New Zealand direct travelled by ship from Glasgow or
London. Two groups boarded their ships in Ireland. In response to the
accusations of anti-Irish prejudice, New Zealand's agent-general, Isaac
Featherston, had appointed Mrs Caroline Howard as an immigration
agent. She proceeded to recruit young women from a workhouse in
Cork, and they reached Dunedin aboard the *Asia* in mid-1874. Their
arrival provoked an outcry about this importation of 'certified scum',
but Mrs Howard was able to arrange for two further sailings before she
was dismissed.[24] The second group of vessels that sailed direct from
Ireland carried a more acceptable group of passengers. These were the
Protestant families from Ulster who came in 1875 and 1878 to Katikati in
the Bay of Plenty as part of George Vesey Stewart's special settlement.

From the 1880s the numbers of Irish began to fall. Between 1891
and the Great War they comprised about one in ten of UK immigrants,
and between the wars the proportion of Irish declined even further.
Moreover, those who did take the long journey from Ireland were overwhelmingly from Ulster. This was partly because from 1921 southern
Ireland was no longer part of the United Kingdom, but even more,
it was because New Zealanders had increasingly learnt the important
distinction between Ulster Protestants and southern Catholics. The
former remained welcome in New Zealand, the latter rather less so.

The story of Irish migration, then, is very different from that of
the Scots. Their numbers were surprisingly low in the early and later
periods of migration to New Zealand, proportionately far fewer than to
Australia. The 1860s and 1870s were decades of significant Irish influx,
in large part explained by the discovery of gold, the exigencies of war,
and the desire of the Irish community to bring out their relatives. After
that the flow declined, and it was only because New Zealanders began to
focus their recruitment on the Protestant north that it continued at all.

Harriet Ritchie came to Canterbury as an assisted migrant with her husband, a blacksmith, and her daughter in 1850 on one of the 'first four ships'. Her husband went off to the Australian goldfields and was not heard of again. To support herself Harriet became matron of Lyttelton Hospital. When Maria Rye, founder of the Female Middle Class Emigration Society, visited in 1863 and spoke of the need for a registry for domestic servants, Harriet became matron of the Christchurch Female Home which provided a registry and accommodation for servants. However, as immigration agents knew well, there was such a demand for servants that turnover was rapid and applications exceeded supply.
CANTERBURY MUSEUM

Finally, let us look at the English. Given that New Zealand has long had a reputation as the 'most English' of Britain's colonies, and that the English were consistently the largest group in the United Kingdom population, it is hardly surprising that they constituted the highest proportion of New Zealand's immigrants. Until 1852 the English were better represented among white people in New Zealand than among the British Isles population as a whole.

Again not surprisingly, four out of five immigrants assisted by the New Zealand Company came from England. The company was based in England, was run by Englishmen, and its head office was in London. The company did not subsidise travel to the port of departure, and 50 of the 65 ships it chartered left from London or nearby Gravesend. English investors in company land often encouraged their employees to emigrate. A. G. Tollemache, the proprietor of Ham House in Surrey, purchased 34 sections in Wellington. In May 1841 the *Lord William*

Richard Seddon, shown here addressing a crowd in his home-town of Kumara in 1877 at the start of his political career, was not a typical English immigrant of the 1860s. He came from the north of England (from St Helens in Lancashire); he had worked previously in an industrial occupation (in the iron workshops), and he arrived in 1866 on the West Coast, a community where the English were a minority among large numbers of Scots and Irish. Yet he was typical in coming to the goldfields after a period on the Victorian diggings. In his later political career as premier, from 1893 to his death in 1906, he was always conscious of those like himself who had migrated from Britain and Ireland. In his provision of old-age pensions, for example, he was determined to ensure that those who had come out in the 1860s and 1870s would live a comfortable old age in 'God's own country'. 1/2-044653-F, ALEXANDER TURNBULL LIBRARY

Bentinck arrived there with four married couples, seventeen children and one single man from his estate.[25] Auckland was a bit different. The English comprised fewer than half of that province's migrants in the years 1840–52, as Irish in particular came across from Australia.

Things changed during the 1850s and 1860s. The English did not stop coming, of course, for in absolute numbers there was a large influx of English people, especially during the 1860s. But as the proportions of Scots and Irish rose, so that of the English fell. Between 1853 and 1870 fewer than half of New Zealand's UK immigrants came from England, and in fact the English were some 18 per cent under-represented in comparison with the population at home. The English were especially few in number among the goldmining communities (making up well under a third of Westland's miners) and among the discharged soldiers. Even Canterbury, 'more English than the English', only gave about half its assisted passages to English migrants, while the numbers of English settling in Auckland remained comparatively low.

The establishment of the central government's assistance schemes did not change things dramatically. Although the English were by far the largest national group they constituted only about half the assisted migrants, and during the 1870s and 1880s the proportion from England (54.6 per cent) was over 10 per cent less than the proportion of English in the UK population. Britain and Ireland as a whole were far more English than New Zealand for most of the nineteenth century. From the 1890s the numbers of English migrants revived proportionately as those from Ireland fell, but right through until the Second World War the percentage of English among New Zealand's immigrants was surprisingly low.

The conclusion that New Zealand's founding immigrant stock is less English than might be expected deserves some discussion. It was not that the English were considered undesirable types by New Zealand immigration authorities – far from it. It probably had rather more to do with conditions at home. Compared with the Irish and the Scots the English were less inclined to leave their homelands in the nineteenth century. Australia, too, had relatively few English migrants. This was partly because England was more prosperous and offered more economic opportunities than Scotland or Ireland. Internal migration was a less drastic route out of poverty than four months of seasickness en route to the other side of the world. The first place the English would move to if things became tough was Manchester or London, where there were jobs to be had, and of course many Scots and Irish also moved to England because it offered jobs or better wages.

The comparatively low representation of the English is even more apparent if we subtract from the English population those who derived from the 'Celtic fringe' of the southwest, especially Cornwall. For much of the nineteenth century that area sent large numbers of migrants to New Zealand, many of whom were rather different from 'Home Counties' English. They descended from the Celts who had been pushed west during earlier invasions of England. They had their own distinct traditions, and a language that was a form of Gaelic, very similar to the language traditionally spoken in Ireland and Scotland. If to the Scots and the Irish we add the 5 to 10 per cent who came from the far southwest, it can be argued that the Celtic fringes of the British Isles provided at least half, if not a clear majority, of those who migrated from the UK to New Zealand in the nineteenth century. In that sense New Zealand's founding Pakeha population is very far from being 'more English than the English'. A high proportion of us in fact have Celtic blood in our veins.

ELIZABETH AND JOHN: THE ENGLISH

Country of origin is a crude measure for explaining the cultural mix of New Zealand's immigrants. Countries are administrative units. They do not tell us about the mix of cultural traditions that came in the baggage of New Zealand's immigrants. It is time to go beneath the country and look at issues of region, occupation and religion. Let us begin digging deeper among the largest single group of immigrants, the English.

Table 5 shows the regions of birth of immigrants to New Zealand from England and Wales as revealed in the death register sample (Wales is included in the English tables because of the small numbers of Welsh immigrants). The regions are a grouping of counties that have been clustered in similar analyses elsewhere;[26] they are as shown on Map 1 (p. viii).

Apart from the consistently low representation from Wales, two significant facts are apparent. First, throughout the nineteenth century three areas of England were especially important in sending people to New Zealand: London and Middlesex; the so-called 'Home Counties' of the southeast (those which border London – Kent, Sussex, Surrey and Hampshire); and the counties of the southwest. This concentration began very early. Even before 1840 over 72 per cent of the immigrants in our sample, which is admittedly small, came from these three areas. In the first major wave of the 1840s almost six out of ten had been born there, and until the end of the nineteenth century these areas constituted almost half of the birthplaces of New Zealand's English settlers.

68

TABLE 5. REGIONS OF BIRTH OF ENGLISH AND WELSH IMMIGRANTS (PERCENTAGES)

Born in	Pre-1840	1840–52	1853–70	1871–90	1891–1915	1916–45
London/Middlesex	28.6	14.8	17.3	16.8	19.5	21.3
Southeast	18.4	21.5	13.0	13.8	11.2	11.8
East	6.1	7.1	7.6	7.0	6.1	7.0
Southwest	25.5	22.8	15.9	17.8	10.0	6.3
Midlands						
East	3.1	3.1	6.2	3.4	4.6	4.4
Central	2.0	5.8	5.4	6.2	5.5	5.0
West	1.0	4.9	5.4	6.3	4.1	2.8
South	2.0	4.6	3.5	6.0	3.0	2.2
Yorkshire	6.1	5.8	8.5	6.6	11.2	9.4
Lancs–Cheshire	2.0	5.2	8.4	7.3	14.6	16.8
Northeast	3.1	1.2	3.4	4.0	4.9	7.7
Northwest	0.0	1.5	2.2	1.2	1.9	1.5
Offshore islands	0.0	0.7	1.6	2.4	1.4	0.8
North Wales	1.0	0.6	0.5	0.5	1.1	0.6
South Wales	1.0	0.4	1.1	0.7	0.7	2.3
	100.0	100.0	100.0	100.0	100.0	100.0
Not stated	28	25	35	76	73	54
Number	126	698	1192	1956	1411	1612

Source: Death registers

It is true that these areas had large populations, and so were likely to be represented well among New Zealand's English. But their strong representation was not simply a reflection of the numbers of people living there. Table 6 shows a regional representation index for each area – that is, the proportion of immigrants to New Zealand born there relative to the number of people born in the area according to the relevant census. Areas with figures over 100 suggests they were over-represented among New Zealand's immigrants.

If anything, these figures highlight the particular importance of London/Middlesex, the southeast and the southwest even more strongly than those in Table 5. These three regions all have figures significantly over 100 for every period of migration up to 1915. Of the other regions, only the northwest and the offshore islands (the Isle of Man and the Channel Islands), both of which had small populations, are over-represented in more than one period. So a disproportionate number of people from three key regions came to New Zealand, and they did so throughout the whole period of migration up to 1945, despite the very different character of the flows at different points in time.

TABLE 6. REGIONAL REPRESENTATION INDICES FOR ENGLISH AND WELSH IMMIGRANTS

Born in	1840–52	1853–70	1871–90	1891–1915	1916–45
London/Middlesex	151	197	179	119	141
Southeast	193	118	122	121	141
East	68	70	67	75	79
Southwest	209	150	180	171	95
Midlands					
East	53	101	58	80	73
Central	102	87	95	83	70
West	77	84	103	88	55
South	99	73	130	93	59
Yorkshire	58	81	62	102	86
Lancs–Cheshire	40	66	55	91	114
Northeast	33	87	98	89	140
Northwest	104	147	86	186	136
North Wales	17	14	15	63	26
South Wales	14	38	23	17	56
Offshore islands	91	266	400	311	800

Sources: Death registers, Census of England and Wales

Nor was this pattern simply a reflection of a general tendency to migrate overseas from those areas. It is true that London/Middlesex, the southeast and the southwest did send large numbers of people to other countries besides New Zealand – to Australia especially, and to the United States and Canada. But those countries also received large numbers from other areas, especially the Midlands and the north.[27] New Zealand was unusual in attracting such a high proportion of its settlers from these three areas alone. They were unusually 'New Zealand-prone'.

Within these areas, certain counties seem to have been especially likely to send people to New Zealand, as can be seen in Table 7. In the southeast, Kent was the home of a large number of migrants – over 10 per cent of settlers in the 1840s. In the southwest, Cornwall and Devon were very significant. London was always important. However, the extent of clustering in the principal counties diminished somewhat over the nineteenth century. In the 1840s, 62.5 per cent came from counties contributing more than 4 per cent of the whole, but the figure dropped to 49.2 per cent for the 1891–1915 period.

TABLE 7. COUNTIES OF BIRTH OF ENGLISH AND WELSH IMMIGRANTS (PERCENTAGES)

Regions/counties	1840–52	1853–70	1871–90	1891–1915	1916–45
London/Middlesex					
London	14.2	16.1	15.4	17.6	19.6
Middlesex	0.6	1.2	1.3	2.0	1.7
Southeast					
Hampshire	5.2	3.7	3.4	2.0	3.3
Kent	10.7	5.6	6.3	4.6	4.1
Surrey	2.5	1.9	1.9	2.6	2.6
Sussex	3.1	1.6	2.3	2.2	1.9
East					
Cambridgeshire	0.4	0.9	0.6	0.7	0.9
Essex	2.1	2.3	1.4	1.9	2.4
Huntingdonshire		0.1	-	0.1	0.2
Lincolnshire	0.7	1.3	2.6	1.8	1.5
Norfolk	2.8	1.2	1.5	0.7	1.4
Rutlandshire	-	-	-	0.1	0.1
Suffolk	1.0	1.8	0.9	1.0	0.5
Southwest					
Cornwall	6.7	6.0	8.0	3.1	1.5
Devonshire	6.8	3.6	4.2	2.8	1.6
Dorsetshire	1.6	0.9	1.0	0.6	0.5
Somersetshire	4.9	4.2	3.0	2.2	2.1
Wiltshire	2.8	1.2	1.5	1.2	0.6
Midlands East					
Derbyshire	1.5	0.9	1.0	1.3	1.4
Leicestershire	0.4	1.6	0.8	1.4	0.9
Northamptonshire	0.3	1.0	0.9	0.7	0.6
Nottinghamshire	0.9	2.6	0.7	1.2	1.6
Midlands Central					
Staffordshire	1.6	1.8	2.1	1.9	2.1
Warwickshire	4.1	3.5	4.1	3.7	2.9
Midlands West					
Gloucestershire	3.3	2.1	3.6	2.0	1.0
Herefordshire	0.3	1.1	0.5	0.6	0.3
Shropshire	0.4	1.0	0.7	0.7	0.6
Worcestershire	0.9	1.1	1.4	0.7	1.0
Midlands South					
Bedfordshire	0.9	0.7	0.9	0.7	0.1
Berkshire	1.2	0.7	1.4	0.7	0.8

Regions/counties	1840–52	1853–70	1871–90	1891–1915	1916–45
Buckinghamshire	0.6	0.6	0.8	0.4	0.3
Hertfordshire	0.7	0.6	0.2	0.3	0.6
Oxfordshire	1.2	0.9	2.7	0.7	0.5
Yorkshire	5.8	8.5	6.6	11.2	9.4
Lancashire/Cheshire					
Cheshire	1.3	1.4	1.2	2.5	2.0
Lancashire	3.9	7.1	6.1	12.1	14.8
Northeast					
Durham	0.3	1.9	2.4	3.1	4.4
Northumberland	0.9	1.4	1.6	1.9	3.3
Northwest					
Cumberland	1.2	1.7	0.9	1.4	1.2
Westmorland	0.3	0.5	0.3	0.4	0.5
North Wales					
Denbighshire	-	-	0.1	0.3	0.3
Flintshire	-	-	0.2	0.1	0.1
Montgomeryshire	0.1	-	0.1	0.1	0.1
Pembrokeshire	0.3	0.3	-	0.1	-
Radnorshire	0.1	-	0.1	0.1	-
Other north Wales		0.3	0.1	0.3	0.1
South Wales					
Glamorganshire	0.1	0.5	0.2	0.4	1.4
Monmouthshire	0.1	0.3	0.4	0.1	0.8
Other south Wales	0.1	0.3	0.2	0.2	0.2
Offshore islands					
Channel Islands	0.6	1.1	2.2	0.7	0.4
Isle of Man	0.1	0.4	0.3	0.6	0.4
	100.0	100.0	100.0	100.0	100.0
Not stated	25	37	76	73	54
Number	698	1192	1956	1411	1612

Source: Death registers

The second important fact about the regional origins of New Zealand's English settlers is that the pattern changed at the end of the nineteenth century. While London and the Home Counties continued to be significant sources of immigrants, the southwest fell away and there was a distinct rise in the numbers who had been born in the north, especially the manufacturing areas of Lancashire, Yorkshire, and the northwest. Closer analysis of the figures shows that the reduction in numbers from the southeast and southwest and the rise in migrants from the north gathered pace after 1904 as assisted migration was reintroduced. By the interwar period well over a third of New Zealand's

Lily Huggan (née Brown) lived for the first 32 years of her life in Halifax, Yorkshire, where she worked in the textile mills. Then in 1922 she emigrated to Wellington with her parents and brother. Seven months later she married another migrant from the north of England, Joseph Huggan, who had come out after serving in France during the First World War. The couple worked for a time in the Petone woollen mills, then opened a general store in Korokoro. During the Depression they served tea there to the unemployed, and became known as the 'mayor and mayoress of Korokoro'. It was an appropriate title for in the 1950s Joe became mayor of Petone, and after his death Lily succeeded him. 1/2-177292; F, ALEXANDER TURNBULL LIBRARY, MORRIE HILL COLLECTION (PACOLL-4814)

English had been born in the north, whereas among the immigrants of the 1870s the figure was less than one in five.

The major point remains, however, that for most of the nineteenth century, or at least for the 50 years of mass migration from the 1840s to the 1890s, the southwest, the southeast and London were very likely to hold the birthplaces of New Zealand's English settlers. How does one explain this long-lasting pattern of geographical clustering? One obvious explanation is that these areas were close to the ports from which the boats left for New Zealand. As Table 8 shows, throughout the period from 1835 to 1890 over 75 per cent of the ships sailing to New Zealand left from either London or Gravesend, and only in the 1853–1870 period did the proportion of boats leaving from Liverpool reach 3 per cent. It is also interesting to note that Plymouth in the West Country was a significant point of departure, especially in the early years. This would have been where many of the migrants from Cornwall and Devon caught the boat south. People living in the Midlands would find it much easier to travel to Liverpool and board a ship going across the Atlantic than to go all the way to London to catch one of the infrequent and far more expensive vessels to New Zealand. But of course the shipping companies followed demand, and had there been an established tradition of travel from the Midlands to New Zealand the ships would have followed. Further, some of the schemes of assisted migration covered the cost of travel to the port of departure. It should also be noted that the predominance of departures from the south of England did not stop the very large numbers who migrated from Scotland.

TABLE 8. PORTS OF ORIGIN OF SHIPS ARRIVING IN MAJOR NEW ZEALAND PORTS BETWEEN 1835 AND 1890 (PERCENTAGES)[28]

	London	Gravesend	Plymouth	Liverpool	Glasgow	Greenock	Other	No.
1835–52	48.4	33.9	10.3	1.3	3.2	1.9	1.0	310
1853–70	41.4	33.5	3.1	3.1	7.6	4.0	7.3	708
1871–90	52.8	24.3	7.4	1.5	6.7	5.4	1.9	1064

Source: http://freepages.genealogy.rootsweb.com/~shipstonz/ships_uk&i.html

Another explanation for the consistent geographical origin of New Zealand's English is that it reflects the areas where recruiting agents were based or concentrated their energies. There is considerable truth in this. There is a very close correlation between the geographical origins of migrants assisted by the New Zealand Company and the location of the company's recruiting agents. Of 74 agents of the company who operated in England, 52 worked in southern England (south of a line from The Wash to Bristol Channel). The level of applications from particular counties reflected in part the number of agents. Hampshire, for example, had eight agents in a population of 355,000, while the West Riding of Yorkshire had four agents working a population of 1,154,000. Not surprisingly, Hampshire's rate of application was over twice that of the West Riding.

This generalisation is true not only at a county level, but even at the level of towns and small rural areas. One of the Hampshire agents was based at Alton. That town supplied 35 per cent of Hampshire's applications, while adjacent districts such as Basingstoke and Alresford supplied very few. In Somerset there were agents at Chard and Langport, and a high proportion of the county applications to the company came from towns in that vicinity.

It seems likely that once patterns of migration from certain areas had been established by the New Zealand Company and its agents a system of chain migration took over, perpetuating the likelihood that these areas would continue to send their sons and daughters to New Zealand. In other words, the network of personal connections, letters back home, and the desire to bring out relatives meant that once one group of migrants from a particular area had settled in New Zealand others were likely to follow. There is no doubt that these personal linkages were crucial in attracting many migrants to New Zealand. Even at the time when applications were being made to the New Zealand Company it is clear that neighbours encouraged neighbours. In May 1841 the Hall family applied to the New Zealand Company from 4 Lyncombe Terrace, Bath, Somerset, and soon after the Mason family from 8 Lyncombe Terrace applied. In July the Vaughans of 25 St James Parade were accepted as emigrants by the company, and the same month their neighbours at no. 27, the Waters family, applied.[29] Once they arrived in New Zealand such migrants would write home and persuade other neighbours to come.

Family networks were even more important in perpetuating patterns of geographical clustering. Let us take the Jackson family, for example. Henry Humphrey Jackson was a Derbyshire farm labourer whose father had a cottage and garden and a mere 3 acres of land. He came out to Wellington on the New Zealand Company ship *Cuba*, and worked as a surveyor for the company. When at the end of the 1840s the company once more advertised passages for farm servants, Henry wrote to his two brothers, George and Sam, and applied on their behalf with a guarantee of their part of the fare. George came out, but Sam changed his mind. Then in the 1850s Wellington province set up a scheme of assistance. Once more Henry encouraged Sam to migrate. By now married, Sam agreed, and a friend of Henry's put up his part of the fare. Even then Henry did not stop acting as an informal recruiting agent, for in 1872, 33 years after he had left home, he was trying to persuade his sister to emigrate.[30]

In this way patterns initially established by the recruitment drives of the New Zealand Company were reinforced by the actions of contented settlers taking advantage of later assistance schemes to cajole or persuade their friends, neighbours, siblings or parents to join them in New Zealand. There can be little doubt that the system of nomination that allowed people to suggest and pay for the migration of other family members served to strengthen regional concentrations.

So New Zealand Company recruitment echoed down subsequent years. Patterns were also reinforced by the practice of recruiting agents going back to old and established stamping grounds. The New Zealand government's agents of the 1870s went to areas first exploited by the New Zealand Company. But they also established new traditions. For example the south Midlands, especially the area around Oxfordshire, was not a particularly happy hunting ground for company agents. But in the 1870s as agricultural unionism affected the area and the New Zealand government developed a good relationship with the union, Oxford became a significant source of assisted passengers. This is reflected in the rise to 6 per cent for the south Midlands among the migrants of the 1870s, as shown in Table 5.

The striking fact remains that certain places in southern England developed long traditions of sending people out to New Zealand. Take Helston in Cornwall, which suffered from overcrowding and the downturn of the tin-mining industry. As Raewyn Dalziel has shown, those who came out with the Plymouth Company to New Plymouth in 1840–43 came from particular townships in the area, of which Helston was one. Eleven families, five of whom were neighbours in one street, migrated with the company.[31] One of those who migrated was 21-year-old seamstress Caroline Julian. With her came her father, an agricultural labourer, her mother, her sister, who was married to a miner, their

Bob Fitzsimmons, heavyweight boxing champion of the world, is remembered through the name of a pub in his home-town of Helston and a statue in his adopted town of Timaru. Here he is photographed, not as a boxer, but as a blacksmith, the trade he learned from his father in Timaru. PRIVATE COLLECTION

three children, another sister as a domestic servant, three brothers who came out as a labourer, a blacksmith and a mason respectively, and three younger siblings – a grand total of fifteen people.[32]

Things did not improve in Helston, and in 1863, taking advantage of Canterbury's assisted passages, ten members of Henry and Grace Penberthy's family came out, as we have already seen in chapter 2. They were probably attracted by the presence of a friend and relative by marriage who was the preacher in the Wesleyan chapel in Christchurch. Nor did the flow from Helston stop then. Bob Fitzsimmons, the 'freckled wonder' who became heavyweight boxing champion of the world, came out from Helston to Timaru with his mother and policeman father in 1873. Today the many cabbage trees and flaxes in Helston may be an accidental echo of the town's New Zealand links, but the presence of 'kia ora' on two doorways is perhaps less coincidental.

While New Zealand Company recruitment undoubtedly had a long and influential echo, this is only part of the story. For a start, the presence of agents did not always guarantee a flow of migrants. The company was well represented in Suffolk and Norfolk, but that area never became a major source of New Zealand immigrants – except among soldiers, who were brought to the country against their will. In the hunt for other explanations let us examine the regional breakdown of particular immigrant flows.

TABLE 9. REGIONS OF BIRTH OF ENGLISH AND WELSH IMMIGRANTS BY PARTICULAR FLOWS (PERCENTAGES)

Born in	Akld 1840–52	NZ Coy	Soldiers 1840s	Soldiers 1860s	Akld 1853–70	Canty assisted	Otago miners	West Coast miners	1871–88 assisted
London/ Middlesex	20.1	14.8	6.1	8.8	18.5	14.0	7.8	12.1	10.5
Southeast	17.2	20.8	18.3	11.8	11.6	12.3	8.5	8.9	16.5
East	7.4	3.3	17.0	18.5	7.9	9.2	6.6	10.3	10.5
Southwest	21.8	16.4	20.0	15.8	16.8	16.9	36.8	26.8	20.7
Midlands									
East	2.1	4.8	3.5	2.0	6.0	8.2	2.0	1.3	3.1
Central	3.6	8.9	4.3	4.4	7.6	4.9	1.8	1.3	6.7
West	4.3	4.7	7.8	5.0	4.8	7.7	2.3	1.3	8.3
South	4.5	4.0	5.7	5.0	2.8	6.6	2.0	0.9	7.4
Yorkshire	6.7	5.6	9.1	9.3	9.5	8.4	6.4	6.3	4.6
Lancs– Cheshire	8.6	3.4	7.0	14.9	8.1	3.2	9.4	11.2	3.9
Northeast	1.7	1.5	0.9	1.4	2.4	3.7	6.6	5.4	2.7
Northwest	0.5	0.8	0.0	1.3	1.4	2.0	3.9	3.1	0.8
Offshore islands	1.2	0.0	0.0	0.7	2.0	0.5	3.9	4.0	2.3
North Wales	0.0	0.0	0.0	0.7	0.3	1.3	1.2	4.0	1.1
South Wales	0.2	0.0	0.4	0.3	0.3	1.1	0.9	3.1	0.8
Not stated	133			3	104				
Number	550	5912	230	688	1495	3093	438	224	6128

Sources: Death registers, Register of Emigrant Labourers, passenger lists

Table 9 shows the regions of birth of the English and Welsh migrants who came to New Zealand in each wave of immigration. As we would expect, a relatively high proportion (52 per cent) of New Zealand Company immigrants came from the southwest, the southeast and London. However, in the years 1840–52 almost 60 per cent of Auckland's immigrants, a higher proportion than the company immigrants, were also derived from these three key areas. These were not people who were recruited, but migrants who paid their own way. So the organised recruitment of the New Zealand Company cannot be the only explanation for the clustered origins of New Zealand's immigrants.

The flow from these areas into Auckland remained strong in the 1850s and 1860s, and similar proportions can be seen in the Canterbury flow in the same years. Since quite a number of Auckland's early settlers came across the Tasman, the pattern is partly the result of the nature of migration to Australia. Paying passengers who went to Australia are hard to track down, but the evidence of those who were assisted to Victoria, New South Wales and South Australia in the 1840s and 1850s shows that the two most important recruitment areas were the southwest and London/Middlesex, two areas that were even better represented among Auckland's immigrants than among the New Zealand Company people.[33]

Several other points about the regional origins of particular flows show up. The considerable numbers from the north who arrived in Auckland in the 1850s and 1860s reflect the 3000 Albertland settlers, many of whom were from Yorkshire. But this influx from the north was temporary. Lancashire and Yorkshire, major centres of the English population, remained poorly represented among New Zealand's assisted migrants, especially those of the 1870s, until new schemes emerged in the twentieth century.

A second obvious point is that there are distinct patterns for the military immigrants and the miners. The discharged soldiers included comparatively few who had been born in London and Middlesex, but relatively large numbers from eastern counties and from Lancashire and Cheshire. This simply reflected the origins of the regiments that came to New Zealand. Walter Tricker was one soldier from the eastern county of Suffolk who settled in New Zealand. He served with the 65th Regiment from 1846 until he purchased his discharge in 1849. He became a farmer near Bulls and would have disappeared into contented anonymity except for the fact that he was condemned to death in 1864 for allegedly killing his neighbour. Tricker became the nineteenth-century equivalent of Arthur Allan Thomas. His supporters in the local community rallied to a remarkable extent and he was released from prison after six years, and ultimately pardoned.[34]

As for the miners, the pattern largely followed the location of mining traditions in Britain itself, with remarkably strong representation from the tin and copper miners of the southwest (almost 37 per cent of Otago's miners came from that area) and the coal miners of the northeast and north Wales. Indeed, the miners of the West Coast were the only migrant group with a representation from Wales that was equivalent to the numbers at home. The Channel Islands and the Isle of Man were also hugely over-represented. In contrast, the miners included comparatively small numbers from the agricultural regions of the southeast. A very large number of the miners came to New Zealand from the Victorian goldfields, and the fact that many had migrated there from the southwest and Wales partly explains the high numbers from those areas.[35]

The case of the miners suggests that occupation may have been a significant determinant of migration from England to New Zealand. Using information taken from the death registers, Table 10 shows the background of immigrants aged 20 and over (including those from Scotland and Ireland), based on the occupation of the father.

One might perhaps be sceptical that a father's occupation can tell us very much at all, particularly from a twentieth- and twenty-first-century perspective, since many people move a long way from the kind of job their father did. This is most obviously true of women. Yet among the migrants of the nineteenth century were many who came from traditional societies where sons did inherit their father's job. It is revealing, furthermore, that the distribution of the occupations of fathers of immigrants was very similar to the pattern revealed by the occupations of the adult male immigrants themselves (e.g., as declared by assisted immigrants). Father's occupation therefore gives us some idea of the class background from which New Zealand's immigrants came.

There are, however, other issues in using father's occupation. The death certificate would show the occupation as recalled by a spouse, child or friend, and was thus not likely to be very reliable. In addition, the information was not provided at all in a large number of cases. We have only included those aged 20 or over, to eliminate migrants who came out as children (usually with their parents) and whose fathers' occupations as stated on the death certificate were more likely to be those in New Zealand rather than in the old country. We have grouped the multitude of fathers' occupations cited in the death registers according to seven major categories: those who worked on the land as farmers or agricultural labourers; labourers; servants; people employed in traditional crafts that had not yet been brought into industrialised or factory modes of production (and which we have called 'pre-industrial'); those who worked in the 'new' occupations created by economic and technological change, especially in factories; gentlemen and white-collar workers; and finally a group of other occupations that includes two of some importance to New Zealand migration – seamen and soldiers.[36]

TABLE 10. OCCUPATIONAL BACKGROUNDS (FATHER'S OCCUPATION) OF ALL IMMIGRANTS FROM THE UK AGED 20 AND OVER (PERCENTAGES)

Occupations	Pre-1840	1840–52	1853–70	1871–90	1891–1915	1916–45	GB census 1851
Agriculture							
Farmers	21.1	28.4	34.1	29.2	19.0	12.4	6.5
Agricultural labourers	2.6	4.6	5.0	5.4	5.3	5.3	20.4
Total agriculture	23.7	33.0	39.1	34.7	24.4	17.6	27.3
Labourers	6.6	7.5	5.9	10.2	5.7	5.8	6.9
Servants	0.0	0.9	0.2	0.1	0.4	0.3	9.3
Pre-industrial occupations							
Building	6.6	6.8	7.4	8.3	10.1	9.6	7.4
Mining	0.0	1.5	2.6	3.4	4.8	7.4	5.2
Transport (traditional)	0.0	1.8	1.1	1.6	1.9	2.5	
Other pre-industrial	23.7	16.9	19.2	17.3	21.8	19.6	17.6
Total pre-industrial	30.3	27.0	30.4	30.5	38.6	39.0	30.2
Industrial	11.8	6.8	5.1	6.6	11.0	15.4	16.0
White collar	19.7	19.6	13.0	11.2	14.3	14.1	10.5
Other occupations							
Soldiers	0.0	2.0	1.4	1.4	0.9	1.9	
Seamen	7.9	2.2	3.8	4.0	3.5	3.7	
Others	0.0	1.1	1.3	1.2	1.2	2.1	
	100.0	100.0	100.0	100.0	100.0	100.0	
Not stated	44	149	360	427	216	229	
Number	120	604	1691	2157	1702	2095	

Source: Death registers

William Shilling, from Faversham in Kent, was one of a considerable number of men who migrated to New Zealand by jumping ship. Shilling did so in 1869 when he deserted the *St Vincent* in Wellington. It was a fortunate decision since the ship was wrecked soon after in Palliser Bay. Here Shilling poses with a Maori family at Karaka Bay on Wellington Harbour, where he became a long-serving pilot. 1/1-020634-G; ALEXANDER TURNBULL LIBRARY

Despite the caveats, the figures suggest several significant factors. In the migration in the years up to 1890, well over a third of the migrants had fathers who had worked on the land, and if we add those whose fathers were described as 'labourers' (who were most likely to be farm labourers) then about two in every five were from an agricultural background. This is important when thinking about the assumptions and desires of those migrants. Coming from a rural background they may well have had landowning aspirations. But it is equally important not to exaggerate the rural origins of Pakeha New Zealanders. Because of the declared preference for farm labourers in many of the schemes of immigration assistance, and because of the rural mythology that has affected so much of New Zealand's understanding of its own past, it is perhaps easy to think of all migrants as farm workers. However, the migrants were not disproportionately from an agricultural background.

Comparing the proportions of those from an agricultural background with the 1851 census of England and Scotland (and noting that these figures exclude Ireland, which was highly agricultural), the proportion of immigrants with a farming background was only slightly higher than in England and Scotland as a whole. In addition, since it is the occupations of fathers we are examining, and one might therefore, strictly speaking, look at the breakdown about a generation earlier, in fact New Zealand's immigrants were slightly less bucolic than might have been expected. Further, from the turn of the century the numbers dropped strongly, so that during the period between the wars no more than one in five came off the farm. Children of rural workers were important among New Zealand's pioneers, but never overwhelmingly so.

On the other hand, throughout this period there were remarkably few people whose fathers had been in the industrial workforce. Right through until the First World War, fewer than one in ten of New Zealand's UK settlers came from this background. New Zealand was not settled by refugees from the smoke stacks and grime of industry. There were, it is true, some migrants whose family members had been attracted into mills from surrounding rural areas, especially in places where factories were established in the country to be close to water-power or coal. Hannah Hadfield's was one such family. Hannah was the daughter of a shoemaker in Glossop, Derbyshire. This is a place of rare rural beauty, but by the 1850s Glossop had 40 cotton mills, and at the age of ten Hannah went to work as a power-loom weaver in one of the mills. The American Civil War disrupted cotton supplies, so in 1865 the Hadfields set off for Christchurch on a Canterbury provincial assistance scheme. They had been sponsored by friends in the colony. Hannah eventually married a rather more typical migrant, Albert Dunstall, a carpenter and son of a farmer of six acres from East Sussex who came out in 1870.[37]

New Zealand was comparatively attractive for those with a white-collar background. In absolute terms the numbers were not great

Walter Mantell was one of quite a number of immigrants in the early years of settlement whose fathers were very respectable white-collar workers. Walter's father Gideon Mantell was a doctor and well-known palaeontologist who hoped that his son would follow his profession. Instead, in 1839, at the age of nineteen, Walter came out with the New Zealand Company to Wellington. He worked as a farmer, clerk, postmaster and overseer of military roads before achieving fame, first as the Crown purchaser of South Island Maori lands, then as a natural history collector for British scientists, especially Richard Owen at the British Museum. 35MM-00129-E; F, ALEXANDER TURNBULL LIBRARY, GENERAL ASSEMBLY LIBRARY COLLECTION (PACOLL-0838), PHOTOGRAPH BY WILLIAM HENSHAW CLARKE

– perhaps one in eight of our nineteenth-century settlers – but this was significantly larger than their numbers at home. These were the troubled middle classes – the children of clerks and professionals who saw new opportunities in the New World. They were particularly attracted to New Zealand in the 1840s, when the propaganda of the New Zealand Company appeared to offer them new opportunities for leadership in a new society.

One who achieved fame was Thomas Brunner. In 1841 Brunner's lawyer father signed him on with the company as an apprentice surveyor. He went to Nelson to lay out sections and roads, but became captured by the hopes of a great interior plain, so desperately needed by Nelson to fulfil its promises to investors and immigrants alike. He

William Brassington, whose father was a stonemason in Nottingham, was himself apprenticed to a mason, and when he migrated to Canterbury in 1863 he quickly set up a yard just south of the Anglican part of the Barbadoes Street cemetery. However, the architect Benjamin Mountfort spotted his talent and invited him to work carving stonework on the provincial council chamber. He later worked on a number of Canterbury's stone buildings, including Canterbury Museum. 10540, CANTERBURY MUSEUM, WILLIAMS COLLECTION

set out to see if it existed. On one journey he was accompanied by two men of similar background – Charles Heaphy, the son of a successful professional watercolourist, and William Fox, son of a rich Durham justice of the peace. On his greatest journey, the longest feat of exploration in New Zealand's European history, Brunner's companions were Maori guides who took him down the west coast and back, a journey that took 550 days. He did not hear a word of English, but with the help of his guides he learned to walk barefoot and eat fern root. At one moment of near-starvation he even ate his faithful dog. It was a long way from the respectable Oxfordshire life of his father.[38]

There were large numbers of people from the category we have called 'pre-industrial'. Until the turn of the twentieth century there were only marginally fewer from this background than from a strictly agricultural background. Who were these people, who were so numerous among the settlers? Very few had a mining background. Rather more came from families that included builders. If they were men who had inherited their father's occupation (which was quite likely), then as builders they were consistently attractive to immigration recruiters. There was always building to be done in a new society, and a number of the schemes of assistance specifically invited applications for builders or carpenters.

A greater number of the emigrants' fathers had worked in pre-industrial crafts – as bakers, blacksmiths, shoemakers, butchers, wheelwrights, sawyers, tanners, coopers and millers. These were craft workers, not yet faced with industrial modes of production. If we add in people involved in traditional transport industries, like carters, then almost one in five of New Zealand's nineteenth-century UK immigrants was born into this pre-industrial world.

It is not entirely clear from our sources where exactly these people lived. In a reaction against the old view that New Zealand's immigrants were overwhelmingly rural, some recent historians have suggested that they were more likely to be from cities.[39] This is at least in part based on Dudley Baines' classification of certain of England's counties as 'urban' on the basis of census figures. But the fact that many immigrants came from counties which included cities does not mean that the immigrants themselves were living in cities. Indeed, apart from Gloucestershire (38.5 per cent), none of the English counties that were significantly over-represented (i.e., by at least 1.5 times) among New Zealand migrants in the 1870s had more than 30 per cent of their population living in urban areas with a population of 20,000 or more. In other words, at least 70 per cent were living in villages or small towns.[40]

When we look at the pre-industrial crafts that are cited as father's occupation in the death registers, some could clearly be pursued within an urban setting – builders, shoemakers, jewellers – while others that were well represented – sawyers, coopers and wheelwrights – were much more likely to be based in a rural setting. Such people depended very much on the agricultural community around them. They may well have had small plots of land themselves. Many would have been part of the village community. They had a simple commercial relationship

86

with the rural hinterland, either providing products such as wheels for the community or processing the products of farms as millers or bakers. It was children from these families, as well as those from a strictly agricultural background, who gave a rural cast to many of New Zealand's immigrant stock.

Interestingly, there are striking contrasts when we compare statistics on the declared occupations of all adult males leaving the United Kingdom with those who were departing for Australasia in the years 1871–76 (years of great migration to New Zealand). Whereas only 9.8 per cent of all emigrants were involved in agriculture, the figure for those leaving for Australia or New Zealand was 32.3 per cent; and while 11.4 per cent of all emigrants were involved in pre-industrial crafts, those heading to Australasia included 19.7 per cent craft-workers. On the other side, industrial workers comprised 12.4 per cent of those leaving the United Kingdom, but only 3.3 per cent of those heading to this part of the world.[41] In other words, New Zealand (and Australian) immigrants were clearly of a more rural character. Of course they were not all rural or small-town people. Obviously those who were born in London (which ranged from about 8 per cent of the English in the case of the Otago miners up to about 20 per cent of those coming into Auckland) arrived with urban experience, as did the substantial numbers coming from Glasgow and, to a lesser extent, Edinburgh.

Finally, it is worth remarking on the surprising number of immigrants whose fathers had been seamen (over 3 per cent). A number of these came from the maritime islands of Scotland. Others may well have followed their fathers and become seamen themselves, and then on a voyage to New Zealand jumped ship.

With this overview in mind, let us look more closely at fathers' occupations among immigrants from England. Table 11 shows the distribution of occupational background in the various immigrant streams, with the occupations of the Great Britain population in 1851 as a comparison (once again, since this excludes Ireland, it underestimates the number of agricultural workers in the UK male workforce). Table 12 shows the declared occupations of the immigrants themselves in the various streams of assisted migrants, so it excludes those who paid their own way.

TABLE 11. OCCUPATIONAL BACKGROUND (FATHER'S OCCUPATION) OF ENGLISH AND WELSH IMMIGRANTS AGED 20 AND OVER (PERCENTAGES)[42]

	Pre-1840	1840–52	Akld 1840–52	1853–70	Akld 1853–70	Otago miners	West Coast miners	1871–90	1891–1915	1916–45	GB census 1851
Agriculture	13.0	28.5	22.6	24.4	25.1	24.3	26.4	26.1	17.7	12.5	27.3
Labourers	7.4	10.0	8.0	6.7	3.1	6.5	5.7	11.8	5.9	5.8	6.9
Builders	5.6	6.9	8.7	8.6	8.5	9.1	6.4	10.4	11.5	9.9	7.4
Miners	0.0	2.4	2.1	3.9	2.2	4.5	17.1	4.7	4.0	6.7	5.2
Total pre-industrial	33.3	30.6	33.8	39.5	36.8	39.7	47.9	36.0	43.5	41.7	30.2
Total industrial	16.7	4.1	5.2	6.7	8.7	4.6	4.3	7.6	11.5	16.0	16.0
White collar	20.4	21.3	19.5	15.8	18.4	17.2	10.0	13.0	15.8	16.9	10.5
Other	9.3	5.5	10.7	6.9	8.1	7.6	6.5	5.5	5.7	7.1	9.1
Not stated	31	89	120	181	242	167	156	220	152	162	
Number	85	380	407	776	1143	796	296	1199	1121	1325	

Source: Death registers

TABLE 12. DECLARED OCCUPATIONS OF ENGLISH AND WELSH MALE IMMIGRANTS (PERCENTAGES)

Occupations	NZ Company	Canterbury assisted	NZ assisted 1871–88
Agriculture	36.1	45.9	34.5
Labourers	13.1	18.2	22.4
Builders	18.9	13.1	15.7
Miners	3.3	0.8	3.2
Total pre-industrial	43.0	28.7	34.3
Industrial	3.5	2.2	3.6
White collar	1.1	2.0	0.5
Other	3.2	3.0	4.6
Not stated	0	18	9
Number	1761	871	1863

Sources: Register of Emigrant Labourers, passenger lists

People with a background in agriculture were important among the English, but not overwhelmingly so, and their numbers dropped fast from the turn of the century. The representation of people with farming origins closely followed the number of people involved with agriculture in the English workforce as a whole. The only immigrant flows with an exceptionally high proportion of people who seem to have been involved in agriculture were those who came as assisted immigrants with the New Zealand Company, Canterbury province or the New Zealand government. Because these figures are based on the migrants' declared occupations, rather than their fathers', the high numbers may partly reflect the preference of the immigration agents for agricultural labourers. In almost every scheme of assistance the publicised male occupations for a free or assisted passage were agricultural labourers, gardeners or shepherds. This may have encouraged individuals applying for such passages to falsify their occupations. It may also reflect the success of the recruiters in attracting those whom they most wanted. The vast majority of these people were neither landowners nor even farmers with tenanted holdings. They were predominantly the third tier in the English agricultural social structure – labourers who were either hired for a period ranging from a day to a season, or lived in tied cottages attached to a farm. Occasionally they might have a couple of acres of freehold, and traditionally they had used common land to hunt for rabbits or gather firewood, but their major source of support was labouring in the fields for wages.

The very low numbers of people with an industrial background is again notable, especially among those who were given assistance, and there was a comparatively high number of English migrants whose fathers were white-collar workers – although as one might expect there were few professionals among the assisted. Most offspring of white-collar workers could afford to come out in cabin class, paying their own way. Finally, there was an even greater representation among the English from those with a pre-industrial background. Over a third of New Zealand's immigrant settlers from England up to 1945 came from this background. Among these people, those with builders as fathers were consistently well-represented, miners much less so – except, as might be expected, among those who came in to the Otago or Westland goldfields. And the numbers of people with craft origins were high among both the assisted immigrants and those who paid their own way.

The builders included several who made distinguished contributions to the colony, such as Charles Carter. He was born up north in Westmorland and trained as a carpenter, but suffered unemployment after moving to London. The experience led him to become a strong advocate for migration to New Zealand. He took the step himself in 1850, and quickly became a successful builder in Wellington and Wairarapa. He served for a time in England as an emigration agent for the Wellington province, then for the New Zealand government at the beginning of Vogel's immigration drive. His record of public service is commemorated in the names of the town of Carterton in Wairarapa and the Carter Observatory in Wellington.[43]

Why were people with an agricultural or pre-industrial craft background so important among England's emigrants to New Zealand? Until the 1890s the two groups comprised about two-thirds of all English immigrants. One reason, as we have noted, was the obvious preferences of the New Zealand government and its agents, who deliberately targeted these people. A second factor, in the 1870s, was the interaction between the so-called 'Revolt of the Field', an uprising of agricultural unions, and the New Zealand offer of free passages. Rollo Arnold has documented the way the New Zealand emigration agents cultivated relationships with rural union leaders, who in turn began to encourage migration to New Zealand as their attempts to raise wages at home faltered.[44]

One person who was crucial in this process was Arthur Clayden, a Berkshire journalist who was involved as an immigration agent for the New Zealand government as early as 1872. He began to work with the National Agricultural Labourers' Union, and as a New Zealand migration agent in Berkshire he reportedly sent about 500 people to the colony. His brother came out in 1877 and Arthur quickly followed. He returned to England in 1879 and published the first of four books advocating emigration to New Zealand, especially for the rural labouring classes. Clayden was convinced that for such people New Zealand was superior to the other colonies on offer. After periods in New Zealand, the loneliness of colonial life finally sent him back to England nine years before his death.[45]

The migration to New Zealand of Clayden's rural labourers was part of a wider 'flight from the land' during the nineteenth century. There were complex causes behind the rural depopulation: the decline of rural cottage industries as many of the processes moved into city factories; a reduction in the use of live-in farm servants (especially in the arable south), which encouraged young people to move to the towns or to emigrate, and the growth of task or piecework and, as a result, recurrent winter unemployment.[46] As the composition of the agricultural workforce changed, so the numbers employed contracted. The number

An important source of English migrants to New Zealand in the 1870s was Kent, where the 'Revolt of the Field' movement of rural labourers' unions was strong. This photo shows The White Horse Inn at Chilham in Kent, where a large group of English were farewelled before sailing to New Zealand in 1879. JOCK PHILLIPS PHOTO

of day labourers (who included shepherds, ploughmen, carters, those in charge of cattle, as well as the general or 'ordinary' labourer mainly engaged in field work) reached its zenith in 1851, then declined markedly. The total number of people employed in agriculture declined by 21.1 per cent between 1861 and 1870, followed by reductions of 16.0 per cent and 8.4 per cent in the succeeding decades.[47] Those who remained in the country found that their options for supplementing their livelihood were being closed up – common lands, for example, were enclosed, reducing the hunting or grazing of pigs. Thus, behind the readiness of England's agricultural labourers to emigrate to New Zealand lay complex changes affecting the availability, continuity and

Ernest and Hannah Hayes in about 1914. Ernest Hayes, the son of a Warwickshire mole-catcher, was apprenticed as a millwright. In 1882 he and his wife Hannah migrated to Dunedin and settled in Central Otago, where he worked for his uncle in a flour-mill. Ernest developed a farm, and to help in his work he began to invent tools, which eventually led on to the establishment of a serious engineering workshop. Among his inventions were the parallel wire-strainer for farm fences and the farm windmill, which was widely used in rural New Zealand. PRIVATE COLLECTION

stability of agricultural employment, especially in the southern counties where the colony found the greatest response to its offers of free passages.

George Smith was a typical example of New Zealand's emigrant agricultural labourers. He was a farm labourer in the Wychwood area of Oxfordshire. There the wages were not high and there was surplus labour. The large forest, a source of wood and game, had recently been cleared. A union was established. When Charles Carter visited in 1872 labourers came out of the fields to meet him. George Smith was one of the ten married men selected for assisted passages, and he sailed with his wife and three children in September that year. The following year George wrote a letter home that was printed in the *Labourers Union*

Chronicle. It spoke in ecstatic terms of this 'sunny land' where there was plenty of work and you could 'get a leg of mutton for sixpence'. His letter helped spark a flood of migration from the area that only halted when seventeen locals lost their lives in the *Cospatrick* fire en route to New Zealand.[48]

As rural depopulation and agricultural depression hit, traditional craft-workers suffered.[49] Those engaged in rural industry found employment opportunities contracting markedly. Rural outwork in the textile industries was reduced as some trades disappeared and others were centralised into large urban mills. Linen manufacture moved to Ireland and Scotland, while straw-plaiting, hosiery and glove-making declined in the face of changing fashions, cheaper imports, and the sewing machine. Small boot- and shoe-manufacturers saw their nearby markets disappear as the population left, while the growing use of imported raw materials encouraged the establishment of large shoe factories in the ports. As rural crafts and trades disappeared this hurt carpenters (including 'hedge carpenters' who serviced farmers' needs), masons, painters, glaziers and plumbers, all of whom featured among those who arrived in New Zealand as assisted immigrants.[50] Employment in blacksmithing and wheelwrighting declined as iron wheels began to be made in factories, millwrights faced rapid technical changes in grain-milling, machine coopering was introduced, fence- and hurdle-makers suffered from imported fencing materials, and the number of sawyers declined rapidly as softwood timbers were imported.

Rural tradesmen and craftsmen therefore responded readily to the offer of free passages to New Zealand, where their skills seemed to be in keen demand in a period of apparently rapid economic growth and development. One who came was William Pike, a wheelwright in Shepherd's Green in Oxfordshire, who emigrated to Christchurch with his wife and four children in 1873. Ten-year-old Ada would later, as Ada Wells, achieve eminence as a great organiser and campaigner for women's suffrage.[51] People like William from a pre-industrial small-town or village world were hugely important among the English immigrants to New Zealand, at least until 1914.

Nor should we forget that the loss of rural work on farms or in crafts hurt women as well as men. Reduced farm incomes lessened the opportunities for young women to obtain work locally as domestic servants, while the loss of crafts like glove-making deprived women of supplementary income. To obtain work young women were often faced with the option of moving to the cities, which could be an uncertain and frightening prospect. When agents came offering free or assisted passages to New Zealand the dangers must have seemed no greater and the possibilities more attractive, especially if brothers or cousins had already headed south.

One other set of statistics that is worth examining before drawing some wider conclusions is that relating to religion. Table 13 shows the religious background of immigrants from England and Wales between 1840 and 1915.

TABLE 13. RELIGIOUS DENOMINATION AT DEATH OF IMMIGRANTS FROM ENGLAND AND WALES (PERCENTAGES)

Denomination	1840–52	1853–70	1871–90	1891–1915	1851 UK census of church 'attendees'[52]	1871 NZ census
Church of England	66.3	61.4	59.5	59.1	49.8	41.8
Presbyterian	7.8	11.6	5.9	11.3	0.1	24.8
Methodist	17.9	17.1	21.8	15.4	15.3	8.5
Other Protestant	3.2	6.5	9.6	9.0	11.2	4.5
Roman Catholic	4.4	3.0	3.2	5.1	3.4	13.9
Jewish	0.5	0.5	0.1	0.2	-	0.5
Not stated	107	155	254	443		
Number	698	1037	1856	1411		

Source: Death registers

Given that they are derived from the denomination of the person who officiated at the funeral or who completed the death certificate, the figures are rough, but they are still suggestive of some trends. They tell us that, compared with their position in England as a whole, non-Conformists, especially Methodists, were very well represented in New Zealand.[53] The Methodist movement, started in the eighteenth century by John Wesley, was a class revolt against the established rural order of Anglican squire and clergy. With lay preachers and open-air services it was a classic religious revival, appealing to those who were less privi-leged in English society. It attracted strong adherence in certain areas, such as the north of England and the far southwest, and it promoted a moral code of hard work and piety. Of course the non-Conformists were a minority of the English, but they were an important minority,

Temple White was the son of the Laceby grocer and emigration agent, John White, who used his Methodist connections to induce many people to come out to New Zealand. John White came out to New Plymouth himself in 1893, bringing Temple, then aged eleven. Subsequently Temple White became the organist and choirmaster at the Wesleyan Methodist Church in Wellington, a position he held for 46 years, during which time he played a leading role in the choral activities of the capital. PACOLL-6388-37, ALEXANDER TURNBULL LIBRARY

and their powerful presence added a distinctive reformist flavour to New Zealand public life.

Behind the broad statistics there lay many particular immigrant flows. The number of Methodists, for example, was affected in the 1860s by the Albertland settlement which drew upon the non-Conformists of the Midlands and Yorkshire. Lincolnshire was a significant Methodist recruiting ground. In 1859 Thomas Ball, a Methodist bookseller in Brigg, led a party of 80 local Wesleyans to Mangonui, where they took up land grants offered by the Auckland province.[54] Between 1874 and 1879 the local agent in Laceby, John H. White, who was also, like many agents, the village grocer, recruited some 2000 largely Methodist migrants. To attract people he drew on his connections with the Methodist chapel and the local temperance society.[55]

The figures also point up the strong Anglicanism of New Zealand's settlers from England in the 1840s. By being so well-represented in these years, they were able to establish Anglican institutions firmly at the start of settlement.

Until the turn of the twentieth century, then, strong continuities defined English immigration to New Zealand. One was the continuing strength of the flow from the southwest and Cornwall in particular. New Zealand Company recruiters had targeted the area and traditions of migration were quickly established, aided by the importance of Plymouth as a port of departure. The Plymouth Company, which sent over a thousand settlers to New Plymouth in 1840–43, as Raewyn Dalziel has described, was based there until it was taken over by the New Zealand Company.[56] Cornwall was an area of massive out-migration in the nineteenth century. It had by far the highest rate of emigration of any English county in the last four decades of the century,[57] and New Zealand was always one of the chosen destinations. More than 6 per cent of New Zealand's English migrants from 1840 to 1870 came from Cornwall, as did some 8 per cent of those in the 1870s and 1880s, and up to 10 per cent of the assisted migrants of that period.

Cornwall was inhabited by people with a Celtic background and in the nineteenth century they were still, in the far west, speaking the distinctive Cornish language. The area had long been known for its mining, and in the late eighteenth and early nineteenth centuries it was one of the first areas exposed to the effects of the industrial revolution, as new technology and demand led to the expansion first of tin- and then of copper-mining. When new supplies of tin, and then copper, began to be exploited overseas, in Malaya and Australia, the Cornish industry suffered from instability and lowering prices. The number of migrants to New Zealand from Cornwall who had a mining background began to rise: in the 1840–52 period about 20 per cent of those of Cornish origin in our sample had fathers described as miners, but then Cornish people with a mining background flooded into the goldfields. Some 30 per cent of Otago's English miners and over 20 per cent of those on the West Coast originated in Cornwall. Many had gone out to the copper mines of South Australia in the 1850s, then moved on to the goldfields of Victoria before crossing the Tasman to the new rushes in the South Island.[58]

John Lawn was a typical example of these trans-Tasman Cornish miners. With his two brothers he had fled the declining Cornish mines in 1857 for the Victorian goldfields. Hearing about the strike in Otago the three bought mining gear and a handcart, and headed for Gabriel's Gully. Within a day they had found 14 ounces of gold. Such success did not keep them here, however. John and his brothers moved back and forth across the Tasman – to the Victorian fields, to Hokitika, to the copper mines of South Australia – before John finally settled at Reefton.[59]

Other miners came direct from Cornwall in the 1860s, when about 50,000 miners left the county for overseas destinations. A number of the Cornish miners on the West Coast had originally come out to Canterbury on assisted passages to work on the Lyttelton–Christchurch railway tunnel. When this was completed in 1867 they crossed over the Southern Alps to the goldmines. And they continued to come – even in the 1870s and 1880s, 8 per cent of the English immigrants to New Zealand were Cornish and about a third of these had fathers who had been miners. Few of those with a mining background would have been exclusively miners. Most mining families also had a small dwelling on what had once been waste land, and subsisted by growing crops and keeping a few pigs.[60]

People with a more exclusively farming background also migrated to New Zealand from Cornwall. In the 1840s about a quarter of the Cornish immigrants in our sample were off the land, while between 1853 and 1870 close to half had this background. Cornwall was an area of small tenanted holdings on which all the family worked. It had been particularly badly hit by pressures of population growth and then by the potato blight of the late 1840s. More than a third of the Cornish people in our samples for the whole period 1840–90 were Methodist; indeed, of those in the 1870s and 1880s, a total of 56 per cent were dissenters. One of these was John Crewes, from Grampound, a small Cornish market town, who came out in 1877 as a missionary for the Bible Christians, a splinter group of Methodists. Crewes was a social worker and temperance advocate in Christchurch before moving to Wellington, where he was the prime mover in the establishment of the zoo.[61]

Elizabeth Horrell (née Moore) was the daughter of a farm bailiff at Topsham, Devon. She married John Horrell, who became a tenant farmer. The farm was not profitable so, spurred on by the local rector who was an advocate for the Canterbury Association, the couple came out to Canterbury on the *Charlotte Jane*, one of the 'first four ships'. Elizabeth was appointed the first woman schoolteacher in Canterbury, but later, with a family that grew to include twelve children, she was kept busy managing the household.
CANTERBURY MUSEUM,
PHOTOGRAPH BY J. M. VERRALL

The rest of the southwest – Devon, Dorset, Somerset and Wiltshire – was also a good source of recruits for New Zealand. There were few miners there and in both the 1840s and the 1870s, if we include labourers, a majority of the migrants from these areas came from an agricultural background, more than for other parts of England. In Devon many of these had come from small-holdings. Further east the completion of the enclosure of land reduced the demand for rural labour. The wool industry that had once flourished in Devon, Somerset and Wiltshire also suffered from mechanisation. Again, builders and pre-industrial craft-workers were quite well represented among the backgrounds of migrants from these areas (although somewhat less than elsewhere). Such families must have been affected by the expanding rail network, which reached the west in the 1840s. Self-employed craft-workers who had provided for the local market now found themselves unable to compete with factory products. As a result of all these factors, schemes of assistance received a warm response in the southwest.

The southeast, especially the county of Kent, provided another continuous source of migrants. Over 10 per cent of England's migrants to New Zealand in the 1840s came from Kent, as did over 6 per cent of those in the 1870s and 1880s – numbers disproportionate to the county's population. And Kent people were better represented among migrants to New Zealand than among those going to other destinations overseas. The area was close to London, a major port of embarkation to New Zealand, and it was a prime area for recruitment by both the New Zealand Company and agents of the provincial and central governments.

The social structure here was very different from that in the southwest. There were a small number of large tenant farmers, and most of the agricultural labour force worked as farm labourers hired by the week or the day. Outside the north, agricultural wages in Kent were among the highest in the country, but being relatively close to London, farm labourers began to compare their wages with those in other parts of the economy. Agricultural wages rose over the course of the nineteenth century, but by less than those for city workers. Kent had suffered from the enclosure movement and the loss of common lands, and it was also among the counties affected by the 'Captain Swing' riots of the 1830s, an uprising of disaffected rural labourers. It is true that as the rail network spread, new fruit and hop-growing industries developed, providing seasonal work. But much of this was short-term employment requiring migration, and in the 1870s, as Rollo Arnold has documented so well, a labourers' union movement sprang up – the so-called 'Revolt of the Field' – in response to farmers' attempts to cut wages. It was led by Alfred Simmons, who was instrumental in directing the frustrations of the rural labour force towards emigration to New Zealand.[62]

So in both the 1840s and the 1870s, the occupational background of over 50 per cent of the Kentish settlers in our sample was either farming or labouring. There were also significant numbers of builders and other craft-workers, who seem to have been especially well-represented in the migrations of the 1850s and 1860s. For such people – among them boot-makers, brewers and rope-makers – proximity to London

Sarah Higgins (née Sharp) came from Lydden, Kent where her father was a labourer. Her mother died and the family came out to Nelson in 1842, but after her older sister died on the voyage Sarah, aged twelve, was left to keep house. Later she married a sawyer, became a midwife and delivered 350 babies. She learnt to write at the age of 74. 1/2-190392; F, ALEXANDER TURNBULL LIBRARY, EDNA HIGGINS COLLECTION (PACOLL-7068)

and major transport routes began to undermine local craft traditions. Those parts of Kent with strong Methodist and dissenting traditions were particularly prone to draw people to New Zealand. Methodism seems to have provided a culture of dissent which helped give focus to resistance and eventual migration.[63] About a third of Kent's migrants in our sample in the period 1840–90 were recorded in the death registers as dissenters, and about a sixth were Methodists. Kent was one of those areas where the new Poor Law was enforced, with so-called 'outdoor' relief no longer provided and only those in a workhouse supported. The prospect of unemployment or a penurious old age had become something to be feared. The thought of independence in a new country where the family could support its dependents on land was an enticing prospect.

The third area of consistent migration to New Zealand was London and Middlesex. The numbers who came from this area were always higher than their representation in the English population, and it was even better represented in the twentieth century than earlier. In the years between the wars over one in five migrants came from the capital. These do not appear to have been the children of recent migrants from rural areas, for throughout the century from 1840 to 1945 very few of the migrants from London and Middlesex had fathers who were farmers. Even if we include those described as labourers, only in the 1870s and 1880s did the proportion of London migrants with farming fathers reach 15 per cent.

Immigrants from this area were disproportionately of three types. Throughout the whole period about 15 per cent had fathers who were builders or carpenters (about twice as high as from other areas). Sophia Anstice, for example, was the daughter of a Marylebone carpenter; she married a salesman and came out to Nelson in 1874 as an assisted migrant. Sent to pioneer in harsh conditions at Karamea, she moved after four years to Nelson and set up a dressmaking business that eventually employed many staff and had branches in Murchison, Takaka and Motueka. She reportedly made use of her London origins by buying material from relatives who had a drapery store in Tottenham Court Road.[64]

The second kind of London migrant came from a background in the skilled traditional crafts. Over one in four of the London migrants during the core years of migration (1853–1915) had fathers who were craftsmen. These were people from a range of crafts serving the urban consumer, among them bakers, bookbinders, jewellers and piano-makers. When we add the builders to this group, until 1915 they comprise well over 40 per cent of the migrants from London and Middlesex. One who came from this background was the eccentric Wellington politician Robert Carpenter. The son of a London cabinet-maker, he trained as a bookbinder. In 1842, when he was in his early twenties, Robert and his wife Harriet came out to Wellington. Finding little demand for bookbinding, Carpenter became a seller of second-hand books and an opinionated provincial politician representing small

James Berry was the son of a London clerk and started work in the city as an insurance clerk. But he did not enjoy it, so in 1925, at the age of eighteen, he came on an assisted passage to New Zealand. He paid off the passage as a farm cadet in Gisborne, then began work as a commercial artist in Wellington, where he found a niche designing stamps and coins. These included most of the 1940 centennial stamps and the coins adopted at the introduction of decimal coinage in 1967. PACOLL-3496-1, ALEXANDER TURNBULL LIBRARY

tradesmen. Harriet made money selling fancy waistcoats.[65] Londoners of this kind were clearly happier in the city.

The third significant group of Londoners were those whose fathers had been white-collar workers; about one in five had this background, a much higher proportion than for migrants from elsewhere in Britain. In the early years a number of these people were from the higher professions, such as clergy or lawyers, while later there were more whose fathers had been clerks or schoolteachers. Henry Wigram, the son of a London barrister, came out to Christchurch for health reasons in 1883 and quickly became a successful businessman. As mayor of Christchurch he was instrumental in establishing the electric tram system, and as an enthusiast for aviation he established the aerodrome that still carries his name.[66] A future mayor of Auckland, John Allum, had himself been a London clerk, although his father had been a porter. Allum was mayor from 1941 to 1953 and was largely responsible for the building of Auckland's harbour bridge, which was known at the time as 'Jack Allum's bridge'. He was a tireless lobbyist for the city and became known as 'His Imperial Highness'. It is perhaps not surprising, given their origins, that Londoners seem to be good for New Zealand cities.[67]

At the other end of the scale, a major continuity was the weak representation, at least until the turn of the twentieth century, of people from the industrial workforce of northern England. This was an area of strong economic growth in the nineteenth century, with vigorous mining and manufacturing industries. Large cities emerged, including Liverpool, Manchester and Leeds, and rural wages also tended to be higher here than elsewhere. Although there was considerable migration overseas from the area, especially during the periodic slumps in the cotton industry, the major focus of emigration was the United States, where industrial skills were in demand. Moreover, the major port taking ships across the Atlantic was Liverpool, close to where the population was concentrated.

So although people from Lancashire and Yorkshire did come to New Zealand in the nineteenth century, their numbers were about half of their proportion of the English population. Recruiting agents seeking labourers in New Zealand's green and pleasant land did not see the area as a likely source of rural labour. However, nineteenth-century migrants from Lancashire included some highly significant people, such as William Hodgkins, the son of a brushmaker in the Liverpool slums. He came to the Otago goldfields via Melbourne and established himself as a lawyer. He became a highly regarded painter and was the father of Frances Hodgkins. The most famous Lancashire son of all, the premier Richard Seddon, was from St Helens, near Liverpool. He was also attracted to the goldfields (of the West Coast), arriving in 1866 after time in Victoria.

From the turn of the century, however, the numbers of migrants from Lancashire grew both in absolute terms and relative to its population, and by the interwar period the county contributed almost 15 per cent of New Zealand's new migrants from England. Among Lancashire-born twentieth-century migrants were two who made a valuable contribution to New Zealand left-wing life: the economist, historian and public servant Bill Sutch, the son of a carpenter and dressmaker, whose family arrived in 1907, and Margaret Thorn, daughter of a Manchester bricklayer, whose family came out in 1912. She became the wife of an MP and a staunch activist for working-class women.[68] The twentieth-century migrants from Yorkshire included another distinguished mayor of Auckland, Dove-Myer Robinson, whose father had peddled trinkets in Sheffield and became a pawnbroker when the family migrated in 1914.

Not surprisingly, few of these people from Lancashire and Yorkshire came from a farming background – less than 10 per cent of those who arrived in the first half of the twentieth century. There were still quite a few children of pre-industrial craft-workers (about 20 per cent of the migrants from the two counties) as well as people whose fathers had been miners and builders (about 5 per cent of each). But more of them (almost 20 per cent) came from an industrial background or had fathers who had worked in white-collar urban jobs, such as schoolteachers, bank officers or insurance agents (roughly 15 per cent). People with such backgrounds were more like those who would flood into New Zealand after the Second World War.

But that was in the future. The immigrants from England who settled in New Zealand during the great migrations of the nineteenth century were people who were essentially victims of the second industrial revolution. Initially, as capitalism, city life and mechanisation took off at the end of the eighteenth century, rural workers and craftspeople had adjusted to the cash economy. People like builders, wheelwrights, even some domestic spinners and weavers, had found additional markets as cash flowed into rural areas. But from about the 1830s, as rail transport improved and increasing numbers of operations were no longer 'put out' into the community but taken into urban factories, labourers and craftspeople faced declining incomes. Agents from a rural English paradise across the seas who offered the chance of land and self-employment received a welcome hearing. Women for whom domestic crafts were no longer a paying proposition were also attracted by the deliberate attempts to court unmarried women. These people, used to the cash nexus and eager to advance, not the down-and-outs or the factory operatives, formed many of New Zealand's founding English.

There is one other migrant flow that deserves mention, that from the offshore islands, especially the Channel Islands. Although not strictly part of England, the Isle of Man and the Channel Islands have been included in our figures. The numbers were not great in the 1840s and 1850s, and in absolute numbers they were never a huge part of the migration to New Zealand. But in the last 30 years of the century there was a quite remarkable flow of people to New Zealand from the Channel Islands of Jersey and Guernsey, especially if we look from the perspective of the sending communities. During those years probably about 3500 people (over 4 per cent of the total population) left those small, rocky islands for New Zealand.

Located off the northwest coast of France, and 60 miles south of England, the Channel Islands, like the Isle of Man, were Crown dependencies. Many of their residents spoke a French patois before coming to New Zealand. Most of them, however, did not come direct, for a high proportion of our sample had married in England before migrating. They had already made one journey before embarking on a longer one. Quite a number of the Channel Island settlers were the children of soldiers or seamen, some of whom may have heard about New Zealand from their itinerant fathers. But the majority were from a pre-industrial background, the sons and daughters of blacksmiths, brick-makers and carpenters.

The Channel Islanders in New Zealand included several who made important contributions to public life in the late nineteenth century, such as James Pope, who was an influential inspector of native schools, and James Arnold, a leading Dunedin unionist and MP. The most eccentric, however, was Henry Poingdestre, who came from the Isle of Jersey to Canterbury and set up a homestead and run called Blue Cliffs. There he lined the paths with gin bottles, wore a white top hat and drove a home-made gig hauled by a mule and an old white mare.[69]

Henry Poingdestre was obviously an unusual immigrant. So too was that son of a Yorkshire Jewish pawnbroker Dove-Myer Robinson, whom we have already met. There were many other English eccentrics, such as Hilda Hewlett, daughter of a London vicar, who, under the pseudonym Grace Bird, was a pioneer aviatrix and came out to New Zealand aged 62 in 1926 to escape 'crowds, convention and civilization'.[70] There was Edward Lofley who arrived from England to fight in

Emilius Le Roy, a sailor, settled in Auckland from the Channel Islands in the early 1850s. He then summoned a fiancée from Guernsey, Catherine Table, and set up a tent- and sail-making business in Queen Street. He also became Captain-Commandant of a naval volunteers unit, and wore the uniform for this photo in 1889. PRIVATE COLLECTION, MRS LORIS MATHEW

the Waikato War and stayed to become a guide in the thermal districts, where he wore a bush-shirt and kilt and a broad-brimmed hat with a feather sticking out of it.[71] The English have always done eccentrics well, and plenty of such people came to New Zealand because here you had the freedom to be yourself. So not all English immigrants by any measure were 'typical.' But if we do try to define the 'typical English immigrant to New Zealand', then he and she were likely to be the children of rural labourers or craftworkers. They left their village worlds when they saw factories and cities arising, and headed across the oceans for a new country where perhaps they could fulfil older hopes of a bit of land and profitable self-employment.

FIONA AND JOCK: THE SCOTS

We have learnt so far that the New Zealand settlers from the British Isles were over twice as Scottish as the homeland population. But who were these Scots? Were they a band of whisky-quaffing Highlanders wearing kilts and blowing bagpipes? If not, where did they come from and who were they?

Some answers can be found in Tables 14 and 15, which provide an overview of the geographical origin of the Scots migrants to New Zealand. Once again, Table 15 shows the comparison between the geographic origins of the people in our sample and the distribution of the population at the closest Scottish census. The regions are as in Map 2 (p. ix). Any figure over 100 implies that people from that area were over-represented among the New Zealand immigrants; any figure under 100 suggests the area was under-represented.

TABLE 14. REGIONS OF BIRTH OF SCOTS IMMIGRANTS (PERCENTAGES)

Born in	1840–52	1853–70	1871–90	1891–1915	1916–45
Far North	6.1	5.9	10.8	3.8	5.2
Highlands	10.3	16.0	9.8	8.7	7.1
Northeast	7.0	10.2	10.4	8.7	10.4
East Lowlands	37.1	32.7	27.9	34.3	33.2
West Lowlands	36.2	26.6	33.2	38.3	39.4
Borders	3.3	8.6	7.9	6.3	4.8
Not stated	6	38	47	43	45
Number	213	745	742	469	738

Source: Death registers

TABLE 15. REGIONAL REPRESENTATION INDICES OF SCOTS IMMIGRANTS

Born in	1840–52	1853–70	1871–90	1891–1915	1916–45
Far North	165	151	292	187	226
Highlands	86	136	91	139	101
Northeast	57	77	78	93	90
East Lowlands	109	97	83	99	99
West Lowlands	127	96	112	92	101
Borders	34	90	87	107	74

Sources: Death registers, UK census

The striking fact here is the number of figures around the 100 mark. This suggests that the places of birth of Scots migrants were not greatly dissimilar from the distribution of the population in Scotland itself. At least in terms of their regional origins, New Zealand's Scots were a microcosm of the home country. Work by Rosalind McClean also suggests that clustering within counties was not a pronounced feature of Scots migration.[72]

The second implication is that during the whole period of settlement a clear majority of Scots migrants – about six or seven out of ten – came from the Lowlands, the most urbanised and industrialised areas around Glasgow and Edinburgh. In the 1840s the western Lowlands (close to Glasgow) were well represented. According to McClean's research this was true of the Otago immigrants despite the Edinburgh or east Lowland base of the Otago Association,[73] and it was even truer among those who came to Auckland. This was probably a reflection of the continuing impact of the organised migration from Paisley in 1842. Even in the 1850s and 1860s Auckland saw a continuing strong influx from the areas around Glasgow.

The Lowland character of New Zealand's Scots is, as we have suggested, rather contrary to the popular image of Scots immigrants, which associates them with Highland shepherds and the kilts and bagpipes of that part of Scotland. There certainly was a good deal of migration out of the Highlands following the clearances by landlords eager to enclose their land for sheepfarming. But much of this occurred before the substantial migration to New Zealand, and when people left the Highlands they tended to go to the United States or Canada, or more often move within Scotland to the urbanising Lowlands. It may well be that some of those who eventually came to New Zealand were the children of ex-Highland dwellers, but Highlanders themselves they were not likely to be.

The only period when there were substantial numbers from the Highlands (and even then under one in six of Scottish migrants to New Zealand) was during the 1850s and 1860s. There appear to have been quite large numbers who came from the Highlands to the gold rushes, especially to Otago (18.4 per cent of Otago's mining Scots were Highlanders, as were 15.4 per cent of those on the West Coast). This was partly a consequence of a Highland influx into the Victorian goldfields.[74] A substantial number of single people also came out from the Highlands under Canterbury's assisted migration scheme. Seventeen

The most famous and influential Highlands settler was John McKenzie. The formative experience of his life came when at the age of five he saw a group of neighbouring crofters evicted from their lands by the landlord. McKenzie's own father was a tenant farmer in Ross-shire, and he himself grew up as a Gaelic speaker. In 1860, as a newly married 20-year-old, he sailed for Otago. Within five years he had managed to acquire a farm just north of Palmerston. After entering politics McKenzie became Minister of Lands in the Liberal Cabinet between 1891 and 1900, where he was known for measures to get more small farmers onto the land, such as attempts to break up large estates and the extensive purchase of Maori land. 1/1-006726-G, ALEXANDER TURNBULL LIBRARY

per cent of the single women, most of whom were recruited as domestic servants, came from the Highlands, as did 25.4 per cent of the assisted single males. Many of these men were recruited to work as shepherds on high-country sheep farms. William Grant was the son of a Ross-shire shepherd who came to Lyttelton with his brother and a sheepdog in 1865. Seeing the dog on the wharf, the owner of Orari Gorge station, Charles Tripp, hired the pair immediately as shepherds. It was the beginning of a highly successful career for William, who became a stock-dealer and owner of high-country runs. Robert Mackay, a Sutherland shepherd, came out with his wife Elizabeth in 1863 and worked on Double Hill station on the Rakaia River. Their daughter Jessie, who was born the following year, grew up hearing tales of Scottish history and legends and in later years became a well-known poet.[75]

TABLE 16. COUNTIES OF BIRTH OF SCOTS IMMIGRANTS (PERCENTAGES)

Region/county	1840–52	1853–70	1871–90	1891–1915	1919–45
Far North					
Caithness	4.2	3.1	1.6	1.2	1.3
Orkney	0.5	0.9	1.2	1.2	0.9
Shetland	1.4	2.0	8.1	1.4	3.0
Highlands					
Argyll	1.9	3.1	1.6	2.1	1.4
Bute	1.9	2.0	1.3	1.6	1.2
Inverness	2.8	4.0	3.6	0.9	2.0
Ross	1.9	4.7	2.4	3.5	2.0
Sutherland	1.9	2.3	0.9	0.5	0.4
Northeast					
Aberdeen	5.6	7.8	8.2	6.8	8.4
Banff	-	0.7	1.2	0.5	1.4
Moray	1.4	1.3	1.0	0.9	0.6
Nairn	-	0.1	0.0	0.5	0.0
East Lowlands					
Angus	5.2	5.4	5.6	7.0	6.6
Clackmannan	0.5	0.6	0.4	0.0	0.3
Dunbarton	1.9	1.4	1.6	2.6	1.7
East Lothian (Haddington)	0.9	0.4	0.1	0.5	0.4
Fife	3.8	4.0	5.0	4.9	6.3
Kincardine	-	0.4	0.9	1.9	0.6
Kinross	-	0.3	0.4	0.2	0.1
Mid Lothian (Edinburgh)	16.9	9.5	8.1	10.6	10.2
Perth	2.8	6.2	2.9	1.9	1.9
Stirling	3.8	3.5	2.4	3.3	2.89
West Lothian (Linlithgow)	1.4	0.7	0.4	1.4	2.02
West Lowlands					
Ayr	8.9	7.9	8.5	4.5	5.9
Lanark	18.8	15.0	20.4	29.3	30.2
Renfrew	8.5	3.4	4.3	4.5	3.3
Borders					
Berwick	1.4	2.0	1.3	1.4	0.3
Dumfries	0.5	2.5	2.4	2.6	1.3
Kirkcudbright	-	0.7	0.1	1.2	0.7
Peebles	-	0.7	0.7	0.5	0.7
Roxburgh	0.9	1.7	1.0	0.7	0.3
Selkirk	-	0.3	0.9	0.0	1.0
Wigtown	0.5	0.7	1.4	0.0	0.4
Total	100.0	100.0	100.0	100.0	100.0
Not stated	6	38	47	43	45
Number	213	745	742	469	738

Source: Death registers

Two other regional characteristics of the Scots migrants are of interest. The first was the relatively poor representation from the more isolated rural areas of Scotland, especially the northeast and the Border areas. A number of Border shepherds were hired for Wairarapa and Canterbury sheep farms in the 1850s, but this was never a big migration. Distance from the major port of Glasgow may have been a factor for these regions.

The exception to this generalisation was the area designated as the far north, which included the county of Caithness and the offshore islands of Orkney and Shetland. The numbers from these areas were not great in the context of the whole New Zealand inflow (a maximum in the 1871–90 period of 10.6 per cent of the Scots migrants), but they were significant relative to the population of those areas of Scotland. In the 1870s and 1880s the far north was over-represented almost threefold. Shetland was especially significant. Its bleak northern islands had seen poor harvests, the collapse of the fishing industry, and then clearances during the 1860s and 1870s. The migration seems to have been sparked by some Shetland seamen who noted the attractiveness of New Zealand and spread the word.

The gold mines attracted many Shetlanders: 6 per cent of Otago Scots miners and a remarkable 16 per cent of the Scots who came to the West Coast were from the Shetlands (almost 20 per cent of Scots-born West Coast miners were from the far north). Some came via the Victorian goldfields. Robert Goudie was born in Lerwick and went to Ballarat before reaching Kaniere on the West Coast in 1870. Thirteen years later he married Barbara Coutts, another Shetlander. Other Shetlanders came direct from their homeland, perhaps encouraged by a series of articles in the *Shetland Advertiser* in 1862 that described the gold discoveries. Migration from the area was further encouraged after the Reverend Peter Barclay based himself as an agent in Lerwick in 1873. A Scot who had served a parish in Napier, he focused his recruitment on single women since the female population of the area was said to greatly exceed the male. By September 1874 he had sent 249 migrants to New Zealand.[76] Death-register figures, however, suggest a reasonably even gender flow from the Shetlands. Many Shetlanders came of their own volition, and they were even better represented among the paying migrants than among the assisted. Chain migration

The most influential Shetland settler was Robert Stout. Son of a merchant in the capital, Lerwick, Stout became a surveyor and set off for Otago as a 19-year-old in the mass migration of 1863. He became a lawyer, a politician who was premier in the 1880s, and eventually chief justice between 1899 and 1926. Stout was a free thinker in religion, an enthusiast and supporter of university education, an intellectual who relished the cut and thrust of debate, and a consistent supporter of Shetlanders whom he encouraged and helped to migrate to New Zealand.
PACOLL-6407-69, ALEXANDER TURNBULL LIBRARY

and perhaps the prominence of a Shetlander, Robert Stout, as premier and chief justice also helped. Shetlanders comprised over 8 per cent of the Scots who arrived between 1871 and 1890, which was over eight times their representation in the Scots population.

Earlier studies of Scots migration have argued that while most nations drew their emigrants from rural areas, Scotland was unusual in sending many people with an urban and industrial background.[77] In addition, it has been claimed that there was a pronounced shift from agricultural to industrial workers among emigrants from England and Scotland in the later nineteenth century.[78] As we have seen, the urban areas of the Lowlands were certainly important sources of migration to New Zealand. However, looking at the occupational background of the Scots (Tables 17 and 18) it can be seen that until the end of the nineteenth century a high proportion, higher than among the English, had fathers who had been involved in agriculture. This may partly reflect families who had moved off the land to centres of urban growth and into urban jobs. But where the actual occupations of the immigrants themselves were obtained – as with those assisted by the Canterbury Association in the 1860s or the New Zealand government in the 1870s and 1880s – the numbers of male migrants who professed to be involved in farming were strikingly high among the Scots. Of course, this follows to some considerable extent from the preference for agricultural labourers in those schemes of assistance. Nevertheless, it seems likely that such schemes helped establish the idea that New Zealand, like Australia, was a good place for people from the land to go, whereas the United States was attractive for people with urban skills.

TABLE 17. OCCUPATIONAL BACKGROUND (FATHER'S OCCUPATION) OF SCOTS IMMIGRANTS AGED 20 AND OVER (PERCENTAGES)

Occupations[79]	1840–52	Akld 1840–52	1853–70	Akld 1853–70	Otago miners	West Coast miners	1871–90	1891–1915	1916–45	GB census 1851
Agriculture	41.0	25.2	44.0	34.5	47.7	37.0	31.0	26.3	17.3	27.3
Labourers	2.0	0.0	4.0	1.0	3.8	5.5	4.5	5.6	6.1	6.9
Builders	7.0	13.0	8.1	9.1	10.5	4.1	8.1	9.6	9.9	7.4
Miners	0.0	1.6	1.7	2.7	5.5	9.6	2.6	8.8	11.2	5.2
Total pre-industrial	18.0	36.6	30.2	31.4	23.2	26.0	32.8	36.7	40.5	30.2
Total industrial	14.0	12.2	4.5	10.8	5.5	6.8	9.4	12.7	16.5	16.0
White collar	18.0	17.1	9.8	12.2	6.3	5.5	10.5	12.4	9.1	10.5
Other	7.0	9.0	7.4	9.9	13.5	19.2	11.7	6.2	10.5	9.1
Not stated	25	39	89	85	0	102	89	40	49	
Number	125	162	509	381	237	175	470	394	575	

Source: Death registers

TABLE 18. DECLARED OCCUPATIONS OF SCOTS MALE IMMIGRANTS (PERCENTAGES)

Occupations	Scots migrants to Otago 1840–50[80]	Canterbury assisted	NZ assisted 1871–88
Agriculture	30.7	73.9	42.9
Labourers	5.6	7.4	13.4
Builders	10.4	9.3	10.9
Miners	0.9	0.7	3.2
Total pre-industrial	33.0	17.2	35.4
Industrial	11.1	0.7	4.3
White collar	18.0	0.5	0.0
Other		0.2	3.9
Not stated		2	0
Number		429	559

Source: Passenger lists

That New Zealand's Scots came from the Lowlands did not mean they had all moved out of farming. Rosalind McClean's work shows that even those emigrants who lived in urban registration districts included a significant minority who lived in rural areas of those districts.[81] The figures of occupational background for those from both the east and west Lowlands up to 1890 suggest that although there were undoubtedly fewer migrants with a farming background than from other parts of Scotland, until 1870 at least 30 per cent of those from the Lowlands came from farming stock, as did over 20 per cent of this group from 1871 to 1890. This does not contradict the view that most of the immigrants from Scotland lived either close to, or even within, cities, in particular Edinburgh and Glasgow, and that many of them were city workers usually employed, if they were men, in crafts, or if they were women, in domestic service. Indeed, 87 per cent of the assisted single women who came from Scotland in the 1870s were described as domestic servants. If we are looking for immigrants with urban experience behind them, there is no doubt that they are to be found primarily among the Lowland Scots and the Londoners. It is hardly surprising that once people from these two places of origin arrived in New Zealand they tended to gravitate to the cities.

On the other hand, until the twentieth century there were few Scots among these city workers who had come from an industrial background, although on average there were slightly more than among the English migrants. Of those whose fathers were involved in industrial work, not surprisingly, most came from the Lowlands. But the numbers were not great. Throughout the nineteenth century no more than about one in eight from these areas had fathers who were working in industrial pursuits. Nor were these necessarily refugees from smoking factories. A high proportion of the Scots migrants from an 'industrial background' had fathers who had been weavers, many of whom may well have worked at home. Mary Parkinson, who was born in Ayrshire in the west Lowlands, was the daughter of a handloom weaver. She married Thomas Cuddie, a cotton weaver. Their first child was baptised by the Reverend Thomas Burns, who persuaded them to sail with him to Otago on the *Philip Laing* in 1848. Despite the loss of her husband and two sons, Mary eventually bought a successful grocery store in East Taieri, and she died a reasonably wealthy woman.[82]

Ann Robertson (née West) was the daughter of a handloom weaver in Perthshire in the eastern Lowlands. She may have worked as a weaver herself, and then as a domestic servant, before she left for the Victorian goldfields. There she married a fellow Scot who brought the family to New Zealand when he enlisted to serve in the New Zealand Wars. Ann successfully ran a boarding house in Tauranga, but when she moved to Rotorua to take over a hotel she became involved in a prolonged legal dispute with another Scots migrant from Glasgow, Robert Graham, which eventually brought her to bankruptcy. However, a government gratuity restored her to comfort and she poured her energies into Rotorua's Presbyterian community. CP 93, ROTORUA MUSEUM

As with the English, there was always a good number of Scots whose fathers had been builders or who were builders themselves, and in total those with a pre-industrial background made up a significant proportion of immigrants, only slightly less than among the English. In addition, there were a striking number of Scots whose fathers had been involved with the sea, either as seamen or fishermen or as shipbuilders. Among the Scots such occupational definitions are hazy and fluid. It seems likely that many of New Zealand's Scots immigrants, especially those from outside the Lowland counties, came from families which had been involved in a number of pursuits. They may well have had a small croft of land, with the father augmenting their income by fishing while the mother knitted and wove. That certainly was the pattern for the surprising numbers who hailed from Shetland. Indeed, among those in our sample who came from the Shetlands, four occupations dominated among their fathers: crofters, farmers, fishermen and seamen. Some 20 per cent of the arrivals from Shetland were the children of seamen.

BIDDY AND SEAN: THE IRISH

The Irish who settled New Zealand were rather different from those who came from the other parts of the British Isles. In terms of occupational background they shared the generally low representation of people with an industrial heritage, as can be seen in Tables 19 and 20. This in large part reflected the low level of industrialisation in Ireland. But compared with migrants from Scotland and England, there were few Irish with a background as builders or miners (even among those who came out to join the gold rushes) and comparatively few from a pre-industrial craft background.

TABLE 19. OCCUPATIONAL BACKGROUND (FATHER'S OCCUPATION) OF IRISH IMMIGRANTS AGED 20 AND OVER (PERCENTAGES)

Occupations	1840–52	Akld 1840–52	1853–70	Akld 1853–70	Otago miners	West Coast miners	1871–90	1891–1915	1916–45
Agriculture	40.6	46.5	60.1	57.1	75.9	81.0	61.1	60.1	52.5
Labourers	4.7	6.5	6.6	4.9	4.6	5.9	11.9	4.9	5.6
Builders	6.3	6.0	4.4	5.3	3.4	2.1	2.7	3.1	6.8
Miners	0.0	0.0	1.3	0.0	2.3	1.7	0.5	1.2	0.6
Total pre-industrial	25.0	19.4	13.3	16.9	8.0	9.7	13.8	14.1	16.9
Total industrial	7.8	5.5	2.8	3.1	2.7	1.3	1.4	4.3	7.9
White collar	14.1	12.4	12.0	13.1	5.3	1.3	7.3	9.8	10.7
Other	7.8	9.7	5.2	4.8	3.4	0.8	4.6	6.8	6.3
Not stated	35	159	90	152	0	196	118	24	18
Number	99	561	406	602	262	434	488	187	195

Source: Death registers

TABLE 20. DECLARED OCCUPATIONS OF IRISH MALE IMMIGRANTS (PERCENTAGES)

Occupations	Canterbury assisted	NZ assisted 1871–88
Agriculture	69.7	68.3
Labourers	17.6	22.6
Builders	4.4	2.5
Miners	0.2	0.1
Total pre-industrial	9.8	7.1
Industrial	1.5	0.5
White collar	0.7	0.1
Other	0.7	1.4
Not stated	1	5
Number	410	1119

Source: Passenger lists

The Irish were strikingly agricultural in origin, especially if one also includes those described as labourers, who were most likely to work in agriculture. Among Irish men who came out as assisted migrants in the 1870s and 1880s, over 90 per cent were either labourers or farmers. Among the single women, 87 per cent were described as servants and another 8.3 per cent as dairymaids. The majority of these people would have been from families which had reasonably small plots of land. If the land was divided among the children, such plots were increasingly less able to provide for the standard of living to which they aspired. The more common practice by the 1870s of impartible inheritance – where the entire property was left to one son, usually the eldest – meant the younger children had no means of support. Migration was the obvious response.

On the whole these migrants from rural Ireland were not the poorest of the agricultural community, nor were they refugees from the potato famine that swept across the central and western counties in the late 1840s and early 1850s. We know this for two reasons. First, the number of immigrants from an agricultural background was actually much lower in the period of the famine than later. During these years no more than 45 per cent came off the land. In the 1840s there was a remarkable number of Irish migrants who either had a white-collar background or whose fathers had been soldiers. The former were probably educated people of Anglo-Irish background, while the latter were likely to be second-generation soldiers who had come out with British regiments.

Some Irish immigrants had fathers who had been weavers, and who would have suffered from the development of factory production.

TABLE 21. REGIONAL ORIGINS OF IRISH IMMIGRANTS (PERCENTAGES)

Born in	1840–52	1853–70	1871–90	1891–1915	1916–45
Connacht	6.3	8.5	6.4	6.8	6.3
Leinster	34.1	19.9	14.9	16.0	12.7
Munster	27.8	31.7	35.2	26.2	19.0
Ulster	31.7	39.8	43.5	51.0	62.0
Not stated	18	45	42	23	15
Number	144	527	748	229	220

Source: Death registers

TABLE 22. REGIONAL REPRESENTATION INDICES OF IRISH IMMIGRANTS

Born in	1840–52	1853–70	1871–90	1891–1915	1916–45
Connacht	37	53	40	45	43
Leinster	141	81	62	65	49
Munster	95	121	136	107	74
Ulster	109	120	127	143	185

Source: Death registers

The second reason we know New Zealand's Irish immigrants were not famine escapees is that the regional breakdowns (as shown in Tables 21 and 22) reveal that in the years of the Great Famine those provinces which suffered most, namely Connacht (the most severely hit) and Munster, were not the regions sending migrants to this country. The provinces are as in Map 3 (p. x). In that period the most significant source of immigrants was Leinster, and particularly the County of Dublin, which was the place of birth of almost 20 per cent of those who came to New Zealand. The explanation for this pattern is the concentration of the Anglo-Irish community in the urban community of Dublin, as well as the fact that the military settlers had commonly been recruited in that area. Interestingly, although the numbers were very small (24), among the migrants from Dublin in our sample for the 1840s not one came from a farming background. Instead civil servants, clergy, gentlemen, lawyers, merchants and soldiers appeared among the fathers' occupations on the death certificates.

It is also revealing that 27 per cent of Irish migrants in those years appear to have been members of the Church of England (or the

John Robert Godley, born in
Dublin and educated at Harrow
school and Christ Church
Oxford, was one of the more
prominent of the Anglo-Irish
elite who came to New Zealand
in the 1840s and 1850s. As high
sheriff of County Leitrim he
struggled with the consequences
of the potato famine and saw
emigration as a possible solution.
A meeting with Edward Gibbon
Wakefield led Godley to launch
the Canterbury Association. He
arrived in Canterbury in April
1850, met the 'first four ships',
and effectively governed the
colony until the establishment
of provincial government and
his own departure in 1852.
This statue was erected in
Christchurch, named after his
college, in 1867. PACOLL-4508-01,
ALEXANDER TURNBULL LIBRARY,
PHOTOGRAPH BY ALFRED CHARLES
BARKER

Church of Ireland as it was known locally). Only 10.7 per cent of the
Irish population of 1834 was of that denomination, but the figures were
very much higher (well over 20 per cent) for Dublin city and suburbs.
The outstanding example of this Anglican Anglo-Irish community
was the leader of the Canterbury settlement, John Robert Godley, but
there were others. Edward Stafford, although born in Scotland, grew
up in the Anglo-Irish environment and attended Trinity College in
Dublin, which was the centre of this culture. Leaving Trinity, Stafford
went first to Australia and then on to Nelson in 1843. Here he joined
his cousins, the Tytlers, who were also part of the Anglo-Irish world.
Stafford married the daughter of William Wakefield, became Nelson's
first superintendent, and was a dominating figure in the first 20 years of
responsible government in New Zealand, serving as premier for a total
of nine years.[83]

TABLE 23. COUNTIES OF BIRTH OF IRISH IMMIGRANTS (PERCENTAGES)

Region/county	1840–52	1853–70	1871–90	1891–1915	1919–45
Connacht					
Galway	4.0	5.7	3.9	3.4	4.0
Leitrim	0.8	0.8	0.6	0.0	0.5
Mayo	1.6	0.2	0.4	1.9	0.5
Roscommon	-	1.3	1.4	0.5	1.0
Sligo	-	0.4	0.1	1.0	0.5
Leinster					
Carlow	-	2.1	0.6	0.0	0.5
Dublin	19.8	6.9	5.8	6.8	4.5
Kildare	0.8	0.6	0.6	1.0	1.0
Kilkenny	2.4	1.3	1.6	1.5	2.5
King's Country	2.4	2.3	0.9	0.5	0.5
Longford	0.8	0.6	0.7	0.0	0.5
Louth	0.8	-	0.0	0.0	1.0
Meath	-	-	0.4	0.0	0.5
Queen's Country	1.6	0.8	0.4	1.5	-
Westmeath	0.8	1.7	1.7	0.5	0.5
Wexford	2.4	1.5	1.0	2.5	-
Wicklow	1.6	1.9	0.9	2.5	1.5
Munster					
Clare	1.6	7.5	4.1	3.9	3.0
Cork	10.3	6.3	9.0	9.2	8.5
Kerry	-	4.2	11.1	4.4	4.0
Limerick	8.7	4.6	4.9	2.4	2.0
Tipperary	4.8	6.3	3.7	2.9	1.5
Waterford	2.4	2.7	2.9	2.9	0.5
Ulster					
Antrim	5.6	12.6	11.7	21.4	27.5
Armagh	4.8	4.4	4.4	3.4	6.0
Cavan	1.6	2.9	2.7	1.5	1.0
Donegal	2.4	2.5	3.6	1.9	1.5
Down	5.6	6.9	5.7	6.3	9.5
Fermanagh	3.2	2.7	1.1	0.5	0.5
Londonderry	4.8	4.0	5.1	8.7	7.5
Monaghan	0.8	0.6	1.3	1.0	2.0
Tyrone	3.2	3.4	7.7	4.4	5.5
Total	100.0	100.0	100.0	100.0	100.0
Not stated	18	50	42	23	19
Number	144	427	748	229	219

Source: Death registers

From the 1850s, as the number of Irish arrivals grew, the pattern of Irish regional origins began to change. Leinster declined as a significant source of migrants, while the two provinces at opposite ends of the island, Munster in the southwest and Ulster in the northeast, became more important. The Munster migration was particularly sparked by the gold rushes: well over 40 per cent of the Irish who came out as miners to Otago and the West Coast were born in Munster (43 and 41.7 per cent respectively, compared with 31.7 per cent for all New Zealand Irish immigrants in those years and 23.8 per cent of Ireland's population). Many had come to the South Island via Australia, so the counties that were well represented among New Zealand's Irish settlers of the period reflected those that sent large numbers to Victoria – especially Counties Clare, Limerick, Kerry and Tipperary.[84] Once the miners reached New Zealand, many settled here.

The Sherlock family is an interesting example of this group of settlers. John Sherlock was a Tipperary farmer, married to Maria O'Rourke of County Kildare. They were due to sail for Australia with their family on Christmas Eve 1852. On the previous day John was wounded by a stray bullet fired in a fight in which he had not been involved. Maria decided the family should continue with the journey, but sadly John died en route. She settled in Victoria and her two sons came across to the West Coast goldfields, where they married Irish women from County Fermanagh and County Galway. In 1867, Maria and her other children followed her sons and settled on the West Coast.

This pattern of families, especially women, following their male relatives to New Zealand was strengthened in the 1870s and 1880s when the New Zealand government offered assisted migration to people nominated by relatives. The Munster Catholic community made a major effort to recruit relatives from home, especially from the counties of Kerry and Cork. Seán Brosnahan has described how with government assistance a 'whole section of East Kerry society' was transplanted from County Kerry to Kerrytown in South Canterbury. The process began when Richard Hoare came out to Otago in 1860 as an assisted immigrant. Two years later he nominated his parents and his three siblings, and they brought other Kerry folk, including Patrick Brosnahan and two other Brosnahans. There were further migrations of relatives on assisted passages following nomination in 1865, 1867,

1870, 1871 and finally in 1874, when Patrick's parents, Hugh and Deborah, falsified their ages in order to qualify for a free passage. The Kerry Brosnahans had completely transferred across the sea and were now the Kerrytown Brosnahans.[85]

There seems to have been a marked increase in Munster immigrants once assisted passages became free in late 1873. The vast majority – almost 90 per cent – of these Munster settlers were Catholic, and consistently over 60 per cent, or almost 75 per cent if we include labourers, were people whose families had been small farmers. Among those people assisted by the New Zealand government between 1871 and 1880 over 42 per cent came from Munster; this compares with its share of the total Irish population in 1871 of 26.6 per cent, and its share of Irish emigration to all destinations of 29 per cent.[86] Among all Irish immigrants to New Zealand in the period 1871–90 over 35 per cent came from Munster.

The Ulster migration had a rather different source. People in authority in New Zealand began to see the northeast of Ireland as an attractive recruiting ground for the hard-working Protestant types who were regarded as desirable settlers. They saw Ulster as likely to provide hard-working families, and also as a good source of unmarried women who might provide both domestic servants and spouses for New Zealand's men. Among all those assisted by Canterbury province in the 1860s almost 60 per cent of the Irish came from Ulster, and among the men the figure was over 60 per cent. Once the New Zealand government got into the act of providing assisted passages, they too looked to the north of Ireland. In all, 45.4 per cent of the Irish given free passages by the New Zealand government in the 1870s and 1880s had been born in the northern province. The government particularly looked to Ulster to recruit married couples and single women, while the single men were more likely to come from Munster.

The Ulster migrants did not come only as a result of organised recruitment. They were also to be found in numbers among those who made their own way to the goldfields, especially the Otago fields. So there were clearly 'push' factors in this Ulster migration. Ulster was a flax-growing area, and the mechanisation of spinning undermined the livelihood of rural women spinners, while the introduction of power looms replaced the handloom weaving that had been the pursuit

Joseph Ward and his family in 1906. Ward's success in eventually becoming prime minister owed much to his remarkable mother, Hannah Barron. She had been born in Cork, Ireland, to a shopkeeper. She married William Ward, and followed him to Melbourne in 1853. William did not do well, so Hannah supported the family by running a shop and lodging house for miners heading to the diggings. Of her eight sons born there, only Joseph survived. William also died and in 1863, only nine months after a second mysterious marriage to John Barron, Hannah headed for Southland, where in Bluff she again opened a shop for miners. A devout Catholic, she eventually owned a successful hotel, and supported Joseph by lending him money for his first stock and station agency and again when he became bankrupt in 1897.
PACOLL-6388-34, ALEXANDER TURNBULL LIBRARY

of men. In addition there was a shift from tilling land to maintaining pastures, which further contracted the need for agricultural labour.[87] So until the twentieth century a consistently high proportion (about 60 per cent) of the Ulster-born migrants to New Zealand came from farming backgrounds, and it was not until the twentieth century that about 10 per cent of people from this area had fathers who had worked in factories or in the shipbuilding industry.

Despite the rural background of so many of the Ulster migrants, the areas that were especially well represented among them were the more

Marianne Smith (née Caughey) was the daughter of a grocer from Portaferry, County Down. Through her brother, Andrew, she met William Smith, who was working in a Belfast drapery store, and the pair married. In 1880, after William's health deteriorated, the couple decided to follow Andrew to New Zealand. Marianne opened a drapery warehouse in Auckland that was soon so successful she was joined by her husband and brother. Soon after that Smith and Caughey moved to a prime site on Queen Street, and its success and Marianne's wealth were made. She remained active in the firm after her husband's death in 1912 and 20 years later, aged 71, she married a retired Methodist minister, which was consistent with the faith that had always been important in her life. F-220117-1/2, ALEXANDER TURNBULL LIBRARY, W. G. CAUGHEY COLLECTION

urban and Protestant counties close to Belfast, namely Antrim, Down and, to a lesser extent, Derry. One immigrant who came from Belfast itself was John McCullough, son of a seamen, an Orangeman and a Presbyterian, who came out to Canterbury in 1880, aged 20. He began a significant career battling for socialism, pacifism and craft unionism which climaxed with his service as the workers' representative on the Court of Arbitration from 1907 to 1921.[88] Ulster Protestantism also sent out sons of a rather different political stripe. One of these was John Ballance, who became the Liberal premier. The son of an Antrim farmer who also spent time in England (in Birmingham), he originally came out to New Zealand because of the ill-health of his wife.[89] A second was the long-serving conservative prime minister William Ferguson Massey, whose father had been a farmer at Limavady, County

Londonderry, before coming to New Zealand in 1869 on the Auckland land grant scheme. William followed a year later, aged fourteen. He later married the daughter of a Scots immigrant family with whom he shared his Presbyterian faith.

Like McCullough, Ballance and Massey, those who came to New Zealand from Ulster were very likely to be Protestant. During the 1870s almost half of the inhabitants of Ulster were Roman Catholic, but less than a quarter of those who migrated to New Zealand from that area appear to have been Catholic. The effect of this was that only 55.9 per cent of Irish immigrants in the 1870s and 1880s were Roman Catholics (to judge from the denomination of the cleric officiating at their deaths).

This is an important finding, because it has long been believed that New Zealand's Irish were overwhelmingly Catholic, as in their home-land. Don Akenson, who pioneered the research into this question, argued that about three-quarters of the New Zealand Irish community was Catholic, which was not much less than in the home population itself.[90] This appears to have been far from the case. At no point from the 1840s on did the proportion of Catholics in the Irish migrant flow reach 60 per cent, and in certain cases, such as those coming into Auckland in the 1853–70 period, the representation of Catholic Irish was under half. Interestingly, however, the character of the Protestant flow appears to change.

In the early years, reflecting the importance of the Anglo-Irish community, especially around Dublin, adherents of the Church of Ireland were very well represented but the numbers of Presbyterians from the north were low. In 1840–52, for example, 27 per cent of New Zealand's Irish immigrants were from the Anglican Church, but only 9 per cent were Presbyterians, not much more than their proportion in the whole Irish population. By the 1870s and 1880s, as the migrants from Ulster increased and as recruiters targeted the Protestant com-munity of the north, a much larger part of the Protestant flow was Presbyterian. In those years the numbers of Presbyterians and mem-bers of the Church of Ireland were about the same (some 19 per cent of the whole), while almost 40 per cent of those arriving from Ulster were of Scots–Irish Presbyterian background. Methodists, too, were significantly over-represented.

From the 1890s these trends – increasing representation from Ulster and of Protestants – became more pronounced, especially once the Irish Free State was established in 1921. By the turn of the century over half of Ireland's immigrants were from the northern province, with over 20 per cent from County Antrim alone, and in the period between the wars the Ulster proportion was over 60 per cent. By then only a third of Irish immigrants were Roman Catholic, with almost the same number being Presbyterian. Although they were from the more urban north, a high proportion of these migrants continued to come from farming backgrounds: 60 per cent of those migrating to New Zealand from Ireland during the interwar years had fathers who were farmers, compared with only 11.8 per cent for the English/Welsh and 15.2 per cent for the Scots.

New Zealanders tend to think of their Irish heritage in terms of re-publicanism, St Patrick's Day and Catholicism, yet almost as important is the heritage from the Protestant community of the north, especially the Scots–Irish Presbyterians clustered in the area around Belfast. In some ways these are New Zealand's least visible immigrants. This is de-spite the fact that the only organised community of Irish settlers, those who came to Katikati in the 1870s and early 1880s, came from Ulster, not to mention those two famous prime ministers, John Ballance and Bill Massey.[91]

KITH AND KIN

If we are to understand the long-term impact of migration we must also work out whether the migrants came alone or in larger groupings, especially families. Families are the vehicles of culture. They teach chil-dren traditions, and their members reinforce each others' accents, reli-gious faiths, ways of doing things. In general, the greater the number of people who migrate as individuals the quicker they will lose their home values. This is especially the case if there is an unbalanced migration of more men than women, which deprives men of the opportunity of get-ting married in the new world. As numerous nineteenth-century social thinkers argued, single men, not tied down by family responsibilities and emotional connections, tended to be a footloose and somewhat unstable crowd. They were attracted to the itinerant character of much early frontier employment, and they developed a loose 'uncivilised' set of social behaviours, from frequenting hotels to gambling.[92]

Certainly Edward Gibbon Wakefield was highly aware of this issue. His scheme of organised settlements was designed to ensure a new world that would be a 'civilised' family utopia. New Zealand opinion-makers continued to be anxious about the surplus of men, and the targeted incentives to migrate offered to women and married couples by the New Zealand Company and provincial and central governments were designed in part to prevent this. In the New Zealand census the gender ratio was among the first questions to be explored.[93] The early censuses certainly did suggest that more men than women migrated to New Zealand. In 1864, for example, the census showed that 61.9 per cent of the European population was male; only 38.1 per cent was female. Our exploration of the death registers confirms this pattern.

TABLE 24. GENDER RATIO (NUMBER OF MALES PER 100 FEMALES) OF IMMIGRANTS FROM THE UNITED KINGDOM TO NEW ZEALAND

	English/Welsh	Scots	Irish	All
1840–52	151.4	143.3	113.4	143.9
1853–70	158.6	136.5	140.6	147.6
1871–90	115.7	119.5	91.3	110.6
1891–1915	146.2	138.1	182.7	147.8
1916–45	104.7	110.3	165.8	110.0

Source: Death registers

TABLE 25. GENDER RATIO (NUMBER OF MALES PER 100 FEMALES) OF IMMIGRANTS FROM THE UNITED KINGDOM TO NEW ZEALAND, AGED 20 AND OVER

	English/Welsh	Scots	Irish	All
1840–52	174.6	184.1	108.5	162.9
1853–70	181.2	150.7	161.9	166.7
1871–90	126.0	136.7	103.3	122.6
1891–1915	143.2	125.1	181.8	142.5
1916–45	95.6	102.5	162.0	103.3

Source: Death registers

Table 24 shows the gender ratio of all immigrants to New Zealand between 1840 and 1945, expressed as the number of males for every 100 females. Thus we learn that between 1840 and 1870 there were over

140 males for every 100 females among those arriving. (In the small sample of those arriving before 1840 the ratio was even higher – 200 males for every 100 females.) Table 25 excludes children, who were likely to comprise a group balanced between boys and girls. Between 1840 and 1870 the ratio of incoming adults was over 160; there were eight men for every five women.

Many of the findings shown in these tables are to be expected. The relatively high gender ratio of the 1850s and 1860s is unsurprising, since this was the period in which the goldminers came flooding into New Zealand along with soldiers. Rather surprising, however, is the comparatively high gender ratio of the 1840s, since much of the migration during this period was under the auspices of the New Zealand Company, which set out to attract families.

We get a partial explanation for this when we break the flows down by year. In the years of high organised company migration, the early and late 1840s, there was certainly a balanced representation of men and women. But in the middle years of the decade, when soldiers came to New Zealand, there was a considerable imbalance. Also of some interest is the fact that the flow into Auckland during the years 1840–52 (with a gender ratio of 122.7) was in fact more evenly balanced than that into New Zealand as a whole. This can be explained by the effects of two particular migration streams: the Paisley settlers who came in as family groups in 1842; and the Fencibles, the group of ex-soldiers who came to Auckland in 1847 accompanied by women and children. Since they comprised about a third of Auckland's newcomers in these years, the Fencibles clearly had a major impact on the gender ratio there.

There were of course some single women who came with the Fencibles, such as Sophia Bates, whose father was a corporal in the 2nd Foot Regiment. At the age of 30, and unmarried, Sophia accompanied her parents to Auckland in 1847. The family settled at the Fencible settlement at Onehunga, where Sophia was appointed New Zealand's first postmistress in 1849. She also taught in the local Anglican parish school.[94]

A second route into the issue of the unbalanced gender ratio of the 1840s is to look at the rates of marriage among the newcomers. A balanced gender ratio can either be caused by a large number of married people and their children entering the country, or by an even number of single men and women. Arguably the social consequences will differ, since married couples are likely to be more protective of their culture than unmarried adults of either sex. Table 26 shows the percentages of immigrants from each part of the United Kingdom who were married on arrival.

TABLE 26. PERCENTAGE OF UNITED KINGDOM IMMIGRANTS AGED 20 OR OVER WHO WERE MARRIED ON ARRIVAL IN NEW ZEALAND

	English/ Welsh males	English/ Welsh females	Scots males	Scots females	Irish males	Irish females	All males	All females	All
1840–52	50.0	83.2	53.1	72.7	53.8	80.9	51.2	80.7	62.4
1853–70	45.4	71.4	38.2	55.7	32.7	49.0	40.3	60.9	48.0
1871–90	53.1	74.6	42.6	66.8	35.5	50.8	47.0	67.1	56.0
1891–1915	45.5	64.9	47.0	61.1	37.8	56.1	44.9	63.1	52.4
1916–45	57.2	67.3	53.3	60.2	33.6	45.1	53.4	63.9	58.5

Source: Death registers

We can now see that the comparatively high gender ratio of the 1840s hides the fact that more than three in every five adults entering New Zealand was married. The total gender imbalance was largely the result of the fact that among the single people, the other 37.6 per cent, there was a much greater number of men than women. Very few single women came in during those years. Indeed, more than 80 per cent of adult women were arriving as wives. Furthermore, it seems likely that many of those single women arrived as part of family groups. They were sisters or aunts or, like Sophia Bates, unmarried daughters. Certainly letters to the New Zealand Company confirmed that many people would only come to New Zealand with relatives. One person requested a copy of the company regulations 'as I have some relatives that are going out to New Zealand and I am desirous to go with them'.[95] The Thomas family refused their embarkation orders unless their brother was accepted,[96] and we have already mentioned the Julian family, who came out with the Plymouth Company and had fifteen in their party of parents, children, in-laws and grandchildren.

Among the New Zealand Company migrants over 87 per cent came as part of a family – 10.4 per cent were couples, 62.8 per cent were parents and children, 2.5 per cent were grandparents, and 11.4 per cent were siblings. Over 4 per cent came with neighbours from the same

These stern-looking ancestors are Elizabeth and Samuel Joll, who left Cornwall in 1841
as a result of the economic depression there and an older brother's authoritarianism. They
came out to New Plymouth on the *Timandra* as Plymouth Company migrants. Like many
of the 1840s settlers they brought a considerable family – in their case five children. During
the 113-day voyage five children on the ship died of illness and five babies were born.
PRIVATE COLLECTION

street. Under 10 per cent came apparently alone. The unwillingness
of single women to come by themselves is understandable. In British
culture family connections were always of great significance to women,
and there is clear evidence that even when families came the women
found the parting harder than the men. To go out to a new country
where there was no family to greet you must have been a very tough
experience. Little wonder tears were shed so often as the boats left
England's shores.

In the 1850s and 1860s the situation changed. As already noted, the
highly male communities of goldminers and soldiers flooded into the
country and the gender ratio rose. For the whole period only two in
every five adult men were married on arrival. Of those coming from
Victoria to join the mining communities of Otago (1861–64) and the

West Coast (1865–70) over 87 per cent were male, and about nine in every ten of these men were unmarried.[97] Nor did those who were married necessarily bring their wives with them. Among the miners it was a common pattern for the men to come first. Once they had established a base or achieved some economic success they would invite their wives and children to join them. Andrew McKenzie, who was from the Highlands of Scotland, migrated with his wife to the early Victorian goldfields. Then in 1862 he came over to the Tuapeka fields, and several months later his wife and three children followed.

Interestingly, whereas in 1865 92.6 per cent of those of both genders coming from Victoria to the West Coast were single, by 1868 and 1869 over 20 per cent were married people arriving without their spouse; many of these were women coming to join their husbands. Nor was it only single men coming into New Zealand in the 1860s. There was also a change among the women. Almost two in every five of the women were unmarried, twice the proportion in the 1840s. This was partly because the provinces deliberately set out to attract single women as domestic servants and to help counteract the surplus of men, and partly because the journey became slightly less intimidating for women, who were now more likely to have relatives to meet them at the wharf and give them support. Once again we should note that being single on arrival did not necessarily mean the immigrant had no relatives in New Zealand.

The comparatively low gender ratio of the 1870s and early 1880s is to be expected, since it followed partly from the deliberate effort by the New Zealand government to attract family immigrants, and also from the incentives offered to single women. Once assistance ended in the mid-1880s, the gender ratio increased again. In the years when there was no assistance, from 1891 to 1904, the ratio was a high 172.7. Once assisted migration returned, in the years 1905 to 1915, with a deliberate policy of attracting families and women, the ratio dropped to 137.9. The fact that it was still so high was largely a reflection of the large numbers of single men who came across the Tasman in the first decade of the twentieth century. By the interwar years, the gender ratio of immigrants was almost even. Schemes of assisted migration were now attracting young families, and the days of the frontier calling miners, whalers or bushmen to New Zealand were long gone.

This postcard was issued
by the New Zealand High
Commissioner's Office in
London about 1913 as part
of an advertising campaign
to attract single women as
domestic servants to New
Zealand. CHRISTCHURCH
CITY LIBRARIES, NEG 1063

There are also some interesting findings when we examine the gender ratios by country of origin. Until the end of the nineteenth century the English appeared to be more male-dominated than the migration flow as a whole. This was not because there were unusually large numbers of single English men. In fact the English were most likely to arrive married. Rather it was because comparatively few unmarried English women were recruited for domestic service. The recruiting grounds for servant women were in Scotland and, increasingly, Ireland. As the provinces sent agents into Scotland to attract domestic servants the numbers of single Scots women rose, before moving closer to the English pattern from the 1870s.

The most interesting story was that of the Irish. During the 1840s there were almost as many Irish women as men coming into New Zealand, and four-fifths of them were married on arrival. This was probably a reflection of their high representation among the Fencibles. But all this changed dramatically in the 1850s and 1860s when the Irish gender ratio became more unbalanced as single men crossed the Tasman in droves to the goldfields. The ratio would have been worse had these years not also seen the arrival of many single Irish women, under half of whom were now married. Provincial governments, especially Canterbury, had discovered Ireland as a source of servants.

Things changed again in the 1870s, when the Irish became by far the most balanced of the national groups – in fact, among all age groups there was actually a surplus of Irish women. There were two reasons for this. One was that Ireland was exceptional among European countries in sending high numbers of women to all overseas destinations during these years. The other reason was the deliberate recruitment of single women and married couples by the New Zealand government, especially from Ulster. One of those who arrived in the late 1870s was Aileen Douglas, the daughter of a miller from County Cavan. She worked as a domestic servant before marrying Frederick Garmson, who had arrived from Australia. Remarkably, she became the secretary of the Christchurch shearers' union, a pre-eminently male organisation. She was also active in support of the rights of working women, although a newspaper once described her as 'the terror of all the women of Christchurch'. Unusually for the times, Aileen Garmson was divorced twice.[98] Not all the single women who came from Ireland in those years were quite such feisty characters.

The passenger lists also show that single Irish men came out in the 1870s, especially from Munster, and presumably including a number who had been nominated. Thereafter, as the number of migrants from Ireland declined, those who did come tended to be men, so that in the twentieth century the Irish arrivals were significantly more masculine than any other national groups. The relatively low level of marriage among Irish immigrants after the 1850s does have some significance. It meant Irish women were more likely to end up marrying non-Irish men, which implies an obvious difference in preserving individual cultures when compared with English migrants arriving as husband and wife.

The distinctiveness of the Irish family pattern is made more evident by our figures on place of marriage. Consistently the Irish were far

'The Buller Lion', Eugene O'Conor was typical of many Irish immigrants of the 1860s in voyaging out to Victoria as a young man, marrying there, and then coming across the Tasman in his early thirties to the Otago goldfields. He eventually moved to Westport and represented Buller in the House of Representatives for 13 years. In the mid 1870s he was also responsible for a special settlement for immigrants at Karamea. Many settlers, however, finding the land swampy and poor, walked off, although O'Conor maintained to the end that it was a success. 35MM-00099-E; F, ALEXANDER TURNBULL LIBRARY

more likely to have been married outside their homeland than other national groups. Almost 40 per cent of the married Irish immigrants between 1853 and 1870 had been wed outside Ireland, 28 per cent in Australia and 10 per cent in England. Even in the years between the wars almost a third of the Irish had been married in England or Scotland. These figures were far higher than for any of the other national groups, among whom well over 80 per cent were married in their homeland (the only exception to this was the pre-1840 period when, because so many of the migrants came from Australia, a quarter of the married UK-born immigrants had wed in Australia).

The Irish pattern suggests the distinctive itineraries the Irish followed in coming to New Zealand. During the gold-rush years a large number came to New Zealand after some years in Australia. It was hardly surprising that some got married along the way. Of the Irish husbands who came to the Otago fields, no fewer than 63 per cent had been married in Australia and only 31.5 per cent brought their wives all the way from Ireland. Of those coming to the West Coast, the numbers who had married in Ireland and Australia were about the same, but interestingly, over 7 per cent had married in Scotland. One of these was James Sharkey, who had been born in County Leitrim in 1831. By the age of 23 he was working as a blacksmith in Glasgow, where he married Catherine O'Hare, who herself had come over from County Down. In 1856 the family, which now included two children, set sail for Melbourne and joined the Victorian gold rushes. In 1863, with three more children, they came out to Dunedin in pursuit of gold, then went on to the West Coast, where James took up his old trade as a blacksmith at Ross.

Later in the nineteenth century this journey via Scotland, or England, became more common. The move across the Irish Sea was the first leg in the migration journey. The Irish pattern also reflects the stage at which people decided to leave their homelands. One of the distinctive elements of Irish emigration was that many Irish left to go overseas as young single people. They often moved in stages, first perhaps to Liverpool or Glasgow, then to Sydney, and only eventually to Auckland. By contrast, those who came from England especially were more likely to be family groups who got on the boat at London having made a single decision to uproot themselves and move to New Zealand.

A third important characteristic that is worth examining is age of arrival. We have to be careful here. Our evidence is derived from the year of arrival as recorded on the death certificates, from which we subtract the stated date of birth. Clearly there is considerable room for error on both counts. More significantly, the date of arrival was only recorded on death certificates from 1876. Any person who arrived in New Zealand and died before that date is not included in the figures, and that is more likely to be true of older people than younger. Thus the figures for the first two periods we have studied, and especially the years 1840–52, will tend to exaggerate the youthfulness of the immigrant flow. After 1876 our figures are reliable across all ages, and obviously they are rather more reliable for the 1860s and 1870s than for the 1840s. Despite these caveats, much can be learned from these figures, which are shown in Tables 27–29.

TABLE 27. PERCENTAGE OF IMMIGRANTS FROM THE UNITED KINGDOM BY AGE GROUP ON ARRIVAL IN NEW ZEALAND

Ages	1840–52	1853–70	1871–90	1891–1915	1916–45
0–14	32.2	18.8	24.8	11.1	10.5
15–24	25.3	34.0	29.3	26.3	22.5
25–34	26.3	28.7	25.4	33.8	32.2
35–44	12.7	12.5	12.7	17.6	19.7
45+	3.5	6.1	7.8	11.2	15.1
Average	21.6	24.6	24.1	29.0	30.6
Number	1057	2462	3446	2109	2568

Source: Death registers

TABLE 28. PERCENTAGE OF MALE IMMIGRANTS FROM THE UNITED KINGDOM BY AGE GROUP ON ARRIVAL IN NEW ZEALAND

Ages	1840–52	1853–70	1871–90	1891–1915	1916–45
0–14	28.7	16.3	23.0	10.9	11.5
15–24	28.1	33.2	29.4	30.4	24.9
25–34	27.4	31.3	26.9	31.0	31.6
35–44	12.2	13.4	12.8	17.6	18.7
45+	3.5	5.9	8.0	10.1	13.4
Average	22.1	25.3	24.6	28.3	29.7
Number	624	1468	1810	1255	1361

Source: Death registers

TABLE 29. PERCENTAGE OF FEMALE IMMIGRANTS FROM THE UNITED KINGDOM BY AGE GROUP ON ARRIVAL IN NEW ZEALAND

Ages	1840–52	1853–70	1871–90	1891–1915	1916–45
0–14	37.4	22.5	26.8	11.4	9.4
15–24	21.0	35.2	29.1	20.3	19.7
25–34	24.7	24.9	23.8	38.0	33.0
35–44	13.4	11.3	12.7	17.5	20.8
45+	3.5	6.1	7.6	12.0	17.1
Average	20.9	23.5	23.5	30.0	31.6
Number	433	993	1636	854	1207

Source: Death registers

The first point to note is the striking change in the proportion of immigrants who arrived in New Zealand as children. According to our figures almost a third of those coming in the 1840s were aged under fifteen, although as explained, the accuracy of this figure might be questioned. However, when we look at the migrants assisted by the New Zealand Company (for which we have comprehensive records) their youthfulness is even more pronounced. Among those who came from England and Wales, 46 per cent were under fifteen, 68 per cent were under 25, and over 80 per cent were under 30.[99] Of course the company only provided assistance for those under 40, and some undoubtedly falsified their ages to obtain that support, but there can be no doubt that the migrants of the 1840s were a remarkably youthful lot.

Using the figures derived from the death register sample, if we look at those aged under 25 (who will be least affected by the 1876 distortion), we find that significantly more of the 1840–52 group were children than were young adults. Many families came out with small children – exactly the kind of people the Wakefield colonisers set out to attract. In the 1850s and 1860s the reverse was the case, with more young adults than children. This reflects the increased flow of single men as soldiers and miners, and single women as domestic servants. In the 1870s the proportion of young children rose once again as the family-centred assisted migration took effect. From that point on, with our figures now reliably accurate, we see a striking decline in the proportions of young children coming to New Zealand. In the 1871–90 period about a quarter of the migrants were children; by the 1920s only one in ten were under fifteen. In large part this was a consequence of the demographic revolution in the home countries. Between 1871 and 1926 the number of children born each year per 1000 English women aged 15–44 fell from 152.1 to 71.9. It was not surprising that this was reflected in the changing age range of New Zealand's immigrants.

On the other hand, as we enter the twentieth century there is a growing number of older people arriving in New Zealand. In the 1870s and 1880s about one in five immigrants were aged 35 or over, but by the interwar years well over one-third were in this age group. Catherine Stewart, who was 40 when she arrived, had been a weaver in Glasgow, married an iron-fitter, and become a feminist. Then in 1921 Catherine and her husband came to Wellington, where she became active in the cooperative movement, and in 1938 she was elected as the sole woman in Parliament. A supporter of John A. Lee, she lost her seat in 1943 and seven years later, at the age of 69, she returned to Glasgow with her sons.[100]

Catherine Stewart and her husband were not the only married couple who migrated in their forties during the interwar years. The

Fred and Nancy Bettjeman. Nancy was one of many women in their thirties or older who came to New Zealand after the First World War. Originally from Glasgow, she had met Fred when she nursed him at a hospital in Surrey. He had been injured at Gallipoli. After the war she came out to join Fred, but faced the ordeal of carving out a home in an isolated soldiers' settlement block in the Mangapura Valley. After a long struggle Fred and Nancy were forced to abandon the farm, and Nancy left as she had arrived – by horse. 1/2-190366; F, ALEXANDER TURNBULL LIBRARY, BETTJEMAN FAMILY COLLECTION (PACOLL-3739)

average age of New Zealand's immigrants rose from under 25 to over 30. Such a change has some consequences for the impact of immigration. Those who arrive young are more likely to adapt quickly to the new society. They lose their accents and their ways of doing things. The relative youthfulness of New Zealand's nineteenth-century migrants must have had an effect in this way. In contrast, the large representation of older migrants in the twentieth century helped perpetuate links with the Old World.

When we examine these changes by gender (Tables 28 and 29), we see that the transformation was most acute among females. In the first three periods there was a significantly higher proportion of women immigrants than men under the age of 25. By the twentieth century, however, the situation had reversed and women were considerably more likely than men to be found among those 35 or over. In 1916–45 a total of 37.6 per cent of women were in that age group, but only 32.5 per cent of men. At least some of these were grandparents who came out with their married children during the 1920s.

TABLE 30. AVERAGE AGE OF IMMIGRANTS FROM THE UNITED KINGDOM ON ARRIVAL IN NEW ZEALAND

	English/ Welsh males	English/ Welsh females	Scots males	Scots females	Irish males	Irish females	All males	All females	All
1840–52	21.0	20.4	23.4	19.2	25.9	24.9	22.1	20.9	21.6
1853–70	24.9	23.0	25.0	23.8	26.7	23.7	25.3	23.5	24.6
1871–90	24.1	23.1	24.6	24.4	26.2	23.7	24.6	23.5	24.1
1891–1915	27.9	29.4	29.2	31.5	29.0	29.7	28.3	30.0	29.0
1916–45	30.0	32.0	29.0	30.6	29.7	31.8	29.7	31.6	30.6

Source: Death registers

Table 30 shows the average age of arrival, grouped by gender and country of origin. The most striking feature is once more the peculiarity of the Irish. Throughout the nineteenth century Irish males appear on average to have been significantly older on arrival than those of other national groups. This is partly a consequence of the fact, already noted, that they were less likely to be married and therefore there were fewer accompanying young children to bring down the average age. But it also follows from their distinctive pattern of migration. Because Irish men often spent time in England or Australia before they came to New Zealand, they were more likely to be rather older and more experienced than other immigrants. By the twentieth century this age differential has disappeared.

So far we have analysed New Zealand's settlers by ethnicity, region, occupation, religion, family status and age. What emerges is a picture of some quite distinct, but highly varied, flows. England was the largest source of New Zealand's immigrants. The English were largely Protestant, with a strong Methodist influence; they arrived early and came in families, and until the end of the nineteenth century they tended to come overwhelmingly from the south of England, with people from a small-town or village background well-represented. Certain areas, such as Cornwall, Kent and the metropolis of London, were especially common places of origin.

The percentage of Scots in the migration flows was over twice the percentage in the total population of the UK. They were to be found in nearly every migratory stream except the military. They too were Protestant, and despite a strong Lowland representation they, like the English, often had family backgrounds as farmers or craft workers. Rather more Scots came as young single adults, especially as miners or servants. Although they were born in all parts of Scotland, New Zealand's Scots included at least one strong regional flow – the influx from Shetland.

As for the Irish, we can see several quite distinct groups. They were divided between largely Protestant Ulster folk, whose numbers became more significant as time wore on, and Catholic people from the south-west of Ireland. Many Irish, especially the Munster people, came across from Australia at an older age. Many arrived in family groups, and by nominating other family members they reinforced these linkages once in New Zealand. But the Irish also included single men, such as miners or labourers, and female domestic servants, especially after the 1850s from the areas around Belfast.

Now that we know our settlers, two big questions remain. The first is, do we simply conclude that the settlers had diverse origins, values and cultures, or are there some larger generalisations that can be made? And second, what happened when these people got to New Zealand? How did these different cultures play out in fashioning a new society? We look at these questions in the following chapter.

4 *The New Land*

TOGETHER OR APART?

OUR MIGRANTS HAVE NOW LANDED. Some are met at the wharf by friends or relatives. Others, such as shepherds or domestic servants, find employers waiting with offers of jobs and a horse and dray to take them off to a new home. Yet others head on foot to the goldfields. Where after their peregrinations did the new settlers spend their lives? Did they cluster together with family members and acquaintances from the old country, and so concentrate particular cultural traditions in one place? Or did they disperse, mixing quickly in communities of different origins? In other words, are distinct ethnic identities to be found in particular areas of New Zealand?

We can partly answer these questions using census figures, which provide us at a provincial level, and from 1878 at a county and borough level, with the proportions of people born in particular countries. The sample of migrants drawn from the death registers allows us to explore the issue from two perspectives. First, looking from the migrants' places of origin we can discover whether high numbers of people from one part of the United Kingdom clustered and then died in close physical proximity. Second, looking from the New Zealand end we can explore whether particular regions received migrants who were disproportionately from one part of the Old World. While the two perspectives are related, each has its own point of interest. The second analysis tells us how far a particular area of New Zealand was ethnically distinctive; the first tells us where the total flow from each source country ended up. It may be that one part of New Zealand, for example, had a very high percentage of Irish among its dead, but that this area did not attract a large proportion of the whole Irish flow to New Zealand.

Once again, the death register figures have to be treated with great caution: the place of a person's death may not have been the same as the place to which they initially migrated, and indeed, given the high transience of the New Zealand population, this was very likely. In addition, the place of birth of a migrant may not necessarily indicate their ethnic identity. Some people, for example, who were born in Scotland actually came out of the Irish community of Glasgow. The small size of samples once one goes beneath country of origin level to region or county of origin also creates large margins of error. Nevertheless, the evidence is worth examining, and it suggests a number of things. Finding out whether people from particular places clustered with their compatriots until their deaths provides an important insight into identity in the new world.

From the outset the evidence suggests that New Zealand was not characterised by extreme long-term clustering of particular groups, nor did particular migratory flows overwhelmingly locate themselves for life in one place. A picture emerges of people from Kent, or the Lowlands of Scotland, or southern Ireland, for example, scattering through the country. They did not stick rigidly to kith and kin. Despite the undoubted importance of family and friends in encouraging people to set off on the long journey, these relationships did not always survive once families got together across the other side of the globe. Take, for example, the Dickinson brothers, whom we met earlier. For Alfred Dickinson, family was obviously important. The son of a tinsmith in Preston, Lancashire, Alfred had a sweets business but decided to migrate to New Zealand with his wife Margaret and their three children. Keen to bring part of the extended family with him, he persuaded his sister and her husband to join the venture. When they were unable to sell their house, Alfred, still anxious for family support, offered a free trip to any of his brothers who were willing to come. George, a carpenter, took up the offer and came out with his wife Martha and their two sons. Arriving in Lyttelton in 1909, the brothers and their families were met by friends from Preston and went to live with them in Sydenham, where others from the north of England were settled. The two brothers started a mobile hardware business, but it did not last long. In fact, they developed a fierce enmity. George and his family moved to Riccarton and the two brothers ended up competing with each other as funeral directors.[1]

Other pressures also broke up family and ethnic clusterings. The instability of the New Zealand economy forced people to move to places where there were jobs. This happened particularly to those who came out in the 1870s and faced the downturn of the 1880s, and to the migrants of the 1920s who then had to face the Great Depression. The large numbers of single male newcomers were often involved in jobs that required a good deal of moving around, such as mining. The high levels of itinerancy among New Zealanders in the late nineteenth century has been well documented by Miles Fairburn, and he is surely correct that this helped break up relationships.[2] The fact that New Zealand lacked large cities of over 100,000 people until the twentieth century also meant it was more difficult for ethnic groups to cluster, for small-town society encourages face-to-face contact with a range of people. In the United States the concentration of ethnic groups was most pronounced in very large cities. For all these reasons, extreme clusterings of culture were not to be found in New Zealand.

Yet interesting groupings are evident. The least concentrated nationality, not surprisingly, was the largest, the English. But even here there are revealing patterns. One interesting fact is that the English were rather more concentrated in urban areas, or at least in boroughs, than were other nationalities. In 1878 a total of 56.6 per cent of those born in the United Kingdom and living in New Zealand boroughs were English, but only 50.9 per cent of those living in counties were English. This is not really surprising given the greater economic development of England over the other countries.

Table 31 shows the distribution at death of all the immigrants in our sample from England and Wales, so it shows where people from those countries were likely to end up. Table 32 shows the percentage of our sample in the different regions who were born in England or Wales. This suggests the extent to which certain parts of New Zealand were English. It tells us, for example, that the most English province of all, at least in the nineteenth century, was Taranaki. This is hardly surprising since the beginnings of European settlement in the area resulted from the activities of the Plymouth Company, which as we have noted drew many migrants from the far southwest of England.

They included some interesting people. Emily Harris was born in Plymouth and came out with her parents on the very first Plymouth Company ship, the *William Bryan*, in 1840. Like many New Plymouth settlers, in 1860, during the Taranaki war, she moved to Nelson, where she became a notable botanical artist. Robert Parris, the son of a Somerset farmer, came to New Plymouth in 1842 and became a leading land negotiator, including during the controversial sale of Te Ati Awa land in 1859. Mary Hood, who was also from Somerset, was another who came out on the *William Bryan*; she eventually managed a successful general store in New Plymouth, and like Parris was active in the Taranaki Philharmonic Society. S. Percy Smith came from Suffolk to New Plymouth as a nine-year-old and subsequently became an important surveyor and one of the country's most influential scholars of Maori history and traditions.[3]

TABLE 31. REGIONS OF DEATH OF IMMIGRANTS FROM ENGLAND/WALES (PERCENTAGES)

Region	1840–52	1853–70	1871–90	1891–1915	1916–45
Northland	0.9	1.8	1.1	2.2	2.2
Auckland	16.0	17.3	14.3	27.2	31.6
Waikato/Coromandel	2.3	4.4	3.8	5.6	8.1
Bay of Plenty	0.9	0.6	1.1	3.5	4.1
Gisborne	0.4	0.8	0.8	2.0	1.7
Taranaki	11.4	2.4	4.5	3.9	2.5
Hawke's Bay	1.4	3.0	6.2	6.5	4.6
Manawatu/Wanganui	5.6	4.1	7.6	6.7	6.5
Wairarapa	2.9	1.8	2.4	1.6	0.5
Wellington	9.7	4.7	8.8	13.8	14.4
Nelson	14.1	3.5	1.6	2.0	1.6
Marlborough	5.3	1.6	1.3	1.4	0.5
Canterbury	20.1	27.6	28.9	16.1	14.7
West Coast	1.0	7.1	2.3	1.6	1.8
Otago	4.3	14.9	12.1	4.3	3.7
Southland	3.6	4.1	3.4	1.6	1.3
	100.0	100.0	100.0	100.0	100.0
Unknown	3	3	552	1	0
Number	696	1189	1955	1410	1622

Source: Death registers

TABLE 32. IMMIGRANTS FROM ENGLAND AND WALES AS A PERCENTAGE OF UNITED KINGDOM-BORN IN EACH REGION OF DEATH (PERCENTAGES)

Region	1840–52	1853–70	1871–90	1891–1915	1916–45
Northland	66.7	66.7	53.6	81.6	67.9
Auckland	47.2	53.4	61.3	75.1	68.8
Waikato/Coromandel	48.5	53.1	65.4	68.7	66.3
Bay of Plenty	75.0	46.7	51.7	75.4	69.1
Gisborne	60.0	56.3	50.0	65.1	77.8
Taranaki	91.9	63.0	76.8	63.2	56.2
Hawke's Bay	50.0	62.1	64.9	63.2	65.5
Manawatu/Wanganui	67.2	54.4	63.5	71.8	69.1
Wairarapa	74.1	70.0	66.7	67.6	42.9
Wellington	77.0	50.9	73.2	70.4	61.6
Nelson	81.7	72.4	68.8	73.7	68.4
Marlborough	74.0	46.3	52.9	83.3	56.3
Canterbury	83.2	57.5	61.3	65.2	61.5
West Coast	58.3	46.9	41.8	63.9	57.7
Otago	27.8	32.8	38.1	38.4	36.4
Southland	75.8	26.1	31.0	37.9	40.4
New Zealand	65.8	48.3	56.2	66.9	62.9
Unknown	3	3	552	1	0
Number	696	1189	1955	1410	1622

Source: Death registers

It was not only among these early settler families that the English were important. Right through until the 1890s, death registers show that the proportion of UK-born people in Taranaki who were from England or Wales exceeded the national average by about 20 per cent. The census of 1878 shows that 73.7 per cent of those in the province who had been born in Britain or Ireland came from England (compared with 53.3 per cent in the country as a whole). The borough of New Plymouth was 78 per cent English. It is worth speculating on the long-term significance of Taranaki's Englishness. Does this, for example, explain the high numbers of young men from Taranaki who volunteered for service in the First World War?[4]

Other places that had a disproportionately high number of English-born in 1878 in comparison with those from Scotland or Ireland included the 'Wakefield' settlements of Wellington (both the province and the city), and the town of Nelson and the associated county of Waimea; settlers in the latter were over 80 per cent English-born. Hawke's Bay, where Napier had many English-born immigrants, also

'The mob' of Atkinsons, Richmonds and Hursthouses, a few of whom are pictured here in the 1880s, were among the more prominent English to settle in Taranaki. Harry Atkinson, sitting in front, established a farm at Hurworth and eventually became premier four times. His second wife Annie is on the left. Jane Maria Atkinson (née Richmond) is on the right. Her older brother had married Emily Atkinson and moved to Taranaki. In 1853 Jane Maria came out on the boat with Harry and Arthur Atkinson. She fell in love with and subsequently married Arthur, who was nine years her senior. Arthur is at the back holding a grand-daughter. He was the intellectual of the group, a lawyer and journalist, and known for his studies of the Maori language. PACOLL-1802-1-63, ALEXANDER TURNBULL LIBRARY, RICHMOND-ATKINSON COLLECTION

attracted comparatively large numbers. All these places – along with Wairarapa – are well represented in Table 32. Canterbury, another 'Wakefield' settlement, had a reputation as 'more English than the English'. Certainly, as the figures in Table 31 show, for the whole period 1853–90 about 28 per cent of the English in our samples died in Canterbury, significantly more than in any other province. In the 1871 census, 62.7 per cent of Canterbury settlers who had come from the United Kingdom had been born in England. But thereafter Canterbury does not seem to have been quite such a strong magnet for English people. Only 16 per cent of our sample of English immigrants who arrived in the two decades before the First World War died in Canterbury, and for the period between the wars the figure was under 15 per cent.

Furthermore, when we look at the place of origin of those who died in Canterbury, after 1891 the province was actually under the national average for people from England. Canterbury's reputation for Englishness can easily be exaggerated. As early as the census of 1878 four other provinces (Taranaki, Hawke's Bay, Wellington and Marlborough) had higher proportions of English, and in 1911 there were three. Christchurch itself had a relatively high proportion of English-born, but by no means the highest in the country, and in the south of the province – in the counties of Geraldine, Ashburton and Waimate – there were fewer English than the national average. Further south, in Otago and Southland, and across the Alps in Westland, the English were in 1878 under 40 per cent of those born in the United Kingdom.

During the twentieth century the 'most English of the English' was overwhelmingly Auckland. As the figures in Table 32 show, the northern province attracted a significantly greater proportion of English among its UK immigrants than did New Zealand as a whole. These Auckland settlers included a number of prominent local politicians. We have already noted Dove-Myer Robinson, who came from Sheffield in 1914, and a fellow mayor of Auckland, John Allum, who came from London in 1909. W. T. Anderton came out in 1921 at the age of 30 as a spiritualist, then became a herbalist and later a Labour MP and cabinet minister. Another was Frederick Young, who came from the East End of London in 1905 and became a union boss and Labour politician in the 1930s, when he was involved in a fierce stoush with another English migrant turned politician, Bill Jordan.[5]

There is little evidence of pronounced clustering of people from particular regions of England or Wales in the New World, although there is the occasional exception. Of those in our sample who came from Cornwall in the 1840s, close to half went to Taranaki and a third to Auckland. But by the 1850s and 1860s Cornish settlers were to be found all over New Zealand – in Auckland, in Canterbury, and in the goldmining areas of Otago and Westland. Fewer than 2 per cent were to be found in Taranaki. There was also a slight tendency for migrants from Kent to end up in Wellington. One of these was Matilda Meech, the daughter of a fishmonger from Rochester. She followed her husband, John Sancto, who was a bargeman, to Wellington in 1855. When he was drowned she married a shipwright, Henry Meech, and together they ran the saltwater baths on the foreshore near Oriental

Dove-Myer Robinson, originally born Mayer Dove Robinson, was the grandson of a rabbi and the son of a peddler of trinkets in Sheffield, Yorkshire. As a youngster he felt the effects of anti-Semitism, and when he reached Auckland in 1914, still a young boy, its absence helped cement his love of the place. He made his political name opposing the pumping of raw sewage into the Waitemata Harbour, and eventually served six terms as a flamboyant mayor of Auckland, receiving support from many of the new English immigrants who arrived in the 1950s and 1960s. *NEW ZEALAND HERALD*

Bay.[6] Henry was from Devon, and there is no evidence that the Kentish Wellingtonians were ever a community. At no stage did the number of Kentish people who died in Wellington reach a third of the total migrants from that county. The strong impression is that precise area of origin did not determine the destination of the English.

The figures in Tables 33 and 34 (taken from the death registers) and the census information support the unsurprising idea that Otago and Southland were for most of the nineteenth century a preferred antipodean home for those migrating from Scotland. In the 1871 census 61.4 per cent of Southland's UK-born residents came from Scotland, while the figure in Otago was 51.5 per cent, which is remarkably close to the death register percentages for the 1853–70 migration, as seen in Table 34. The 1871 census revealed no other province where the number of Scots reached 21 per cent of those born in the UK.

TABLE 33. REGIONS OF DEATH OF IMMIGRANTS FROM SCOTLAND (PERCENTAGES)

Region	1840–52	1853–70	1871–90	1891–1915	1916–45
Northland	1.4	1.1	0.9	1.1	1.8
Auckland	18.3	9.7	8.1	19.0	22.4
Waikato/Coromandel	4.1	2.0	1.7	5.1	6.6
Bay of Plenty	0.0	0.5	0.8	2.6	2.3
Gisborne	0.9	0.4	0.8	2.1	0.8
Taranaki	2.1	1.2	1.9	4.3	3.0
Hawke's Bay	2.3	1.2	3.4	6.8	3.9
Manawatu/Wanganui	5.5	3.4	5.6	4.3	3.9
Wairarapa	2.3	0.8	1.1	0.9	1.1
Wellington	4.1	3.5	2.4	10.3	15.9
Nelson	9.1	1.1	1.5	1.3	1.5
Marlborough	4.1	2.0	1.5	0.9	0.7
Canterbury	7.3	16.8	18.6	16.7	16.4
West Coast	1.8	4.2	3.0	2.4	2.8
Otago	33.8	36.4	35.6	16.9	12.9
Southland	3.2	15.8	13.1	5.6	4.1
	100.0	100.0	100.0	100.0	100.0
Unknown	0	0	209	1	0
Number	219	745	742	469	738

Source: Death registers

TABLE 34. IMMIGRANTS FROM SCOTLAND AS A PERCENTAGE OF UNITED KINGDOM-BORN IN EACH REGION OF DEATH

Region	1840–52	1853–70	1871–90	1891–1915	1916–45
Northland	33.3	24.2	17.9	13.2	24.5
Auckland	17.0	18.8	13.2	17.5	22.1
Waikato/Coromandel	27.3	15.3	11.1	20.9	24.6
Bay of Plenty	0.0	26.7	13.8	18.5	17.5
Gisborne	40.0	18.8	18.2	23.3	16.7
Taranaki	4.7	19.6	12.2	23.0	30.1
Hawke's Bay	25.0	15.5	13.4	22.2	25.7
Manawatu/Wanganui	20.7	27.8	18.0	15.3	19.1
Wairarapa	18.5	20.0	11.8	11.8	38.1
Wellington	10.3	23.6	7.7	17.3	31.0
Nelson	16.7	13.8	25.0	15.8	28.9
Marlborough	18.0	36.6	23.5	16.7	31.3
Canterbury	9.6	22.0	15.0	22.4	31.3
West Coast	33.3	17.3	20.3	30.6	40.4
Otago	68.5	50.2	42.6	49.7	57.6
Southland	21.2	62.8	45.2	44.8	57.7
New Zealand	20.7	30.3	21.4	22.2	28.6
Unknown	0	0	209	1	0
Number	219	745	742	469	738

Source: Death registers

Annie Cleland Millar, shown here with her husband John Millar, was the fourteenth child of a Glasgow moulder who came out to Invercargill in the 1870s when she was in her twenties. John was a baker, but also an alcoholic, so Annie quickly became the main breadwinner. She managed a private hotel, then leased two highly successful tearooms, and eventually A. C. Millars Limited became the leading bread bakers in Invercargill.
PRIVATE COLLECTION

The dominance of the Scots in Southland, even more than in Otago, is notable. Among the Invercargill Scots of the period was Thomas Fleming, who was born in Lanarkshire in 1848 and came out to Bluff with his parents in 1861. He purchased an Invercargill flour-mill in 1876 and soon took over other Southland mills. Eventually an oatmeal plant, the source of much New Zealand porridge, was based in Gore, while Fleming stayed in Invercargill, where he became mayor.[7]

The concentration of Scots in the far south did not stop. Even in the 1911 census 46.6 per cent of the UK-born in Otago were Scots, as were 43.6 per cent of those in Southland, while in the 1920s, as Table 34 shows, a clear majority of migrants to those provinces were Scottish. There is no doubt that if you visited Otago or Southland up to 1930 you would have encountered large numbers of people speaking with a Scots accent.

The Scots were not only to be found in the south, however. Most of the censuses up to the First World War showed that in nearly every province at least 15 per cent of those born in the United Kingdom were from Scotland. There were small places like Turakina where there was a substantial Scots community, but the only local-government district outside Otago or Southland where the Scots were unusually numerous was Whangarei County (31.4 per cent in 1878), which reflected the organised migration to Waipu. The only district with a small number of Scots was New Plymouth, while most other places had their quota of about 15 per cent of the UK-born.

The death register information shown in Tables 33 and 34 confirms that although many Scots went south in the nineteenth century, this was by no means an overwhelming flow. Only a third of those who migrated to New Zealand from Scotland in the 1840s went to Otago, with 18 per cent going to Auckland. Even the settlement of Christchurch, sponsored by the Anglican Canterbury Association, brought out some Scots on the first four ships. John Anderson and his wife Jane arrived aboard the *Sir George Seymour* in 1850 and spent their first night ashore with an earlier Canterbury Scots family, John and William Deans, at Riccarton. Later Anderson established a highly successful engineering and construction firm and was responsible for bringing out the province's first Presbyterian minister.[8]

In the 1850s and 1860s the arrival of Scots miners and the efforts of both Otago and Southland to attract assisted migrants from Scotland did make the southern provinces the favoured choice of the Scots, with over half the Scots population of New Zealand (52.2 per cent) showing on the death registers from those regions. But Canterbury also made efforts north of the border, with schemes to give assistance to Scottish domestic servants and to shepherds, about a quarter of whom came from the Highlands. The superintendent of Canterbury, William Rolleston, keen to encourage the migration of Highland shepherds and crofters to help develop the inland high country, agreed to pay £5 for each collie dog brought in by its master.[9] Some early Scots runholders were like Allan McLean of Waikakihi in South Canterbury, who made it 'a sine qua non for those wishing to work on Waikakihi' to be from Scotland.[10]

A number of these Scots came to Otago before moving north, which perhaps explains why the whole of the east of the South Island, including

This model of John Deans is in his cottage at Riccarton, which is now a suburb of Christchurch. He was originally from Riccarton, Ayrshire, in Scotland, and came out to Nelson in 1842. His brother William was already in New Zealand, having arrived with the first New Zealand Company settlers in Wellington in 1840. The brothers leased land at Putaringamotu Bush, which they renamed Riccarton. They also named the local river the Avon after a river in the Scottish Highlands, and a property they temporarily held Morven Hills, after a Highland range. In 1852 John returned to Riccarton, Scotland, to marry Jane McIlraith, whom he had met ten years before. After his early death in 1854, Jane became a stalwart of the Presbyterian church. PHOTO JOCK PHILLIPS

Marlborough, tended to be a bit more Scottish than the North Island. There was a particular cluster around Amuri and Cheviot. James Little, for example, came out as a shepherd to the Corriedale station in Otago before leasing land near Hawarden in North Canterbury. Helen and Stewart Gibb, who came from Forfarshire in 1863 and worked as a married couple at Teviotdale station in North Canterbury, eventually moved to Cabbage Tree Flat near Motunau. After Stewart's death Helen planted gorse seeds carefully imported from Forfarshire, and set up an accommodation house which made her known as 'the queen of Cabbage Tree Flat'.[11]

Of the Scots who arrived in the 1870s almost half (48.7 per cent) died in Otago and Southland. Thereafter the pattern changed. Under a quarter (22.5 per cent) of those who came in the 1891–1915 period died in the far south, and only about one in six (17.0 per cent) of interwar migrants did so. Instead the Scots eventually moved (either when they first migrated or later) to the urban provinces further north – Auckland, Wellington and Canterbury. By the interwar period each of these three larger provinces was the place of death of more Scots than Otago. Wellington saw the most striking change since it had a very low proportion of Scots among its UK immigrants in the 1870s; as Table 34 shows, this rose to almost a third by the interwar years. In other words, although the far south of New Zealand was always far more Scottish than other parts of New Zealand, it was never the only place to which the Scots moved, and increasingly during the twentieth century they settled, like migrants generally, in the more populous areas further north.

The Irish had their own distinctive story. The first notable fact is that they tended to be rather more strongly represented in the counties of New Zealand than in the boroughs. In 1878 they made up 23.9 per cent of the UK-born in the counties, as against 19.1 per cent in the boroughs – a not surprising reversal of the English pattern given the more rural character of Ireland in the nineteenth century. The second point of interest is that the Irish tended to go to certain areas at particular times. In the 1840s and 1850s Auckland was overwhelmingly the place to which the Irish gravitated, as Tables 35 and 36 suggest. Well over half went there, and they were also well represented in the Bay of Plenty and Waikato, immediately to the south. Some came as soldiers, but many came across the Tasman from New South Wales to take up commercial opportunities. They included the father of Thomas Russell, the great commercial entrepreneur, and Patrick Dignan from County Galway, who came out to New South Wales in 1839 and on to Auckland two years later. There he achieved financial success through his Clanricarde Hotel in Albert Street.[12]

During the 1860s the Auckland area remained an important magnet for the Irish, and again Irish soldiers and soldier-settlers were significant. But the overall pattern changed and the South Island, which had received less than 17 per cent of the Irish in the 1840s, began to attract larger numbers. Indeed, almost 60 per cent of the Irish in the death register sample arriving in the years 1853–70 died in the South Island. From the 1890s Auckland attracted a lower proportion of Irish than the country as a whole.

TABLE 35. REGIONS OF DEATH OF IMMIGRANTS FROM IRELAND
(PERCENTAGES)

Region	1840–52	1853–70	1871–90	1891–1915	1916–45
Northland	0.0	0.8	1.4	0.9	1.8
Auckland	56.3	20.3	14.8	16.5	31.2
Waikato/Coromandel	5.6	5.9	3.4	5.2	8.3
Bay of Plenty	1.4	0.8	1.8	1.7	6.0
Gisborne	0.0	0.8	1.3	2.2	0.9
Taranaki	1.8	1.5	1.6	5.2	4.6
Hawke's Bay	3.5	2.5	5.2	9.1	4.6
Manawatu/Wanganui	4.9	3.0	5.5	7.4	8.3
Wairarapa	2.1	0.6	2.0	3.0	1.8
Wellington	7.7	5.3	5.7	14.8	12.8
Nelson	1.4	1.5	0.4	1.7	0.5
Marlborough	2.8	1.3	1.4	0.0	0.9
Canterbury	8.5	22.2	28.1	18.7	12.8
West Coast	0.7	12.1	5.4	0.9	0.5
Otago	2.8	17.4	15.4	8.3	4.6
Southland	0.7	4.0	6.6	4.3	0.5
	100.0	100.0	100.0	100.0	100.0
Unknown	1	0	198	0	0
Number	143	527	757	230	218

Source: Death registers

TABLE 36. IMMIGRANTS FROM IRELAND AS A PERCENTAGE OF UNITED
KINGDOM-BORN IN EACH REGION OF DEATH (PERCENTAGES)

Region	1840–52	1853–70	1871–90	1891–1915	1916–45
Northland	0.0	12.1	28.6	5.3	7.5
Auckland	34.0	27.9	25.5	7.5	9.1
Waikato/Coromandel	24.2	31.6	23.5	10.4	9.0
Bay of Plenty	25.0	26.7	34.5	6.2	13.4
Gisborne	0.0	25.0	31.8	11.6	5.6
Taranaki	3.5	17.4	11.0	13.8	13.7
Hawke's Bay	25.0	22.4	21.6	14.6	8.8
Manawatu/Wanganui	12.1	17.8	18.6	13.0	11.8
Wairarapa	17.4	10.0	21.6	20.6	19.0
Wellington	12.6	25.4	19.0	12.3	7.4
Nelson	1.7	13.8	6.3	10.5	2.6
Marlborough	8.0	17.1	23.5	0.0	12.5
Canterbury	7.2	20.6	23.8	12.4	7.2
West Coast	8.3	35.8	38.0	5.6	1.9
Otago	3.7	17.0	19.3	11.9	6.1
Southland	3.0	11.2	23.9	17.2	1.9
New Zealand	13.5	21.4	22.4	10.9	8.5
Unknown	1	0	198	0	0
Number	143	527	757	230	218

Source: Death registers

Thomas Russell was born a Wesleyan in Cork, Ireland in 1830 and came out to New South Wales as a three-year-old. In 1840 the family moved to Kororareka and then Auckland, and when his father headed to the Californian gold rushes Thomas was left to provide for the family. He did this highly successfully by becoming a lawyer and very quickly a leading member of Auckland's business elite. PRIVATE COLLECTION

The most famous South Island flow was to the Westland gold rushes. In the census of 1878 over 40 per cent of those born in the United Kingdom and living on the West Coast came from Ireland, while Table 36 shows a similarly high representation of Irish on the West Coast in these years. Most were miners who came across from the Victorian diggings. One was Hugh Cassidy from County Donegal, who arrived in Hokitika in 1864 from Victoria, and achieved fame by establishing a Cobb and Company coach service. Among the women was the prostitute Barbara Weldon, from County Limerick. She arrived in Dunedin in 1861 and only reached the West Coast because, being considered 'the most drunken and disorderly woman' in Dunedin, she was given a one-way ticket to Hokitika, where she again quickly became notorious.[13] Few of the Irish women on the coast were of her ilk. Many were wives who followed their husbands to the diggings; others came out in the 1870s on the back of assisted passages.

One of the latter was Ann McNamara from County Clare, who came to avoid an arranged marriage. Her brothers purchased the ticket from a family friend who had bought one for her sister, who had then changed her mind. After arriving in 1879 Ann married an Irish miner and had six children. When her husband died she supported herself by running hotels at Blackwater and Waiuta. Despite the names of her hotels, the Rose and Thistle and the Empire, Ann was a strong member of the Irish Catholic community of the coast.[14]

Given the legendary nature of the West Coast Irish, one needs to be careful about exaggerating their role. Even among the UK immigrants who arrived in the 1860s and 1870s fewer than two in every five who died on the West Coast were Irish. They never dominated the area. Further, although the Irish who came to the coast tended to be Catholics from Munster, for the Munster migrants as a whole the West Coast was not the overwhelming destination of choice. Fewer than one in five of our sample of Munster people who arrived during the period 1853–70 died on the West Coast. Many may have initially gone there and moved on, but even so the figure is revealing. During the next period, the 1870s and 1880s, fewer than 5 per cent of the Munster migrants died on the West Coast. By the time of the 1911 census the proportion of Irish among the UK-born people living in Westland was down to 34 per cent. Our sample also shows that the UK immigrants who arrived after 1890 and died on the West Coast were about half as Irish as in the rest of the country, and of those arriving from the United Kingdom in the interwar years and dying on the coast under 2 per cent were from Ireland. So the clustering of Irish on the West Coast was very strongly time-bound and was never overwhelming.

Further, the sample suggests that fewer Irish arriving in the 1850s and 1860s died on the West Coast than in Auckland, Otago or Canterbury. The Canterbury story is interesting. In the 1871 census Canterbury had a significantly lower proportion of Irish than New Zealand as a whole, and our sample for 1853–70 confirms this. But by 1878 the province had almost exactly the national average of about 22 per cent of UK-born, and by 1911 there were significantly more Irish-born there than in New Zealand generally. The flows had begun among Ulster people of the 1850s and 1860s, almost a third of whom died in Canterbury; then in the 1870s Canterbury was the most popular choice

Joseph Ivess was a Munster Irishman who through his newspapers had strong links with two centres of Munster settlement, the West Coast and South Canterbury. Born in County Limerick in 1844, he came to Melbourne with his parents in 1852. He moved to Hokitika in 1868 and became manager of the Irish Catholic newspaper, the *New Zealand Celt*, whose owner John Manning was convicted for expressing sympathy with the 'Fenian' nationalists in the paper. Ivess started newspapers at Inangahua and Greymouth before moving to Ashburton, where he set up a local paper as well as papers at Temuka, Banks Peninsula, and later Timaru. *WEEKLY PRESS*, 22 NOVEMBER 1911, P. 40, CANTERBURY MUSEUM; PHOTOGRAPH BY STANDISH AND PREECE

for Irish migrants, both from Ulster and from Munster – over a quarter of our sample of Munster-born died in Canterbury, and almost 10 per cent in fact died in South Canterbury.

Among those from Munster who settled in South Canterbury was Thomas O'Driscoll from County Kerry. He came out to Timaru in 1866, one of eight members of his immediate family who migrated. He became the publican of the Hibernian Hotel, and on Boxing Day 1879 achieved brief notoriety when he persuaded fellow members of the Hibernian Society to attempt to prevent members of the Protestant Orange Lodge marching through Timaru. He was fined for riotous assembly and disturbing the peace. O'Driscoll was able to elicit support from about 150 members of the local Irish Catholic community because there was a clustering of Munster Irish in this area and in North Otago.[15]

Thus, in the census of 1878 the borough of Oamaru and the counties of Selwyn, Ashburton, Geraldine, Waimate and Waitaki had strong

Irish representation, as did Tuapeka and Vincent counties in Otago. We have already noted the particular movement of Kerry Irish to Kerrytown in South Canterbury. There are several other patterns that deserve comment. The death registers show a relatively high percentage of Irish in the Bay of Plenty among the migrants of the 1870s and 1880s, possibly reflecting Vesey Stewart's organised migration of Ulster people to Katikati. There also appears to have been a good representation in Wairarapa, although the numbers were low. Finally, the census suggested relatively high numbers of Irish in Nelson province (25.9 per cent of British/Irish-born in 1871). Examination of these figures reveals a striking contrast between those parts of the province that were on the West Coast and those in Tasman Bay. In 1878, for example, Waimea County had only 6 per cent Irish among its UK-born, whereas Inangahua County had 43.2 per cent. In those years the West Coast certainly had strong Irish representation. But the popular image of this region as *the* Irish part of the country does need to be qualified, in the same way as does the image of the southern Scots or the Canterbury English. It ignores the overwhelming extent to which the Irish gravitated to Auckland in the 1840s, and the increasing importance of Irish migration to Canterbury in the last three decades of the nineteenth century.

THE LEGACY

We began this study in the expectation that an exploration of the national, regional, religious and class origins of immigrants from Britain and Ireland might explain some of the enduring characteristics of New Zealand society. We now turn to this issue. Inevitably we leave the solid evidence of tables and graphs and enter the dangerous but fascinating world of speculation.

It may be that much of the settlers' cultural baggage was left at the dockside in London or Glasgow, and that the kinds of immigrants New Zealand received is of no great long-term importance. The act of migration itself often provided a moment when the migrant shook off older habits and looked to a new world that was worth going to precisely because it was different. Those who stayed in New Zealand, as distinct from the considerable numbers who took one look and fled back home, usually believed that success would come from integration into the new society. It is fascinating to read settlers' letters and see how often they proudly noted their adoption of New Zealand customs, eating meat three times a day or going to the beach at Christmas.

Colonial culture was not very sympathetic to newcomers who showed their Old World roots too strongly. There was a stock distinction between the 'new chums' and the old. The 'old chums' were tough and adaptable. The 'new chums' were yet to be 'colonised' or have 'the lime juice' squeezed out. In his book *Philosopher Dick* George Chamier recalled one such newcomer, describing the 'look of helplessness and suffering on his pale and meagre features'.[16] From ribbing by colonials through to jibes about 'homies' or 'poms' in the twentieth century, some New Zealanders made the perpetuation of Old World customs a source of at best joking and at worst overt hostility. Distinct cultural traditions were also weakened by the extensive mobility in nineteenth-century New Zealand. As we have already noted, there were few enclaves of tight ethnic clustering. True, there were English in Taranaki, Scots in Southland and Otago, Irish in Auckland and the West Coast. But these places were never ethnically exclusive, and the concentration of ethnic groups did not last for very long. All these factors were likely to dilute the distinct traditions brought by migrants from particular parts of the United Kingdom.

Further, we know that a high proportion – probably over a third – of migrants who had been born in the United Kingdom came to New Zealand via Australia. They arrived here, not straight from the suburbs of Glasgow or the mines of Cornwall, but after a few years on the sheep stations of New South Wales, the goldfields of Victoria, or working in the suburbs of Sydney or Melbourne. Here they would have picked up elements of a colonial culture which they brought with them when they went on to cross the Tasman. Many New Zealand words, such as 'jokers' for men or 'sheilas' for women, first became established terms in Australia; indeed, H. W. Orsman's *Dictionary of New Zealand English* includes 700 words (from a total of 6000) that are shared with Australian English – the same number as are derived from Maori and almost twice the number from British regional dialects.[17] There was often a continuing flow back and forth across the 'ditch' which kept

The great Australian writer Henry Lawson, photographed in Wellington in 1894. Lawson was probably the most famous writer to contribute to *The Bulletin*, a radically nationalist magazine that appeared in Sydney in the 1880s. Lawson's short stories mythologised the characters of the Australian outback and had a considerable following in New Zealand. Typifying that continual migration back and forth across the Tasman in the late nineteenth century, Lawson came to New Zealand twice to live, in 1894 and 1897, but on neither occasion was it a success and he returned to Australia. PA COLL-8674, ALEXANDER TURNBULL LIBRARY

cultural influences alive. Arguably, until the First World War there was an Australasian culture – earthy, democratic, and infused with a mythology about the 'bush' or frontier.[18]

It is also true that the cultural traditions and the institutional framework of New Zealand were heavily shaped from 1840 by the power of the British Empire. This was the result of direct political and economic influence as well as control of such institutions as the press and book publishing. The capital of the Empire was London, and the values of the Empire largely expressed an English 'home county' upper- or middle-class set of values. The telegraphed news that New Zealanders read in their papers usually had the byline 'London', and the values of the Empire were continually being reinforced by visiting agents of that Empire, whether they were governors or army officers. Many of the

This sketch appeared in the *School Journal* produced for use in New Zealand schools in 1908, accompanied by a poem, 'The Band of the Red, White and Blue'. Among its lines were the following: 'There waves the Flag of Britain, / The old "Red, White and Blue" / . . . We're fighting for the Shamrock, / The Thistle, and the Rose. / "rat-tat-a-too, rat-tat-a-too" / Three cheers for the Red, White and Blue'. Through such propaganda the separate cultures of the British Isles were moulded into one loyalty to the Empire. ALEXANDER TURNBULL LIBRARY; *SCHOOL JOURNAL* 2, NO. 4 (1908): 57

important institutions of New Zealand, such as the form of government, the legal traditions and the court system, owe a great deal to Imperial power.

This suggests that there is no simple correlation between the numbers of immigrants from particular countries, regions or backgrounds and the size of their long-term impact on New Zealand's values and institutions. Other factors besides Imperial power gave the English an influence in New Zealand that was greater than their numbers. People from an upper- or middle-class background had advantages of money and confidence when they arrived in New Zealand, and the English consistently had greater numbers of migrants whose fathers had been in white-collar jobs than the Scots and especially the Irish. They were more literate, more able to use the press. For example, in the years

1840–52 a total of 21.4 per cent of the English had fathers who were white-collar workers, compared with 17.1 per cent of the Scots and 14.1 per cent of the Irish.

Those years were especially important because they were the time when many of the traditions and institutions of the new society were being established. People who come early get a chance to set enduring patterns in place. In the 1840s the English came proportionately in greater numbers than later. In addition to their strong middle-class character, these early English migrants had a long-term advantage in coming predominantly in family groups, with the married couples still in their twenties. There is little doubt that family helps to perpetuate culture, and the fact that these first generations were often in ruling positions until the 1870s helped extend their influence.

It is interesting to see how quickly the largely English Wakefield settlers introduced certain practices into Wellington. Louis Ward tells us that 'Christmas Day, 1840, was celebrated in the good old English style. Fat bullocks were slaughtered and dressed with evergreens, and festivities were held.'[19] To the few Scots in their midst this would have been a strange ritual, for celebration of Christmas was not part of their culture.[20] Thereafter, however, it was very much part of New Zealand's. Soon after, about a year after the colonists reached Wellington, cricket enthusiasts got into action with the formation of a cricket club and games played on Thorndon Flat.[21]

So despite the proportionately smaller number of English in the New Zealand population when compared with that of the United Kingdom, there is no doubting their huge cultural influence in this country. Because they were a majority, the English rarely set themselves apart from society in their own exclusive institutions. Albion clubs were few. They did not have to establish such refuges because the English were the dominant group, and the institutions they enjoyed became established as the ruling institutions for the whole society.

The first generations of English migrants introduced a wide range of important governmental practices. In Wellington in the 1840s English immigrants, notably William Fitzherbert, William Rhodes, Charles Clifford, Frederick Weld and Isaac Featherston, pushed for a constitution embodying representative government, and the English were among the leaders in the first Parliament which pressed for and gained responsible government in 1856. The English continued to dominate New Zealand politics. Of 764 MPs from 1854 to 1890 whose birthplaces are known, only 30 were born in New Zealand, but 382, exactly half, were born in England, and they made up 60 per cent of those born in the United Kingdom.[22] Not surprisingly, the New Zealand Parliament often followed English precedent.

In the first session in 1854 it passed the English Acts Act, which adopted seventeen English statutes; the Trade Union Act of 1878 followed English precedents, and the Criminal Code Act of 1893 followed the English code. The idea of a loyal opposition and a neutral civil service were also English in origin, while the courts were largely English in structure and often drew on English precedents. The *Dictionary of New Zealand Biography* database of prominent New Zealanders includes 3688 people born in the British Isles.[23] Of these 66.2 per cent were from England, yet among those born in the UK who are classified as making a mark in the field of public administration, 77.2 per cent were born in England.

The English settlers introduced a wide range of other cultural practices that became important to New Zealand life. Obviously the religious faiths of New Zealanders showed a heavy influence from English churches. Right through the nineteenth century over 40 per cent of New Zealanders belonged to the Church of England, whose early establishment owed much to the Yorkshire-born missionary Samuel Marsden and the first bishop, George Selwyn, who had been educated at Eton and Cambridge University. The considerable number of English migrants who had a Methodist background also helps explain why over 10 per cent of New Zealanders in the 1901 census were of that faith. The Gothic style of so many Anglican churches was the work of architects such as Benjamin Mountfort, who arrived in Christchurch in 1850 on one of the 'first four ships' and designed many of Christchurch's Gothic revival public buildings. Frederick de Jersey Clere, the son of an Anglican clergyman from Lancashire, arrived in 1877 at the age of 21 and designed over a hundred churches, mainly in the Wellington diocese.

Educated English settlers also brought a tradition of scientific exploration. There were geologists like Frederick Hutton, born in Lincolnshire to another clergyman father, who arrived in 1866. There

'The home of Mr and Mrs William Bishop, Maitai Valley'. Charles Heaphy's watercolour of 1844 shows that within two years of arrival in Nelson, an English couple had succeeded in replacing the New Zealand bush with the lawn and flowering shrubs of the 'English garden'. A-144-011, ALEXANDER TURNBULL LIBRARY

were botanists like the missionary William Colenso and Thomas Kirk, who arrived from Coventry in 1863 and eventually became conservator of forests. Middle- and upper-class English settlers also brought the desire for an 'English' garden. For the artist Sarah Greenwood, who came with her physician husband to Nelson from London in 1843, the establishment of an 'English' garden was the essence of bringing order and civilisation to a Nelson swamp. The writer Lady Barker had similar feelings when she and her husband Frederick Broome, son of a Shropshire vicar, moved to a Canterbury outback station after emigrating in 1865.

Robert Heaton Rhodes, who was born in New Zealand to an English family but as a teen attended school in England before studying at Oxford University, established a very English garden near Taitapu, including the characteristic English spring bulb, the daffodil.

Kathleen Nunnerly, born in Leicestershire, England, was a highly successful tennis player in England before she migrated to Wellington in 1894. From 1895 to 1907 she won thirteen national singles titles. The gold medals she won at the championships were turned into the Nunneley (sic) Casket, which was awarded to the winning women's provincial team. Kathleen Nunnerly did much to raise the level of tennis in New Zealand. MNZ-0947-1/4; F, ALEXANDER TURNBULL LIBRARY, MAKING NEW ZEALAND CENTENNIAL COLLECTION (PACOLL-3060)

It was bulbs from this garden that subsequently formed the basis of the famous flowering daffodils in Hagley Park, Christchurch. A similar desire to establish a sense of home led the English to introduce English trees and English grasses. Following the establishment of acclimatisation societies in England in 1850, similar societies in New Zealand in the 1860s brought in English birds, rabbits and trout.

The establishment of municipal rather than church cemeteries, such as the Bolton Street cemetery in Wellington, the Symonds Street cemetery in Auckland and the Barbadoes Street cemetery in Christchurch, followed English legislation in 1853. Public parks were also an English institution.[24] In the early 1870s old boys of English public schools introduced the game of rugby to sit alongside cricket and horse-racing, which upper-class English had introduced in the early 1840s. Lawn tennis, rules for which were established in England in 1874, quickly followed. According to the *Dictionary of New Zealand Biography* database, 68.2 per cent of the UK-born people who were distinguished for sporting achievement were born in England.

Many of these cultural traditions were introduced by English people from a middle- or upper-class background and received reinforcement from the institutions of Empire. There were other practices with a less elevated origin. The fact that a number of the English migrants had previously been involved in the union movement, and indeed saw migration as an alternative to agitation at home, helped establish unionism in New Zealand. There were some who had been involved in Chartism, a movement for political and social reform in England in the late 1830s and 1840s, and they pressed labour causes in New Zealand. William Griffin, for example, campaigned for shorter working hours in Auckland in the 1850s, while London-born Charles Rae became active in the Knights of Labour.[25] John Lomas, a coal-miner from Barnsley, was given a free passage in 1879 and within five years had become the founder of unionism among the country's coal-miners.[26] Besides unions there were other voluntary organisations carried in the cultural baggage of English settlers, such as mechanics' institutes, building societies and friendly societies, which all expressed a working-class aspiration to improve oneself. Voluntary fire brigades and local militia were also English institutions.

The food eaten by non-Maori New Zealanders largely followed the traditional English diet, with an emphasis on meat, potatoes and cereals, together with bread, cakes and puddings. Despite the abundance of fish in New Zealand waters, this was not widely consumed since in English culture it was rejected as poverty food. Fish and chips, which became popular in England in the mid-nineteenth century, was a conspicuous exception, although the dish may have appeared in Scotland at much the same time. Favourite English vegetables like cabbage and sprouts were popular in New Zealand in spite of a Mediterranean climate that might have led to greater consumption of tomatoes, zucchini and eggplants.[27] Beer, and to a lesser extent gin, also became the alcoholic drinks of choice in New Zealand as in England, although to be fair they were also popular among the Scots and the Irish.

That English culture and values were hugely influential in New Zealand is clear, but what of the particular regional cultures that came out with the settlers? This is much harder to prove. The most revealing evidence of regional influences has been uncovered by researchers into the origins of the distinctive dialect of English to be found in New Zealand. They conclude that the most obvious source was the language spoken by people in London and the southeast of England. While they concede that there is a possible Australian influence, a consequence of the fact that many migrants spent time in Australia,[28] this is unproven. More likely is the direct effect of the large numbers of immigrants from those areas, who in our figures consistently comprised over 30 per cent of all immigrants from England and Wales between 1800 and 1945.

David Thomson has suggested that demographic patterns in New Zealand, such as size of family and age of marriage, may reflect as much the practices of the particular communities from which migrants came as any alleged effect of the New World frontier.[29] However, when we explore this in detail the suggestion does not appear to be sustainable. The pattern that emerged in New Zealand very quickly was for women to marry at an early age. According to evidence from Canterbury the average age of women's first marriage in the 1850s was about 22, rising to 23 in the subsequent decades. In England the age range of first marriage for women, based on the 1861 census, was from about 23 years to 26, but the counties that had the lowest average age were not places that sent large numbers to New Zealand. They were clustered in the mining and industrial areas of the north of England. Conversely, the counties that did send people to New Zealand in numbers tended to be those where the age of first marriage was among the highest – London, Devon, Middlesex, Surrey, Sussex, Cornwall and Devon all had an average age of 24.9 years or over.[30] The New Zealand pattern is clearly not explained by the regional traditions. Completed families in New Zealand also tended to be unusually large, and here there is a little more evidence of cultural continuity. England's rural communities tended to be among those who were the latest to adopt family limitation, and so tended to have larger families. Such areas were well-represented among New Zealand's immigrants – but this is not, of course, proof that cultural traditions explain this pattern, and even the evidence of larger family size is not overwhelming.[31]

As for other effects from specific regions of England, the evidence here is suggestive rather than conclusive. Raewyn Dalziel has shown how rural settlers from Cornwall and Devon brought with them distinctive patterns of protest which they used in the first few years after their arrival in New Plymouth. For example, they practised the ancient tradition of charivari, shaming a local minister who had offended their moral norms by making a loud brouhaha outside his home.[32] In a more general sense the large Methodist representation in the areas that sent people to New Zealand strengthened the impact of that denomination in New Zealand. As we would expect, Taranaki, with its large numbers of Cornish immigrants, was disproportionately Methodist.

Other possible impacts of English regional cultures are more speculative. For example, does the high number of migrants from Cornwall explain the adoption of meat pies and Cornish pasties as an unusually favoured food item in New Zealand? Such influences are hard to prove. Reluctantly we are left with a series of broader generalisations about the effect of English culture in New Zealand which have more to do with the undue influence of upper-class Englishmen and Imperial institutions than with the precise regional origins of New Zealand's English.

The consistently high representation of the Scots in the New Zealand immigrant population is worth exploring. The Scots had the advantage that there was a strong clustering in Otago and Southland which made it easier for their culture and values to perpetuate themselves. Certainly in the early years of settlement, especially while the first generation remained dominant, there was evidence of Scots cultural traditions. The Presbyterian church became entrenched as a dominant force in the south, and Highland shepherds for a time continued to speak Gaelic. There were places where Scots funeral traditions hung on. These included a wake with drinking of the dram, a kisting ceremony during which the body was placed in the coffin accompanied by prayers from the local minister, and the absence of prayers at the graveside. Gaelic crosses were carved into headstones above inscriptions which told of the person's Scots birthplace.[33]

From the mid-1860s Caledonian societies were established in most small communities of Otago and Southland, and in other parts of the country. These operated partly as charitable institutions, but they also

'The emigrants'. William Allsworth's 1844 oil painting was supposed to show James MacKay and his family about to leave for New Zealand from their ancestral Highland home of Domdruan. In fact, James MacKay was not a Highland laird at all. Later research has shown that he was the son of an Aberdeen merchant, had spent the years before leaving for New Zealand in London, and his name was actually Macky, not the Highland MacKay. His Highland origin was a New World invention. MUSEUM OF NEW ZEALAND TE PAPA TONGAREWA

deliberately fostered Scots culture. They taught Scots literature and history, and held Caledonian Games which encouraged Highland traditions such as the playing of bagpipes and Highland dancing. There were also history competitions, with such subjects as 'Give a brief sketch of the rise of Wallace, his exploits and his manner of death'. The games were often held on the traditional Scots holiday of New Year's Day.[34] Arguably, given the comparatively low numbers of Highlanders among New Zealand's immigrants, such activities were as much about confirming a sense of Scots identity as perpetuating activities the migrants had enjoyed at home. Highland culture became an 'invented tradition' for Scots from the Lowlands just as it did at home. In Waipu, where the first generation of settlers were Highlanders, the Highland Games were established after that generation had died out.[35]

So these Highland traditions did not essentially stem from High-landers, and they did not survive as exclusively Scots pursuits. Tanja Bueltmann has shown that in the 1880s in Oamaru 7000 people regu-larly attended the first day of the Caledonian Games, which was New Year's Day. But by the 1890s numbers had dropped to 3000, and from the end of the nineteenth century Caledonian Games were increas-ingly being upstaged by organisations like athletics clubs which were promoting alternative activities such as running and cycling. What remained from the Caledonian Games were certain activities like Highland dancing and the playing of bagpipes, which continued to be seen at public events.

The general pattern seems to be that, once the first generation had died, elements of Scots culture did not long survive if they remained exclusive to people of Scots heritage. As Tom Brooking has argued, the Scots did not establish their own schools – which might have been hotbeds of Scots culture – early on. They put their energies into public education for all, and the exclusive Presbyterian schools were not nor-mally established until the early twentieth century, and then they were largely for paying middle-class children. Their culture was very similar to that of the private Anglican schools, and they were not mechanisms for ensuring the transmission of 'Scottishness' to a later generation.[36] This is a very different pattern from that of the Irish Catholic parochial school system.

So Scots separatism did not last in New Zealand. However, because the Scots were consistently present in considerable numbers, and since they were widely accepted as 'British' and arrived as confident members of the British community, some of their traditions made the transition to general acceptance. There are two good examples: holi-days and country shows. Alison Clarke, in her delightful book *Holiday Seasons*, showed that the Scots who came to New Zealand never ob-served Christmas. Their observances were twofold: holidays preparing for the Presbyterian communion, and New Year's Day, a time of jollity and group revelry. In New Zealand the communion days, because they were tied so closely to the exclusive Presbyterian church, did not spread to wider society and died out. But New Year's Day did spread. Events held on that day, such as the Caledonian Games, began to attract wider audiences outside the Scots community, and New Year's Day adjusted itself to New Zealand's summer season. By the end of the nineteenth century in labour laws and common practice New Zealanders were recognising New Year's Day as a public holiday, while in England it remained a day of work. Even then, however, the exclusive Scots custom of 'first footing' – entering homes as the first visitors in the new year, carrying a bottle of spirits and a cake – was not continued in New Zealand beyond isolated examples in heavily Scots areas in the first generation. It was not a custom that could find relevance in the new colonial environment.[37] In some places, especially among sawmillers, St Andrew's Day was also observed as a half-holiday until the end of the nineteenth century. But again this was not a practice that managed to gain support beyond occasional clusterings of Scots, such as in North Canterbury. St Andrew's Day, like St George's Day, disappeared from New Zealand culture.

The country show is a slightly more complex story. Agricultural and Pastoral Associations and the shows they sponsored had first emerged in Scotland in the eighteenth century, and were then picked up by people in England who were keen to encourage agricultural improvement. As early as 1842, only four years after the first Royal Show in England, a show was held in the Bay of Islands, and they became widespread during the 1870s. These shows became a general community event attended by the whole rural and small-town community. Yet there was much in the show that derived from Scotland. The animals on display, especially the Clydesdale horses and the Aberdeen Angus cows, were Scottish in origin; so too were many of the sheepdogs. And from the 1890s Highland dancing became accepted as an essential part of any show day, while in the twentieth century many shows had pipe bands playing alongside the brass bands that were of English origin.[38]

In other words, Scots traditions made a long-term contribution where they could reach out beyond the Scots themselves and win support among other New Zealanders. The same was true with respect to language. There is little evidence of Gaelic-speaking lasting for very long outside the occasional isolated area, such as the Hokonui Hills.[39] Unless Highland shepherds had only their dogs to talk to, they began to learn English. For example, Kenneth McIntosh was a Gaelic-speaking ploughman who worked on a farm near Inverness. In 1858 he married Grace Cruickshank, a dairymaid on the same farm, and soon after they came out to Canterbury on assisted passages. On the journey Grace taught her husband English so that by the time he arrived he would be practised in the language which they both accepted would be the mode of conversation in their new land. Kenneth did not give up his Scots connections. He established a Clydesdale stud on the basis of two horses imported from the homeland, and in 1904 he returned to Scotland for a visit and persuaded some friends to come out. But the Scots connection did not extend to continuing the language of his early years.[40]

On the other hand, the burred 'r' that can still be found in Southland clearly carries echoes of the Scots pronunciation, and certain New Zealand words such as 'wee' for little or 'crib' for bach, or the addition of 'ie' in terms such as 'footie' are evidence of a Scots influence. In literature too there were a few initial years when Scots traditions found a home in New Zealand. There were Burns Clubs, and some poets who modelled themselves on the master, such as Dugald Ferguson and to a lesser extent David McKee Wright. Jessie Mackay, it may be recalled, was born in New Zealand to Scots parents and her father managed a station on the upper Rakaia. Educated at home, she grew up with the myths and legends of Scotland and this infused her later poetry, which featured ballads with a strange mixture of Scots and Maori stories. Jessie Mackay was an important figure in early twentieth-century New Zealand, but it could be argued that it was her feminism rather than her Scottish literary style that made a long-term difference to New Zealand life.[41]

The general pattern appears to be that where Scots practices could establish a following outside the Scots community they had a long-term place in New Zealand; where they remained within Scots enclaves they died out. The pattern holds for food, where scones and porridge became essential items of the New Zealand diet, but haggis did not. Some flora and fauna of Scots origin established themselves, such as salmon, which was introduced by the Scots and flourished in some South Island rivers, soon attracting anglers of all ethnic backgrounds. Gorse was also planted by Scots migrants to remind them of home and quickly became only too well domesticated. We have already mentioned Helen Gibb, who in order to fence her land at Cabbage Tree Flat near Motunau in Canterbury wrote home to Forfarshire for

The Flemings factory in Gore, which supplies most of the oats used in New Zealand porridge. Flemings was begun by Thomas Fleming, who came out from Lanarkshire in 1861.
PHOTO JOCK PHILLIPS

gorse seeds. When they arrived they were so precious she would not let anyone else do the planting.

What of the contribution from particular parts of Scotland? Our research has shown that the vast majority of Scots were not Highlanders, but from around Edinburgh or Glasgow. Apart from Londoners these were the most urban of New Zealand's settlers, and it is arguable that their Lowland values, rather than the more obvious Highland traditions of dancing and pipe-playing, had a more substantial impact on New Zealand life. Since so many of them grew up in or close to big cities, Lowland migrants understood the institutions of capitalism and the value of investment for long-term gain. They played important roles in the economic development of the country. Jim McAloon has documented in detail the importance of the Scots in a range of colonial economic activities. John Logan Campbell was the most well-known Scot of the Auckland merchant class. Not surprisingly, the Dunedin entrepreneurs, like the clothing magnates John Ross and Robert Glendinning, or the Burt brothers who established a nationwide plumbing firm, were Scottish.[42] The *Dictionary of New Zealand Biography* database suggests that Scots were over-represented among those noted for business success (25.1 per cent compared with the 21.3 per cent that was the Scots' representation among all UK-born in the database), but not overwhelmingly so. In addition, the Scots who settled in such numbers in Dunedin had the real advantage that gold made that city the centre of economic growth at a crucial moment in the formation of the New Zealand economy.

The *Dictionary of New Zealand Biography* database also suggests that the Scots were slightly over-represented among those noted for their contribution to education (23.4 per cent of all UK-born New Zealanders), and rather more strongly represented among those involved in science (24.0 per cent) and health (26.8 per cent). Scots Calvinist insistence on Bible-reading may be one influence here, but perhaps more pertinent was the fact that the Scottish enlightenment, with its roots in Lowland Scotland, especially Edinburgh, encouraged education. The most Scots part of New Zealand, Otago, saw the first New Zealand high school for girls, which opened in 1871 after a battle by Learmonth Dalrymple, the daughter of an iron-merchant from Angus. The first headmistress was another Scot, Margaret Gordon Burn, daughter of an accountant from Edinburgh. Two years earlier the country's first university had opened in Otago. The Scots education system of 1872, which set out to provide compulsory, free and universal education in public primary schools, was the model for New Zealand's 1877 Education Act. A Scots-born prime minister, Peter Fraser, masterminded the 1944 Act that effectively introduced free secondary education to New Zealand. The fact that Otago had for a long time the only medical school in the country, and the strong links that school established with Edinburgh, help to explain the continuing impact of Scots-born people in both the health and scientific fields.

Some specific groups who clustered in particular areas may have had a disproportionate effect. To cite one example, although in the 1850s and 1860s migrants from the Border region of Scotland were under-represented in the whole Scots flow, there appear to have been quite a number from that area who were sons of farmers and who themselves became farmers in Canterbury and Otago. In the Amuri district of North Canterbury, for example, John Tinline and George

Margaret Burn (née Huie) was born in Edinburgh in 1825 and came out to Geelong, Victoria, with her mother following the death of her father in 1852. She married a teacher who suffered sunstroke, forcing Margaret to support herself and her three children. She did this by opening the Geelong Ladies College. A strict Presbyterian, she was appointed the first principal of Dunedin's Girls' Provincial School (later Otago Girls' High School), arriving six weeks before the school opened in 1871. She retired thirteen years later with the school's reputation firmly established. *OTAGO WITNESS*, 25 DEC. 1918, P. 33, HOCKEN LIBRARY

Rutherford became important landowners. They had been school-mates at Jedburgh, Roxburghshire, the Border county that includes the Cheviot Hills. In the early 1850s Tinline began running sheep in the Amuri, and he persuaded Rutherford to come across from Australia to join him at the end of the decade. Subsequently other Scots, both land-owners and shepherds, followed and, in a reference to Robert Burns' description of Scotland, the area became known as 'the land o' cakes'.[43] There is some evidence that Border patterns of allowing sheep to graze rather than rounding them up into enclosures every evening provided the model for this practice in the South Island sheep stations, a practice very different from what happened in Australia.[44]

Perhaps too the strong Shetland migration may have encouraged the spread of knitting in New Zealand society, although the northern isles were not the only places where knitting traditions were strong.[45] As with the English, it is hard to nail down the Scottish regional origins of significant New Zealand practices. This is not, of course, to deny that at least in the first generation after initial settlement, say until the 1880s, anyone visiting the southern parts of the South Island or isolated places like Amuri county in North Canterbury, Turakina near Wanganui, or Waipu in the far north would have heard and seen plenty of evidence of a Scottish presence.

Turning to the Irish, it is immediately obvious that the national group is not a particularly helpful unit for examining the perpetuation and impact of cultural traditions. As we have seen, the Irish were divided along both geographical and religious lines – between Protestants and Catholics, and between Ulster folk and those from the south, especially Munster. The Ulster Protestants were a significant presence in New Zealand – almost 10 per cent of the total migrants from the United Kingdom in the 1870s, and again in the first decade of the twentieth century. Because they had easy routes of assimilation into the Anglican and Presbyterian churches, and they tended to identify with the values and institutions of the British Empire, they were a less visible minority. Yet they did contribute one significant institution: the Orange Lodge. In the New Zealand setting this became less a place for Ulster folk to hide out and preserve Old World memories than a vehicle for instilling 'British principles' in the wider community. English and Scots were encouraged to join. The tendency of Ulster migrants, therefore, appears to have been to encourage the replacement of narrow ethnic loyalties with a more inclusive patriotism towards the Empire.[46]

The Catholic southerners are a more interesting subculture. Compared with other New World societies, especially Australia, the proportion of Catholic Irish settlers in New Zealand was never very high. Many of the men, especially those who arrived in the 1860s gold rushes, tended to be highly itinerant, while many of the single women found themselves working in Protestant households. These factors made it difficult for some southern Irish to sustain their own cultures, or for the cultures to have an impact on the wider society. Yet there were countervailing forces. Irish Catholicism had always placed great importance on the family, and the early migrants made extensive use of the device of nominating family members and friends to come and join them in New Zealand. The very fact that Irish Catholics were living in a society dominated numerically and culturally by English and Scots Protestants encouraged them to look to each other for psychological support, especially where there was some initial hostility towards them, as in Canterbury. Once the Irish took over ruling positions within the Catholic church, the church encouraged cohesion. From the 1860s it established parochial schools which were in effect protectors of the faith, but also a mechanism for perpetuating Irish Catholic culture.

Lyndon Fraser's work on the community in both Canterbury and the West Coast has shown that Irish Catholics in the nineteenth century had a very high rate of marriage within their group. In Christchurch from 1860 to 1889 over 95 per cent of Irish Catholic men and over 70 per cent of the women married Irish spouses, and the figures were similar on the West Coast.[47] There was also some geographical clustering among the Irish Catholics. As we have seen, this was never extreme at the provincial level. Even in the most Irish area, the West Coast, they never comprised more than 35 per cent of the UK-born population. But Fraser has also shown that while New Zealand never saw the large-scale ethnic clustering that occurred among the Irish in Liverpool or Boston, for example, there was some small-scale concentration. Numbers of Irish Catholics began to take up residence around the Church of the Blessed Sacrament in Barbadoes Street in eastern Christchurch.[48] There school, church and protective institutions like the Hibernian Society ensured that Irish Catholics could mix daily with their own. There was also some concentration of Irish within particular occupations. They were always well-represented among the police force (over 40 per cent of the UK-born police in the *Dictionary of New Zealand Biography* database were from Ireland) and among publicans, for example. So Irish Catholic culture and values were kept alive in New Zealand.

Yet, in contrast to the Scots, the culture did not manage to extend beyond its own confines into the wider society. Few specifically Irish traditions became adopted by other New Zealanders. For example while New Year's Day was universally adopted, St Patrick's Day never attained that status, and after considerable interest in the late nineteenth century celebration of the day dropped away. Further, the Irish Catholic community did not seriously challenge the dominant British values of New Zealand. The curriculum in Catholic schools

Potato pickers, South Canterbury. This was an area that attracted considerable numbers of Irish immigrants, and potato picking would have been a familiar pursuit. However, it is not known if these men were Irish, and there are few other signs of Irish traditions in the farming practices of New Zealand. WAIMATE HISTORICAL MUSEUM

was broadly similar to that found in Anglican or state schools, and the Catholic boys' schools adopted the English game of rugby remarkably early, although they tended to maintain their own separate teams after school.

While small pockets of anti-British republicanism emerged in the early twentieth century around such journals as the *Green Ray* in Dunedin, this was never on the same scale as in Australia, where the much larger Irish Catholic community promoted a radical republican nationalism in the highly popular journal *The Bulletin*.[49] When the First World War broke out there was tension over the conscription of Catholic priests, but the extent of real Irish Catholic dissent was minimal, again far less than across the Tasman. A few Irish resisted conscription, especially on the West Coast, but in general the evidence is that the proportion of Catholics who volunteered was very similar to those of other religions and origins.[50]

This is not to deny, of course, that people of an Irish Catholic background have had a major influence in New Zealand – from politicians like Mickey Savage to rugby players like Sean Fitzpatrick and writers like Dan Davin and Vincent O'Sullivan. The claim is simply that specifically Irish Catholic practices and traditions have not radically impacted on New Zealand culture or the behaviour of Protestant New Zealanders.

In general then, the shaping power of the individual national groups from the United Kingdom reflected the power and numbers of each group. The English, as the most numerous, earliest and most socially prestigious, clearly had the greatest impact on New Zealand. The Scots, confident, economically successful, and arriving in substantial numbers, were able to achieve the acceptance of some of their traditions, and felt little need to sustain their culture in a separate enclave. The Irish Catholics, relatively few in number, arriving with few class or economic advantages, did sustain their own identity through creating places of refuge from the larger society. However, they had little influence on the way New Zealand developed.

All this is not to deny that through most of the nineteenth century, Pakeha New Zealand was largely a community of first-generation immigrants from Britain and Ireland. Among adults there was not a majority of New Zealand-born non-Maori until 1896. So nineteenth-century New Zealand must have been a place where people were continuously aware of the different ethnic and cultural origins that made up the settler community. There were different accents, distinct patterns of religion, patterns of eating and drinking, and different death customs and holidays. It was less that these local traditions got left on the dock in Britain than that, having come here, they did not survive far into the second generation in the New World.

Why did the separate national, and indeed local, cultures that settlers brought to New Zealand not have a more visible long-term impact on Pakeha practices? We have already noted several factors. One was the absence of large cities, with the four main centres not much more than about 50,000 people before 1900, and a majority of settlers living in communities of under 5000. In large cities like Liverpool or Chicago people from a particular ethnic community could band together, attend their local ethnic church, eat their own foods, talk their own language.

In New Zealand most people lived in 'face-to-face' communities where people from different backgrounds interacted daily.

Another factor was the high level of itinerancy in nineteenth-century New Zealand, which broke up enclaves of migrants from particular groups. In *State Experiments in Australia and New Zealand*, William Pember Reeves noted, 'The country people in the colonies move about. . . . I do not mean only the classes whose work keeps them always moving – the drovers, mail-carriers, hawkers, waggoners. . . . Artisans and general labourers seem to share in the readiness to shift their ground.' In his earlier book, *The Long White Cloud*, Pember Reeves also argued that settlers in New Zealand became 'a British race in a sense in which the inhabitants of the British Isles scarcely are' because they lived together, met daily and intermarried.[51] There is no doubt that there was considerable intermarriage between people from different parts of the British Isles. To take just one example, Mary Jane Tripcony, a domestic servant in Cornwall, and Thomas Moses, a Cornish farm labourer, married and in 1878 came out to New Zealand, bringing their daughter and son. In New Zealand that daughter, Annie, met and eventually married Henry Hampton, whose father had been a farm labourer in County Down, Northern Ireland. So Cornish woman and Ulster man were joined in marriage.[52]

The actions of the New Zealand state also encouraged the disintegration of particular identities. The introduction of compulsory and universal education in 1877 was important. Migrants who came out as children and attended state schools, rather than Catholic parochial schools or private Anglican schools, were quickly exposed to people from different backgrounds. Marriage outside the founding group often followed. Further, at the end of the nineteenth century, when the South African War highlighted New Zealand's military role in the British Empire, there was a strong infusion of Imperial culture into the schools and the community in general. All New Zealanders going to school were exposed to stories of British (but largely English) heroes, they read English poets like Wordsworth and Milton, and they were encouraged into English upper-class institutions such as Boy Scouts.

The importance of the Empire was constantly reinforced. At Waipawa at the turn of the century locals could drink at either the Imperial Hotel or the Empire Hotel, and play tennis at the Empire

This headstone in the Warkworth cemetery records a marriage across two British cultures. The husband, Nathaniel Wilson came from Glasgow, Scotland, while his wife, Florence, came from Roche in Cornwall. PHOTO JOCK PHILLIPS

Gardens or rugby on the Empire Paddock! Further, they began to attend Imperial celebrations, such as a Grand Gala Day to celebrate the coronation of the King in 1902, in place of St Andrew's or St Patrick's or St George's day. The concert at the end of the Grand Gala Day included such songs as 'Red, White and Blue', 'His Majesty the King', 'When the Empire Calls', 'Rule Britannia', and 'God Save the King'.53 So a sense of Imperial identity helped to expunge the different cultures of Great Britain, and became an important ingredient in the emergence of a sense of New Zealand identity as the 'Empire's finest'.

As suggested earlier, this Imperial ideology also tended to strengthen the dominance of upper-class English traditions over regional ones. By the 1920s, when Alan Mulgan, the grandson of a Church of Ireland minister who came to Katikati with the Ulster Protestant immigrants of the 1880s, wrote a book called *Home*, he conceded that it was Westminster Abbey and Lords cricket ground that he yearned to see. Growing up, he recalled, 'Ulster was a shadowy place. England and English things were always before my eyes.'[54]

While recognising the speedy dissolution of local and national traditions (with the exception of those from England), it is perhaps worth going beyond nation and reconceptualising our findings in ways that provide added meanings. There are two other interesting approaches. One is to look across all national groups in the search for broad generalisations about the kinds of people who came to New Zealand. The second is to reconceptualise the settlers into cultural, and particularly religious, groupings. Let us begin with the latter perspective.

We have already seen that it makes no sense to look at the Irish as one national group. Irish Catholics and Irish Protestants had quite distinct cultures. The settlers who came to New Zealand, at least until the First World War, came from communities in which religion was hugely important, and they carried these values to the New World. In New Zealand only slightly less than at home the church remained the major community institution, a place to which many people went regularly to meet their neighbours, discuss common issues and have their moral values continually reinforced in prayer, song and sermon. At the end of the nineteenth century between 30 and 40 per cent of New Zealanders went to church weekly (the Anglicans were the poorest attenders, the Methodists the best, with the Catholics and Presbyterians in the middle). But in the five-yearly census over 90 per cent gave a Christian denomination to which they belonged, and when it came to funerals or Christian holidays New Zealanders proclaimed a religious adherence.[55] The language of public discourse was Christian and ministers had no hesitation in entering into public debate on both political and moral matters. Christian morality infused family life, as well as social behaviour in and out of the workplace. Religion, in sum, formed a complete worldview for many colonists, and this was especially true for women.

If religion was important, then the perspectives of the different denominations took on real significance. We have already noted that the Catholic church formed the heart of the identity maintained by migrants from southern Ireland. What was Irish and what was Catholic was not always easy to distinguish. Among New Zealand's Protestants there was one central division – between the Anglicans and the more puritanical denominations. About 40 per cent of New Zealanders were Anglican. A large majority of these were English, but there were also some who came from northern Ireland and a very few from Scotland. In England Anglicanism was the established church, supported by both the state and large land-holdings. It was therefore not required to be evangelistic, or heavily dependent upon increasing its numbers to survive. It was the respectable church to which many of that first generation of upper/middle-class English settlers belonged. It was a relatively relaxed faith, not activist, and increasingly expressing a slightly sentimental ideology of the family.

The other Protestant churches were rather different. The largest was the Presbyterian church, which found its strongest support among the Scots, but also claimed up to 20 per cent of the Irish, almost all from the north. The Presbyterians had emerged during the Reformation as followers of John Calvin. They expressed a suspicion of popish ceremony and a strong belief in personal moral virtue. The English also included smaller Protestant groups of a seventeenth-century Puritan background, such as the Baptists and the Congregationalists, and one larger group, the Methodists, who had emerged in the eighteenth century in revolt against the alleged 'decadence' and moral backsliding of the established Anglican church. Together these 'low' Protestant groups comprised over 35 per cent of the population of nineteenth-century New Zealand (Presbyterians 23 per cent, Methodists about 10 per cent, the others in total about 3 per cent). They were much more activist and evangelical than the Anglicans. They were used to trying to convert people, and they held to strong moral views of correct behaviour.

As we have noted, religion tended to be most strongly supported by women, who were more regular churchgoers than men, and religion was more systematically maintained in the cities, where there were churches and denominational institutions such as Sunday schools. So a final cultural grouping worth considering is the largely male communities to be found in the more isolated rural areas of New Zealand. These were the goldminers, the timber-fellers, the navvies, the high-country shepherds. Patterns of swearing, yarning, going on a spree with drinking binges, even fisticuffs were to be found in this group. Their culture was largely derived from the itinerant workers of Britain, 'those who slept rough', but in New Zealand the high numbers of unmarried men and the seasonal, itinerant nature of much labour allowed such traditions to flower in rural areas. Such people were often a long way from church and family. The pub, an institution that was brought from Scotland, Ireland and England alike, was a more accessible gathering point. So arguably it was among these people that inherited ethnic and religious traditions dissolved fastest. In work gangs, or yarning in the men's quarters of large stations, or socialising in the pub, it was easy for Cornish miners, Scots shepherds and Irish ex-soldiers to establish relationships and develop a vigorous colonial culture. Cultural change was not restrained by family, by churches or by other ethnic or religious institutions.

One way of looking at the culture – and indeed to some extent the politics – of New Zealand at the end of the nineteenth century is to segment society not according to strict national group of origin, but according to these four religious/ethnic divisions. There were the largely southern Irish Catholics; the largely English Anglicans; the low-church Protestants, who had a strong Scots component mixed with northern Irish Protestants and some English Protestants, especially the Methodists; and the culturally and ethnically mixed blokes of the frontier. The division can be seen being played out in the tumultuous battles over temperance during these years. Obviously the frontier blokes and the southern Irish Catholics were not enthusiasts for temperance, for drinking alcohol was a central ritual of their cultures. Indeed, to some extent they were the target of the campaign to outlaw alcohol. The leading protagonists of the change were without doubt the low-church Protestant churches. Scots Presbyterians played a major role. Some of the earliest electoral districts to vote against licensing were areas of Otago and Southland where there were heavy Scots Presbyterian majorities: Clutha in 1894, Mataura in 1902, Invercargill and Oamaru in 1905, and Bruce in 1908. It is of interest that Scots-born Members of Parliament supported an 1872 bill to take licensing out of the hands of local JPs by fourteen to three, and an 1876 bill to give it to local electors by eleven to two.[56]

Leonard Isitt was the public face of the prohibitionist movement in New Zealand at the end of the nineteenth century. Born in Bedford, England, he was brought up as a Methodist and came out to New Zealand in 1875 aged 20. He served as a Methodist missioner in Lawrence, the old goldmining centre, and the sight of widespread drunkenness made him a committed opponent of alcohol. He started and edited the paper the *Prohibitionist* and was an outstanding public orator. Isitt eventually became a Member of Parliament. 1/1-014096; G, ALEXANDER TURNBULL LIBRARY, S. P. ANDREW COLLECTION (PACOLL-3739)

Among the English, the Baptists and Congregationalists were consistently supporters of prohibition. Sir George Fowlds, the Auckland Congregationalist, was among its strongest adherents. The Methodists were equally ardent, with L. M. Isitt and T. E. Taylor leading the fight in Parliament. But the Anglicans were always ambivalent, with Bishop Julius of Christchurch in 1899 supportive of local no-licence, but the Otago synod in 1901 declaring prohibition 'irrational'.[57] It is revealing that in the two parliamentary votes mentioned above the English, who would have been predominantly Anglican, divided eight in favour and eighteen against in 1872, and twelve in favour and eighteen against in 1876. It is also apparent that in the agitation for women's suffrage, which was closely associated with the battle against drink, leading roles were played by low-church women. Feminists like Kate Sheppard, Margaret Sievwright and Jessie Mackay all had non-Conformist Scots

Although she was born in Liverpool, Katherine Sheppard (née Malcolm) was the daughter of Scots parents and her early religious education came from an uncle who was a minister in the Free Church of Scotland. She came out to New Zealand aged 21, married a grocer soon after, joined a Congregational church in Christchurch and became active in support of temperance. The visit of an American evangelist, Mary Leavitt, led her to become a founding member of the New Zealand Women's Christian Temperance Union. Thus began her public career as the leading women's temperance worker and promoter of women's suffrage.
S6/1, CANTERBURY MUSEUM.
PHOTOGRAPH BY H. H. CLIFFORD.

family backgrounds. Interestingly, of those in the *Dictionary of New Zealand Biography* who were characterised as active in 'reform', no less than 57 per cent of the UK-born were Methodists, Presbyterians and Baptists. Of course these cultural boundaries were never watertight. As the agitation for temperance developed, even some Catholics, such as Bishop Cleary of Auckland, came out in support. But the larger framework remains relevant.

It is perhaps easy to underestimate the extent of Protestant–Catholic animus in the first three decades of the twentieth century. Francis Bennett, who was from a good Protestant background, recalled the merciless ribbing his father received for supporting the Catholic Joseph Ward over the Protestant Bill Massey. One conspiratorial local even suggested that the Temuka railway station had been painted green to please the local Catholics.[58] In politics Protestant–Catholic conflict saw fierce debates over schooling, the conscription of Catholic priests during the First World War, and some Irish Catholics' alleged support for the Irish rebellion of 1916. The period saw the emergence of the Protestant Political Association, which accused Catholics of extracting privileges, supporting enemies of the Empire and influencing the public service. They succeeded in getting legislation passed in 1920 which banned Catholic teaching on marriage. Two years later the Auckland Catholic bishop, James Liston, was charged with sedition for allegedly describing the 'martyrs' of the Easter Rising in Dublin as 'murdered by foreign troops'.[59] So for some 30 years Protestant–Catholic feelings ran high in New Zealand. In a sense this cultural/religious conflict was a second-generation migrant ethnicity playing itself out, with larger loyalties of religion and Empire emerging out of the original national groupings.

A second approach to understanding the wider impact of the immigrants from the British Isles is to explore the experiences or cultural values that were common to a very large number of the settlers, and cut across the various ethnic and religious divisions. For a start there is the simple fact that a high proportion of the United Kingdom immigrants from all areas came to New Zealand with the assistance of governments, provincial and national. Did this encourage a subsequent willingness to turn to the state? One has to remember that once the assisted immigrants landed they were not deserted by the government. They were often housed in immigration barracks, and immigration officers took responsibility for giving them advice and helping them into work. The new Labour Department bureaux that were established in the 1890s grew out of the older immigration bureaux. The involvement of the state in public works followed naturally from its involvement in immigration.

The one form of state activity which colonial New Zealanders resisted for a considerable time was any type of public welfare that replicated the old British Poor Law. David Thomson has suggested that this too was derived from New Zealand's immigrant origins. Under the old Poor Law, British localities had provided some support in the form of work or money to the unemployed, and increasingly had paid pensions to the old. But from the 1830s there was a strong ideological reaction against these practices. The unemployed were only to be supported if they were incarcerated in workhouses, while there were attacks on pensions for the elderly and an insistence on thrift and individual or family responsibility. Thomson suggests that those who came here brought these new attitudes with them and ensured hostility to public relief in the colony. Families were expected to provide for their own needy and sick. Attitudes varied in different parts of Britain. Some areas that sent many people to New Zealand, such as Scotland, London and the West Midlands, never did have strong traditions of public welfare, while the southeast was an area where an especially strident change had taken place and opposition to the old Poor Law was most marked. The practice of minimal welfare that prevailed for much of the second half of the nineteenth century in New Zealand may well have been affected by these immigrant origins.[60]

When in the last decade of the century it became clear that family and voluntary systems were unable to cope with issues of sickness and old age, New Zealanders, many of them either migrants of the 1870s or the children of migrants, were quite ready to turn to the government to provide assistance once again. How far the extent of government involvement in the economy in New Zealand in other respects was a legacy of immigrant attitudes, or whether it was a consequence of other factors such as size, is a question that remains to be explored.[61]

From whatever parts of Britain and Ireland the immigrants came, they tended to share quite similar occupational backgrounds. As we have noted, many settlers came from a largely rural world. The number of migrants whose fathers had been farmers or farm labourers was not disproportionate to the home population; however, when one adds the large numbers of children of village or small-town craft-workers, then many of the new immigrants from all ethnic groups would have understood the significance of independent land ownership. If they had not themselves suffered, they would have seen tenant farmers who had lost their leases when holdings were brought together and enclosed; they would have seen agricultural labourers lose allotments and rights to common lands; and if they had come from Ireland they would have seen the social costs of uneconomically small holdings.

The security and independence that came from ownership of a decent plot of land would have been a major value for many migrants to New Zealand, and it is one of the reasons for the appeal of the country.

William Hall-Jones was in many respects a typical English immigrant to New Zealand. The son of a cabinet-maker in Kent, he came out to New Zealand as a builder with his wife in 1873. He eventually settled in Timaru, and became its MP in 1890. In Parliament he promoted the breaking up of large estates for farm settlements and a 'non-contributory' form of pension, an idea that was enacted with the passage of the 1898 Old-Age Pensions Act. In 1906, following Richard Seddon's death, Hall-Jones became the first leader to be designated 'Prime Minister'. 1/1-001433; G, ALEXANDER TURNBULL LIBRARY, HERMAN JOHN SCHMIDT COLLECTION (PACOLL-3059)

Certainly the opportunity to own land quickly was at the heart of the propaganda pushed by New Zealand's immigration agents. The emphasis subsequent New Zealand governments gave to providing for land-ownership for the Pakeha population – often at the expense of the Maori population – and the long-term priority given to home ownership were among the consequences of these attitudes. The Liberal government at the end of the nineteenth century, which set out to break up the large estates, purchase more Maori land, offer assistance to settlers and loans for housing, included a number of people who had migrated to New Zealand in the previous 30 years (Richard Seddon and John McKenzie among them).

The other side of this regard for independent property ownership was a fear of large cities. The settlers who came to New Zealand tended to be from rural areas or small towns. London was an important source of migrants, but the heavily industrialised cities of the north were not.

Many of those who came had suffered economically when their pre-industrial craft traditions had come under threat from the products of the factory. Admittedly, when people came to New Zealand they did not all rush into frontier isolation. More often they settled in coastal communities, usually with a port, like Auckland, Dunedin, Oamaru and New Plymouth. But these were relatively small places, very different both in scale and in character from industrialised cities like Manchester and Birmingham. There remained a deep suspicion that such urban conglomerations might develop in New Zealand, a dislike of factories and terrace housing, and a desire to perpetuate through suburban sections a less urban atmosphere and culture.[62]

This is not to say that the settlers from Britain and Ireland were anti-capitalist or yearned for self-sufficiency. Many had lived near London or Glasgow and participated fully in the capitalist economy. But as we have seen, a good proportion of them had been craft-workers, people like builders and blacksmiths, whose style of work was as small, self-employed independent operators. When they left the homeland for the New World it was often because their independent economic lifestyle had come under threat. What they brought to New Zealand was a respect for self-employment. The small skilled operator, not the industrial magnate, was their model of success. Arguably this remained the New Zealand ambition for much of the twentieth century.

As small self-employed operatives, many of the New Zealand migrants were not highly specialised individuals. Urban and industrial work requires a high degree of specialisation since it depends on an intensive division of labour. The large majority of New Zealand settlers did not come from this background. Their families would have depended on a range of skills. Agricultural labourers, for example, would have turned their hands to many different tasks on the land, from ploughing to caring for animals. They would often have had small allotments or common rights where they would grow vegetables. They might well have kept a pig and gone hunting for rabbits on the common. The women were equally adaptable – knitting or weaving for their own needs, doing domestic service in their teenage years, perhaps sewing for the market through the 'putting out' system. They might have had sellable skills as glove-makers or hatters.

This versatility was especially characteristic of people in certain

This Shetland woman is knitting as she carries peat on her back. She would also have worked on her croft, growing vegetables and perhaps minding her sheep, while her husband was out on the water fishing. This versatility would have been typical of the many people from the Shetland Islands who came to New Zealand. ALEXANDER TURNBULL LIBRARY, ROBERT STOUT COLLECTION (PACOLL 5367-2-02)

areas that sent many people to New Zealand. In the southwest of England there were many who had worked part-time in the mines but also grown crops; in the counties of the southeast such as Kent there was seasonal work on the fruit and hop orchards; in the far north, especially in Shetland, men combined fishing and digging peat with work on a croft, while the women earned money knitting; in the area around Belfast people combined weaving linen with agricultural work. In other words many of New Zealand's settlers were highly versatile individuals, often used to seasonal patterns of employment and fully expecting to have to travel at times to find work. It is arguable that these characteristics, which many New Zealanders have subsequently claimed as part of the 'national character' – versatility, a jack-of-all-trades 'number 8 fencing wire' attitude, a willingness to go on the road – have as much to do with the background of New Zealand's immigrants as of the unspecialised conditions in nineteenth-century New Zealand.

Such versatility was as important for the women as for the men. There was, it is true, a long-term trend for women to cease employment in the fields, and in England especially the agricultural unions that encouraged migration sought to work against women being employed out-of-doors for fear that this would lower wages.[63] The New Zealand view that a woman's place was in the home may have derived in part from such inherited attitudes. But the rural women who came to New Zealand also had long experience of 'making do'. Whether through growing food on allotments, making clothes, or sending the youngsters out to hunt for rabbits, they had learnt ways of providing for the household when their labourer husbands suffered periods of low or nil employment. In New Zealand the tradition of 'making do' was not lost, and it became a noted characteristic of housewives in the Depression.[64]

The rural culture of nineteenth-century Britain and Ireland left other marks in New Zealand. For example, the agricultural labourer had traditionally supplemented the family table with hunting on the common land and occasional poaching on the lord's estate. Increasingly these rights came under pressure as commons were enclosed and poachers punished. Hunting and shooting pigs in the New Zealand bush, an unrestricted right, became one of the characteristic privileges of colonial males. As the Irish settler John Gilmore wrote home, 'There is plenty of game here to shoot. The licence is only £2.'[65] The introduction of other traditional British game such as deer followed from these Old World aspirations. Similarly, we have already noted how the institution of the pub and the culture of those who 'slept rough' had origins in most parts of rural Britain and Ireland.

We began this project in the expectation that if we could discover exactly where New Zealand's United Kingdom settlers came from we would learn something about the origins of New Zealand culture. The analysis has led us from regional distinctiveness to nation to religious groupings, and finally to characteristics that were shared across many of the groups of people who came from Britain and Ireland. Each level of analysis has borne fruit. The large numbers from the southeast of England help to explain our accent; the large numbers of Scots explain

In New Zealand, as long as they had access to the land anyone could hunt for pigs or birds and later for deer. In Britain and Ireland the privilege of hunting was governed by game laws which restricted these rights to the élite. This encouraged considerable resentment and poaching among the rural folk. So when immigrants from the United Kingdom settled in New Zealand they often spoke enthusiastically of the experience of hunting wild boars.
ILLUSTRATED NEW ZEALAND HERALD, 1876

our enjoyment of the New Year; the body of low-church Protestants from Scotland, Northern Ireland and England helps to explain the long battle for temperance in New Zealand and the quest for moral respectability; and the fact that so many of New Zealand's migrants from whatever country had small-town rural origins explains the pervasiveness of a rural mythology.

Yet as we move from the village to the whole United Kingdom, it is easy to forget the extent to which, for the first half-century of settlement after 1840, white New Zealand must have been a patchwork of many different cultural traditions as people at first found homes close to family or fellow-countrymen. Journeying from South Canterbury with its clusterings of southern Irish to Dunedin with its Scots, the nineteenth-century traveller must have been confronted with a number of contrasts – of religion, of personal habits, of foods, of accents.

At one level, as we have suggested, New Zealand's Pakeha were highly monocultural. Over 90 per cent came from the United Kingdom, which shared traditions such as Christianity, the English language, a taste for beer and bread, and a certain commitment to a Westminster style of government. Barring a few thousand people from Germany, Scandinavia, China and, from the turn of the century, Dalmatia, New Zealand's founding Pakeha were overwhelmingly from Britain or Ireland. Yet many of them were people who had particular ways of speaking and eating and thinking that had been learnt in their local communities. Nineteenth-century Britain and Ireland had yet to be fully integrated into one BBC world. Although most of New Zealand's Scots and Irish spoke English, rather than Gaelic, they did so with marked accents. So nineteenth-century Pakeha New Zealand would have been a more diverse society in its culture and habits than it subsequently became. By the interwar period several generations of schooling, the social control of the state, and the enforced discipline of war had helped to squeeze out many of these regional traditions, and a sense of New Zealand as the most loyal and 'English' of the dominions had become established. It may be that as New Zealand once more confronts a more radically multicultural future, there is value in contemplating its multicultural past.

Appendix: Sampling Methodology

TABLE 37. MAJOR STATISTICAL SOURCES

	Death registers	Passenger lists	Other
1800–39	☒		
1840–52	☒		
Auckland	☒		Alexander, *Royal NZ Fencibles*[1]
NZ Company			Register of Emigrant Labourers
Discharged soldiers			Hughes, *Discharged in New Zealand*[2]
Scots			McClean, 'Scottish Emigration'
1853–70	☒		
Discharged soldiers			Hughes, *Discharged in New Zealand* Nominal rolls
Auckland	☒		
Canterbury assisted		☒	
Otago miners	☒	☒ (from Victoria)	
Westland miners	☒	☒ (from Victoria)	
1871–90	☒		
Assisted		☒	Guthrie, *Patrick Henderson Shipping Company*[3]
1891–1915	☒	☒	
1916–45	☒		
Assisted			*AJHR*[4]

Table 37 shows the range of sources which were used to compile the statistical data used in this study. There were some sources where all the available data was analysed and there was no need for sampling. This was the case with the Fencibles and the discharged soldiers. There were others, such as the Canterbury provincial immigrants, where the sources possessed sampling frames or a frame could easily be created. In such cases random table numbers were used to extract a sufficiently large number of cases to produce results with a high level of confidence.

For the Registers of Deaths we found it necessary to adopt an alternative approach. The many thousands of entries in the scores of volumes were arranged by district and by month. So we began by deciding on our periods of analysis, which were defined by date of arrival: 1840–52, 1853–70, etc. We then drew on the published data relating to the number of deaths in each year in New Zealand to establish the average number of deaths per month for each year. The next step was to estimate the range of years for which the registers would have to be consulted to obtain a good sample of immigrants for each period of arrival. Thus, for the period 1840–52 we consulted the volumes from 1876 to 1922 on the assumption that a one-year-old arriving in 1852 could live to the age of 70, i.e. 1922. To obtain the sample we decided to select consecutive months in every second year within the range of years defined. For the selected months we took all those in all districts who had died in that month, had been born in the United Kingdom, and had arrived within the defined period. For example, for the years 1840–52 we took all those UK immigrants who died in January 1876, followed by all those who died in February 1878, and so on. The result was the creation of considerably larger samples than would normally be required.

We gained comfort in the value of this method when we checked our findings, where possible, against the published findings of the New Zealand census. There was a remarkable level of consistency.

Notes

1. SETTING OFF

1 *Paisley Advertiser*, 19 Mar. 1842.
2 *Ibid.*, 9 Apr. 1842.
3 Hazel Petrie, 'Mixed origins', MS-Papers-4280-030, Alexander Turnbull Library (ATL).
4 Val Wood, 'Recording my Murphy family', MS-Papers-4280-041, ATL.
5 Elspeth Mairs, 'Wallis, Mary Ann Lake 1821–1910', *Dictionary of New Zealand Biography (DNZB)*, updated 7 Apr. 2006, http://www.dnzb.govt.nz/
6 Elsie Locke, 'Small, Mary Elizabeth 1812/1813?–1908', *DNZB*, updated 7 Apr. 2006, http://www.dnzb.govt.nz/
7 J. A. B. Crawford, 'Porter, Thomas William 1843–1920', *DNZB*, updated 7 Apr. 2006, http://www.dnzb.govt.nz/
8 See David Hastings, *Over the Mountains of the Sea*, pp. 20–1; also Rosalind McClean, 'Reluctant leavers?', in Tom Brooking & Jennie Coleman (eds), *The Heather and the Fern*, pp. 103–16.
9 *Appendix to the Journals of the House of Representatives (AJHR)* 1886, vol. 2, F-1, p. 13.
10 William Pember Reeves, *The Long White Cloud*, pp. 399–400.
11 A. W. Shrimpton & Alan E. Mulgan, *Maori & Pakeha*, pp. 266, 272; Guy H. Scholefield, *New Zealand in Evolution*.
12 Keith Sinclair, *A History of New Zealand*, p. 153.
13 John Stenhouse, 'God's own silence: secular nationalism, Christianity and the writing of New Zealand history', *New Zealand Journal of History (NZJH)*, vol. 38, no. 1, 2004, pp. 52–71.
14 R. H. Silcock, 'Immigration into Canterbury under the Provincial Government', MA thesis, University of Canterbury, 1963; N. J. Northover, 'The Control of Immigration into Canterbury, 1850–1853', MA thesis, University of Canterbury, 1951; P. M. O'Regan, 'The Control of Immigration into Canterbury, 1854–1870', MA thesis, University of Canterbury, 1953; L. G. Gordon, 'Immigration into Hawkes Bay, 1858–1876', MA thesis, Victoria University of Wellington, 1965; L. Khan, 'Immigration into Wellington Province, 1853–1876', PhD thesis, Victoria University of Wellington, 1968; John Morris, 'The Assisted Immigrants to New Zealand: A Statistical Study,' MA thesis, University of Auckland, 1973.
15 W. H. Oliver, *The Story of New Zealand*. See also Keith Pickens, 'The writing of New Zealand history: a Kuhnian perspective', *Historical Studies: Australia and New Zealand*, vol. 17, 1977, pp. 384–98. It is revealing that Oliver has recently come to discuss the Cornish heritage, but purely as a part of his own autobiography, concerning its impact on himself, not in the context of the substantial Cornish migration to New Zealand and its possible impact on this society at large. See W. H. Oliver, *Looking for the Phoenix*.
16 See especially J. C. Beaglehole, 'New Zealand since the war, 4: politics and culture', *Landfall*, vol. XV, no. 2, 1961, pp. 138–52; R. M. Chapman, 'Fiction and the social pattern', *Landfall*, vol. VII, no. 1, 1953, pp. 26–58.
17 Jock Phillips, 'Of verandahs and fish and chips and footie on Saturday afternoon', *NZJH*, vol. 24, no. 2, 1990, pp. 107–23.
18 Patrick O'Farrell, 'How Irish was New Zealand?', in Sarah Briggs, Paul Hyland & Neill Sammells, *Reviewing Ireland*, p. 100.
19 Phillips, 'Of verandahs', p. 133.
20 Erik Olssen, 'Where to from here? Reflections on the twentieth-century historiography of nineteenth-century New Zealand', *NZJH*, vol. 26, no. 1, 1992, p. 69.
21 On the Chinese, see J. Ng, *Windows on a Chinese Past*, and Manying Ip (ed.), *Unfolding History, Evolving Identity*; on the Indians, Kapil N. Tiwari (ed.), *Indians in New Zealand*; on the Dalmatians, Andrew Trlin, *Now Respected, Once Despised*; on the Germans, James N. Bade (ed.), *The German Connection*; on the Dutch, Hank Schouten, *Tasman's Legacy*.
22 Susan Butterworth with Graham Butterworth, *Chips Off the Auld Rock*; Maureen Molloy, *Those Who Speak to the Heart*.
23 See especially Michael King, *Being Pākehā Now*.
24 Rollo Arnold, *The Farthest Promised Land*, p. 103.
25 Raewyn Dalziel, 'Popular protest in early New Plymouth: why did it occur?', *NZJH*, vol.

20, no. 1, 1986, pp. 3–26; R. Dalziel, 'Emigration and kinship: migrants to New Plymouth 1840–1843', *NZJH*, vol. 25, no. 2, 1991, pp. 112–28.
26 Charlotte Macdonald, *A Woman of Good Character*.
27 Donald Akenson, *Half the World from Home*.
28 Lyndon Fraser, *To Tara via Holyhead*; Alasdair Galbreath, 'The invisible Irish? Re-discovering the Irish protestant tradition in colonial New Zealand', in L. Fraser (ed.), *A Distant Shore*, pp. 36–54. See also the other essays in Fraser's collection, and Patrick O'Farrell, *Vanished Kingdoms*.
29 L. Fraser, *Castles of Gold*.
30 R. McClean, 'Scottish Emigration to New Zealand, 1840–1880: Motives, Means and Background', PhD thesis, University of Edinburgh, 1991; Tom Brooking, *Lands for the People*; Brooking & Coleman (eds), *The Heather and the Fern*.
31 Brad Patterson (ed.), *The Irish in New Zealand*; B. Patterson (ed.), *Ulster–New Zealand Migration and Cultural Transfers*.
32 Margaret Galt, 'Who came to New Zealand? New light on the origins of British settlers, 1840–1889', *New Zealand Population Review*, vol. 21, nos 1 & 2, May/Nov. 1995, pp. 50–71.
33 James Belich, *Making Peoples*, p. 320.
34 Tony Simpson, *The Immigrants*.
35 J. G. A. Pocock, 'British history: a plea for a new subject', *NZJH*, vol. 8, no. 1, 1974, pp. 3–21; see also Raphael Samuel, *Island Stories*.
36 Information from Rebecca Lenihan, PhD candidate based at the Irish–Scottish Studies Programme at Victoria University of Wellington.
37 The sample sizes for the main datasets were: 1840–52, 1061; 1853–70, 2464; 1871–90, 3446; 1891–1915, 2109; 1916–45, 2571.
38 The numbers were: Auckland 1840–52, 2318; Auckland 1853–70, 2751; Otago miners, 1765; West Coast miners, 906.
39 Register of Emigrant Labourers Applying for Free Passage to New Zealand (Colonial Office (CO) 208/273), Public Record Office (Kew).

2. THE EBBS AND FLOWS OF MIGRATION

1 See Imre Ferenczi & Walter F. Willcox (eds), *International Migrations*.
2 See Hastings, *Over the Mountains of the Sea*; Charles R. Clark, *Women and Children Last*.
3 Quoted in Akenson, *Half the World from Home*, p. 14.
4 For example, of those arriving between 1840 and 1852, 65% were assisted by the New Zealand Company; of those arriving 1871–91, the assisted represented 32% of the gross immigration numbers and 75% of the net migration figures for those years; and of those arriving 1904–15 the assisted represented 34% of gross migration.
5 Margaret Francis, 'Alabaster, Ann O'Connor 1842–1915', *DNZB*, updated 7 Apr. 2006, http://www.dnzb.govt.nz/
6 Erik Olssen, 'Allen, Ernest John Bartlett 1884–1945', *DNZB*, updated 7 Apr. 2006, http://www.dnzb.govt.nz/
7 From 1 April 1921 New Zealand adopted a new method of classifying arrivals, so the figures from that year only include people intending to reside more than a year. In 1933 a change was made to end the year on 31 March, not 31 December. Therefore the figures for 1933 cover the fifteen months from 1 January 1933 to 31 March 1934. Thereafter the 31 March year is used.
8 Belich, *Making Peoples*, p. 131.
9 See Robert McNab, *Murihiku and the Southern Islands*, and F. G. Hall-Jones, *Kelly of Inverkelly*.
10 Ernest Dieffenbach, *Travels in New Zealand*, pp. 38, 62; Edward Shortland, *The Southern Districts of New Zealand*, p. 300.
11 Don Grady, *Guards of the Sea*.
12 J. Busby, *Despatches of the British Resident in New Zealand 1833–1840*. See also R. P. Wigglesworth, 'The New Zealand Timber and Flax Trade 1769–1840', PhD thesis, Massey University, 1981.
13 Trevor Bentley, *Pākehā Māori*.
14 See L. L. Robson, *The Convict Settlers of Australia*. Many observers record the presence of runaway convicts, including the missionary Thomas Kendall in 1815, the artist Augustus

Earle in 1827, and the scientist Charles Darwin in 1835 (see Jack Lee, 'I have named it the Bay of Islands...', p. 162). The Sydney Herald (30 Mar. 1837) asserted that there were 200 to 300 convicts in New Zealand.

15 Harrison M. Wright, New Zealand, 1769–1840, pp. 22–3, 26.
16 Caroline Fitzgerald (ed.), Letters from the Bay of Islands; Peter Adams, Fatal Necessity, p. 26.
17 J. M. R. Owens, 'New Zealand before annexation,' in W. H. Oliver & B. R. Williams (eds), The Oxford History of New Zealand, p. 50.
18 Eric Richards, Britannia's Children, pp. 117–49.
19 A. D. Gayer, W. W. Rostow & A. J. Schwarz, The Growth and Fluctuation of the British Economy, 1790–1850; Norman Gash, Aristocracy and People, especially pp. 210–12.
20 There was no official data for the country as a whole until 1853. The New Zealand figures were compiled for us by Sue Upton using shipping lists and the New Ulster Gazettes. The figures of departures from the United Kingdom are derived from 'General reports of the Colonial Land and Emigration Commissioners' in British Parliamentary Papers, passim.
21 Kathleen A. Coleridge, 'Revans, Samuel 1807/1808?–1888', DNZB, updated 7 Apr. 2006, http://www.dnzb.govt.nz/
22 Margaret Brown, 'From Keillour to Kapiti', in Colleen P. Main (ed.), Our Lesser Stars, pp. 63–93.
23 Dalziel, 'Emigration and kinship', p. 120.
24 Janice C. Mogford, 'Whisker, Alexander 1819–1907', DNZB, updated 7 Apr. 2006, http://www.dnzb.govt.nz/
25 Alexander, The Royal New Zealand Fencibles 1847–52.
26 Wood, 'Recording my Murphy family', MS-Papers-4280-041, ATL.
27 See especially David Thomson, A World without Welfare.
28 Violet Ward, 'Immigrants and Immigration in the Auckland Province, 1792–1876', MA thesis, University of Auckland, 1943.
29 Sarah Jane Lander, 'The salt of the earth that simply endured', MS-Papers-4280-065, ATL.
30 Among the many works on Waipu see Molloy, Those Who Speak to the Heart, and N. R. McKenzie, The Gael Fares Forth.
31 Sir Henry Brett & Henry Hook, The Albertlanders.
32 This is one reading of the fact that the gross migration from Australia for 1861–70 was 132,901 but the net gain was only 55,911, while the gross migration from the British Isles was 69,247 and the net gain 63,420. Of course it is likely that some of the British migrants may have moved on to Australia, but the contrast remains instructive.
33 Elizabeth Jessie Beer, 'George Beer: the saga of his family', MS-Papers-4280-097, ATL.
34 S. W. Grant, 'Russell, William Russell 1838?–1913', DNZB, updated 7 Apr. 2006, http://www.dnzb.govt.nz/
35 Neill Atkinson, 'Garrard, William George 1832–1835?–1906', DNZB, updated 7 Apr. 2006, http://www.dnzb.govt.nz/
36 AJHR, 1873, D2, pp. 16–19.
37 Vicki Joy Fissenden, 'Success or defeat: an immigrant's account', MS-Papers-4280-052, ATL.
38 Ellen Ellis, 'Chemis, Annie 1862–1939', DNZB, updated 7 Apr. 2006, http://www.dnzb.govt.nz/
39 Arnold, The Farthest Promised Land, pp. 2–17.
40 New Zealand Parliamentary Debates (NZPD), 1888, vol. 43, pp. 188–9.
41 Geoffrey Blainey, 'Hannan, Patrick (1840–1925)', Australian Dictionary of Biography, http://www.adb.online.anu.edu.au/biogs/A090184b.htm
42 Coral Dickinson, 'The Dickinson brothers', MS-Papers-4280-060, ATL.
43 Dorothea Kenney, 'Of British descent', MS-Papers-4280-020, ATL.
44 Kathryn Peacocke, 'Ranstead, William 1859–1944', DNZB, updated 7 Apr. 2006, http://www.dnzb.govt.nz/
45 Quoted in Stephen Constantine, 'Immigration and the making of New Zealand', in S. Constantine (ed.), Emigrants and Empire, p. 136.
46 See Katie Pickles, 'Pink cheeked and surplus: single British inter-war migration to New Zealand', in L. Fraser & K. Pickles (eds), Shifting Centres, pp. 63–80.
47 AJHR, 1920–34, D9.
48 Val Wood, War Brides, p. 17.
49 See Marjory Harper, Emigration from Scotland Between the Wars.
50 V. C. Goodall, 'Flockhouse', pp. 26–35.

3. THE SETTLERS

1   The national figures do not include the Channel Islands and the Isle of Man, and hence they do not add up to 100%.
2   William D. Jones, *Wales in America*; Carol Bennett, *In Search of the Red Dragon*.
3   James Jupp (ed.), *The Australian People*, pp. 738–41.
4   *Ibid.*, p. 666.
5   Louis E. Ward, *Early Wellington*, p. 350.
6   Henry Brett, *White Wings*, vol. 1, pp. 21, 25; G. L. Pearce, *The Scots of New Zealand*, p. 48.
7   Alexander Marjoribanks, *Travels in New Zealand*, pp. 25–6.
8   *AJHR*, 1873, D1, p. 48.
9   Gaynor Kirkby (comp.), *Passenger Lists, Victoria, Australia Outwards to New Zealand Part 3, 1866–1870*.
10 T. J. Hearn, 'McQueen, Charles 1836–1906', *DNZB*, updated 7 Apr. 2006, http://www.dnzb.govt.nz/
11 T. J. Hearn, 'Ewing, John 1844–1922', *DNZB*, updated 7 Apr. 2006, http://www.dnzb.govt.nz/
12 CO 208/171/229, Alston to McEwan and Millar, 17 Aug. 1840.
13 Quoted in Fraser, *To Tara via Holyhead*, p. 37.
14 See http://cust.idl.com.au/pt39/emnz1.html
15 Jupp, *The Australian People*, p. 451.
16 Christine Little, 'The Donovan story', MS-Papers-4280-079, ATL.
17 Hugh Laracy, 'Kennedy, Martin 1839/1840?–1916', *DNZB*, updated 7 Apr. 2006, http://www.dnzb.govt.nz/
18 Alasdair Galbreath, 'A forgotten plantation: the Irish in Pukekohe, 1865–1900', in Patterson (ed.), *The Irish in New Zealand*.
19 See Macdonald, *A Woman of Good Character*.
20 Figures calculated from a table in Fraser, *To Tara via Holyhead*, p. 46.
21 Charlotte Macdonald, 'Crowe, Ellen 1845-1847?–1930, *DNZB*, updated 7 Apr. 2006, http://www.dnzb.govt.nz/
22 Richard P. Davis, *Irish Issues in New Zealand Politics 1868–1922*, p. 31.
23 Dulcie Innes, 'Scant rest in the gloaming', MS-Papers-4280-072, ATL.
24 Charlotte Macdonald, 'Howard, Caroline Cadette 1821–?', *DNZB*, updated 7 Apr. 2006, http://www.dnzb.govt.nz/
25 Rex Evans & Adriene Evans, *The Descendants of John and Ann Howell*.
26 For example, Jupp, *The Australian People*.
27 Dudley Baines, *Migration in a Mature Economy*.
28 This table is derived from a list of ships from the United Kingdom to New Zealand compiled by Gavin Petrie from many sources. He warns that this list is not definitive, and that some of the ships did not carry passengers. However, in total his list includes over 2000 ships, and it is clearly a valuable indication of migrant shipping. Sourced from http://freepages.genealogy.rootsweb.com/~shipstonz/ships_uk&i.html
29 Paul Hudson, 'English Emigration to New Zealand, 1839–1850: An Analysis of the Work of the New Zealand Company', PhD thesis, University of Lancaster, 1996.
30 Donald Hansen, 'Cutting colts and biting dog tails', in Main (ed.), *Our Lesser Stars*, pp. 40–5.
31 Dalziel, 'Emigration and kinship', p. 120.
32 Madge Malcolm, 'Girls all the way', MS-Papers-4280-011, ATL.
33 See especially John McDonald & Eric Richards, 'The great migration of 1841: recruitment for New South Wales in British emigration fields', *Population Studies*, vol. 51, 1997, p. 339; Jupp, *The Australian People*, pp. 283, 293–4, 303–7.
34 Beaglehole, Diana, 'Tricker, Walter Pettit 1823?–1907', *DNZB*, updated 22 Jun. 2007, http://www.dnzb.govt.nz/
35 Robin Haines & Ralph Shlomowitz, 'Immigration from the United Kingdom to colonial Australia: a statistical analysis', *Journal of Australian Studies*, no. 34, 1992, pp. 43–52; Jupp, *The Australian People*, pp. 48–54, 327, 389–92, 401, 842; P. J. Payton, *The Cornish Miner in Australia*.
36 A detailed listing of the occupations in their groups is available from the authors.
37 Thelma Dunstall, 'I birthed him myself', in Main (ed.), *Our Lesser Stars*, pp. 174–7.
38 See especially Nancy M. Taylor (ed.), *Early Travellers in New Zealand*.
39 For example, Belich, *Making Peoples*, pp. 316–20, 333–4.
40 Baines, *Migration in a Mature Economy*, pp. 334–5.

41 N. H. Carrier & J. R. Jeffery, *External Migration*, tables 11 and 12.
42 The figures for the Otago and West Coast miners include all miners in our sample, the vast majority of whom were 20 or over. The table does not show servants who were normally under 1 per cent of the total. They are included in 'other occupations'. This is also true of all subsequent tables.
43 G. H. Sutherland, 'Carter, Charles Rooking 1822–1896', *DNZB*, updated 22 Jun. 2007, http://www.dnzb.govt.nz/
44 Arnold, *The Farthest Promised Land*. He noted (p. xi) that, 'The circumstances of the time gave New Zealand a larger share of this outflow [of English rural labourers] than any other receiving area.'
45 Rollo Arnold, 'Clayden, Arthur 1829–1899', *DNZB*, updated 22 Jun. 2007, http://www.dnzb.govt.nz/
46 John Saville, *Rural De-population in England and Wales, 1851–1951*; and Brian Short, 'Rural demography, 1850–1914', in E. J. T. Collins (ed.), *The Agrarian History of England and Wales, Volume VII, 1850–1914 (Part II)*, Chap. 21, p. 1236; W. A. Armstrong, 'Labour 1: rural population growth, systems of employment, and incomes', in G. E. Mingay (ed.), *The Agrarian History of England and Wales, Volume VI, 1750–1850*, pp. 641–728; Roger Schofield, 'British population change, 1700–1871,' in Roderick Floud & Donald McCloskey (eds), *The Economic History of Britain Since 1700, Volume 1: 1700–1860*, pp. 60–95.
47 Lord Eversley, 'The decline in the number of agricultural labourers in Great Britain', *Journal of the Royal Statistical Society*, Jun. 1907, pp. 267–319; W. A. Armstrong, 'The flight from the land', in G. E. Mingay (ed.), *The Vanishing Countryman*, pp. 57–75; Alan Armstrong, *Farmworkers in England and Wales*; and Peter Dewey, 'Farm labour', in Collins (ed.), *The Agrarian History of England and Wales, Volume VII, 1850–1914 (Part I)*, pp. 848–9.
48 Arnold, *Farthest Promised Land*, pp. 116–33.
49 E. J. T. Collins, Jennifer Tann & J. A. Chartres, 'The agricultural servicing and processing industries', in Mingay (ed.), *The Agrarian History of England and Wales, Volume VI, 1750–1850*, pp. 384–544; see p. 396. For the earlier part of the nineteenth century, see E. A. Wrigley, 'Men on the land and men in the countryside: employment in agriculture in early nineteenth-century England', in Lloyd Bonfield, Richard Smith & Keith Wrightson (eds), *The World We Have Gained*, pp. 295–336. See also J. A. Chartres & G. L. Turnbull, 'Country craftsmen', in Mingay (ed.), *The Victorian Countryside, Volume 1*, pp. 314–28; Mingay (ed.), *The Vanishing Countryman*, pp. 133–41; and W. A. Armstrong, 'The countryside', in F. M. L. Thompson (ed.), *The Cambridge Social History of Britain, 1750–1950*, pp. 87–153.
50 On rural crafts and trades, see Chartres & Turnbull, 'Country craftsmen', in Mingay (ed.), *The Victorian Countryside*, pp. 314–28; and J. A. Chartres, 'The retail trades and agricultural services', in Collins (ed.), *The Agrarian History of England and Wales, Volume VII*, pp. 1150–1212.
51 Philippa Fogarty, 'Wells, Ada 1863–1933', *DNZB*, updated 22 Jun. 2007, http://www.dnzb.govt.nz/
52 There were also 20.2% attending 'other' denominations.
53 Note that the immigration figures include Welsh, but the census figures cover only England. However, given the small number of Welsh in our sample, the comparison remains valid.
54 Neva Clarke McKenna, 'Ball, Thomas 1809–1897', *DNZB*, updated 22 Jun. 2007, http://www.dnzb.govt.nz/
55 Arnold, *Farthest Promised Land*, pp. 135–63.
56 Dalziel, 'Popular protest in early New Plymouth', pp. 3–26; 'Emigration and kinship', pp. 112–28.
57 Baines, *Migration in a Mature Economy*, p. 152.
58 Jim Faull, *The Cornish in Australia*.
59 R. G. Lawn, 'Lawn, John 1840–1905', *DNZB*, updated 22 Jun. 2007, http://www.dnzb.govt.nz/
60 Arnold, *Farthest Promised Land*, pp. 211–25; Philip Payton, 'The Cornish and the dominions: a case-study in sub-national Imperial contact', unpub. paper, Jul. 1998; Jupp, *The Australian People*, pp. 227–34.
61 Mollie Chalklen, 'Crewes, John 1847–1925', *DNZB*, updated 22 Jun. 2007, http://www.dnzb.govt.nz/
62 Arnold, *Farthest Promised Land*, pp. 182–210.
63 Barry Reay, *Rural Englands*, p. 164.
64 C. B. Malone, 'Anstice, Sophia 1849–1926', *DNZB*, updated 22 Jun. 2007, http://www.dnzb.govt.nz/

65   Kathleen A. Coleridge, 'Carpenter, Robert Holt 1819/1820?–1891', *DNZB*, updated 22 Jun. 2007, http://www.dnzb.govt.nz/
66   Gordon Ogilvie, 'Wigram, Henry Francis 1857–1934', *DNZB*, updated 22 Jun. 2007, http://www.dnzb.govt.nz/
67   Graham W. A. Bush, 'Allum, John Andrew Charles 1889–1972', *DNZB*, updated 22 Jun. 2007, http://www.dnzb.govt.nz/
68   Brian Easton, 'Sutch, William Ball 1907–1975'; and Elsie Locke, 'Thorn, Margaret 1897–1969', *DNZB*, updated 22 Jun. 2007, http://www.dnzb.govt.nz/
69   William Renwick, 'Pope, James Henry 1837–1913'; Erik Olssen, 'Arnold, James Frederick 1859–1929'; and Philippa Graham, 'Poingdestre, Henry 1832?–1885', *DNZB*, updated 22 Jun. 2007, http://www.dnzb.govt.nz/
70   Pat Irene Winton, 'Hewlett, Hilda Beatrice 1864–1943', *DNZB*, updated 22 Jun. 2007, http://www.dnzb.govt.nz/
71   Barbara Cooper & Brian O'Brien, 'Lofley, Edward 1838-1840?–1889', *DNZB*, updated 22 Jun. 2007, http://www.dnzb.govt.nz/
72   McClean, 'Scottish Emigration to New Zealand, 1840–1880', pp. 150, 157.
73   See McClean, 'Scottish Emigration', p. 120. Note that McClean's figures relate to place of last residence, not place of birth.
74   Donna Hellier, '"The humblies": Scottish highland migration into nineteenth century Victoria', in Patricia Grimshaw, Chris McGonville & Ellen McEwan (eds), *Families in Colonial Australia*, pp. 9–18.
75   Noel Crawford, 'Grant, William 1843–1910', and Heather Roberts, 'Mackay, Jessie 1864–1938', *DNZB*, updated 22 Jun. 2007, http://www.dnzb.govt.nz/
76   *AJHR*, 1875, D2, p. 35; *Ibid.*, D1, p. 10. See also Butterworth with Butterworth, *Chips Off the Auld Rock*, especially pp. 62–6. They also suggest an even flow of men and women in the 1870s.
77   Excludes servants (always under 1%).
78   McClean, 'Scottish Emigration to New Zealand', pp. 320, 325.
79   T. M. Devine (ed.), *Scottish Emigration and Scottish Society*.
80   Charlotte Erikson, 'Who were the English and Scots emigrants to the United States in the later nineteenth century?', in D. V. Glass & R. Revelle (eds), *Population and Social Change*.
81   McClean, 'Scottish Emigration to New Zealand', p. 201.
82   Janet C. Angus, 'Cuddie, Mary 1823–1889', *DNZB*, updated 22 Jun. 2007, http://www.dnzb.govt.nz/
83   Edmund Bohan, *Edward Stafford*.
84   Jupp, *The Australian People*, p. 562; see also Fraser, *Castles of Gold*, pp. 32–5.
85   Seán G. Brosnahan, *The Kerrytown Brosnahans*.
86   Kerby A. Miller, *Emigrants and Exiles*.
87   Liam J. Kennedy, 'The rural economy', in Liam Kennedy & Philip Ollerenshaw (eds), *An Economic History of Ulster 1820–1940*, p. 5.
88   Melanie Nolan, *Kin*.
89   Timothy L. McIvor, *The Rainmaker*.
90   Donald Akenson, 'The Irish in New Zealand', *Familia: Ulster Genealogical Review*, vol. 2, no. 5, 1989, pp. 7–12.
91   See especially Alasdair Galbreath, 'New Zealand's "Invisible Irish": Irish Protestants in the North Island of New Zealand, 1840–1900', MA thesis, University of Auckland, 1998.
92   There is a huge literature on this issue. See, on New Zealand, Jock Phillips, *A Man's Country?*; Charlotte Macdonald, 'Too many men and too few women: Gender's fatal impact in nineteenth century colonies', in Caroline Daley & Deborah Montgomerie (eds), *The Gendered Kiwi*, pp. 17–35.
93   For example, *Census of New Zealand*, 1871, pp. iv, v.
94   Kay Morris Matthews, 'Bates, Sophia Ann 1817–1899', *DNZB*, updated 22 Jun. 2007, http://www.dnzb.govt.nz/
95   CO 208/19/410, PRO (Kew).
96   CO 208/5/28, PRO (Kew).
97   Figures drawn from Kirkby, *Passenger lists, Victoria, Australia outwards to New Zealand*. The figure for Otago male arrivals was 87.7% unmarried, and for the West Coast male arrivals 91.3%.
98   Suzanne Starky, 'Garmson, Aileen Anna Maria 1861-1863?–1951', *DNZB*, updated 7 Apr. 2006, http://www.dnzb.govt.nz/
99   CO 208/272 and 273, PRO (Kew).

100 Roberta Nicholls, 'Stewart, Catherine Campbell 1881–1957', *DNZB*, updated 7 Apr. 2006, http://www.dnzb.govt.nz/

4. THE NEW LAND

1 Coral Dickinson, 'The Dickinson brothers', MS-Papers-4280-060, ATL.
2 Miles Fairburn, *The Ideal Society and its Enemies*.
3 Moira M. Long, 'Harris, Emily Cumming 1836/1837?–1925'; Ian Church, 'Parris, Robert Reid 1816?–1904'; Judy Hanline, 'Hood, Mary 1822?–1902'; Giselle M. Byrnes, 'Smith, Stephenson Percy 1840–1922', *DNZB*, updated 7 Apr. 2006, http://www.dnzb.govt.nz/
4 Malcolm McKinnon (ed.), *Bateman New Zealand Historical Atlas*, plate 78.
5 Switzer Hudson, 'Anderton, William Theophilus 1891–1966'; Neill Atkinson, 'Young, Frederick George 1888–1962', *DNZB*, updated 7 Apr. 2006, http://www.dnzb.govt.nz/
6 Hilda McDonnell, 'Meech, Matilda 1825?–1907', *DNZB*, updated 22 Jun. 2007, http://www.dnzb.govt.nz/
7 J. F. Fleming, 'Fleming, Thomas 1848–1930', *DNZB*, updated 7 Apr. 2006, http://www.dnzb.govt.nz/
8 Peter Lowe, 'Anderson, John 1820–1897', *DNZB*, updated 7 Apr. 2006, http://www.dnzb.govt.nz/
9 Sheila S. Crawford, *Sheep and Sheepmen of Canterbury, 1850–1914*, p. 63.
10 John Wilson, *Waikakahi*, p. 42.
11 Suzanne Starky, 'Little, James 1834–1921'; Jo-Anne Smith, 'Gibb, Helen 1838–1914', *DNZB*, updated 7 Apr. 2006, http://www.dnzb.govt.nz/
12 Hugh Laracy, 'Dignan, Patrick 1813/1814?–1894', *DNZB*, updated 7 Apr. 2006, http://www.dnzb.govt.nz/
13 Francis Minehan, 'Cassidy, Hugh 1840–1922'; Anne Hutchison, 'Weldon, Barbara 1829-1837?–1882', *DNZB*, updated 7 Apr. 2006, http://www.dnzb.govt.nz/
14 Kathleen C. McDonald, 'O'Donnell, Ann 1857-1860?–1934', *DNZB*, updated 7 Apr. 2006, http://www.dnzb.govt.nz/
15 Seán Brosnahan, 'The "Battle of the Borough" and the "Saige O Timaru": sectarian riot in colonial Canterbury', *NZJH*, vol. 28, no. 1, 1994, pp. 41–59.
16 Alexander Bathgate, *Waitaruna*, p. 77; George Chamier, *Philosopher Dick*, p. 151.
17 H. W. Orsman (ed.), *The Dictionary of New Zealand English*, p. viii.
18 Rollo Arnold, 'Some Australasian aspects of New Zealand life', *NZJH*, vol. 4, no. 1, 1970, pp. 54–76; J. O. C. Phillips, 'Musings in Maoriland – or was there a *Bulletin* school in New Zealand?', *Historical Studies*, vol. 20, no. 81, 1983, pp. 520–35.
19 Ward, *Early Wellington*, p. 75.
20 See Alison Clarke, *Holiday Seasons*.
21 Ward, *Early Wellington*, p. 78.
22 Database of MPs compiled by Susan Butterworth and available at the Ministry for Culture and Heritage.
23 The database was compiled by working parties, so it is based on many people's subjective judgements. It is not 'scientific', but its size makes it a valuable source.
24 See Te Ara, *Settler and Migrant Peoples of New Zealand*, pp. 134–6.
25 Herbert Roth, 'Griffin, William 1810/1811?–1870'; Herbert Roth, 'Rae, Charles Joseph 1819-1821?–1894', *DNZB*, updated 7 Apr. 2006, http://www.dnzb.govt.nz/
26 Len Richardson, *Coal, Class & Community*.
27 Ray Bailey with Mary Earle, *Home Cooking to Takeaways*; Tony Simpson, *A Distant Feast*.
28 Elizabeth Gordon, Lyle Campbell, Jennifer Hay, Margaret Maclagan, Andrea Sudbury & Peter Trudgill, *New Zealand English*, esp. p. 256.
29 David Thomson, 'Marriage and the family on the colonial frontier' in Tony Ballantyne & Brian Moloughney (eds), *Disputed Histories*, pp. 119–41.
30 N. F. R. Crafts, 'Average age at first marriage for women in mid-nineteenth century England and Wales: a cross-section study', *Population Studies*, no. 32, 1978, p. 22.
31 On these issues see Ian Pool, Arunachalam Dharmalingam & Janet Sceats, *The New Zealand Family from 1840*, pp. 62–69. The authors drew heavily on the research presented in this book.
32 Dalziel, 'Popular protest in early New Plymouth', pp. 3–26.
33 Debra Powell, 'It was hard to die frae hame': Death, Grief and Mourning among Scottish

Migrants to New Zealand, 1840–1890', MA thesis, University of Waikato, 2007.
34 Tanja Bueltmann, unpublished paper, 'Keeping up the name of Scotland', Jun. 2007.
35 Molloy, *Those Who Speak to the Heart*; Hugh Trevor-Roper, 'The invention of tradition: the Highland tradition of Scotland', in Eric Hobsbawm and Terence Ranger (eds), *The Invention of Tradition*, pp. 15–42.
36 Tom Brooking, 'Sharing out the Haggis: the special Scottish contribution to New Zealand history', in Brooking & Coleman (eds), *The Heather and the Fern*, p. 54.
37 Clarke, *Holiday Seasons*, pp. 73–85.
38 These conclusions are based on reading a dozen histories of particular New Zealand A & P shows.
39 Brooking, 'Sharing out the Haggis', p. 54.
40 Lynne Richards, 'A colonising achievement', MS-Papers-4280-078, ATL.
41 Heather Roberts, 'Mackay, Jessie 1864–1938', *DNZB*, updated 22 Jun. 2007, http://www.dnzb.govt.nz/
42 Jim McAloon, 'Scots in the colonial economy', in Brooking & Coleman (eds), *The Heather and the Fern*, pp. 87–102.
43 W. J. Gardner, *The Amuri*, pp. 115–17.
44 We are grateful to Robert Peden for this information.
45 In *The Loving Stitch*, Heather Nicholson makes it clear that knitting was a widespread practice among rural communities throughout the British Isles.
46 Based on discussion with Patrick Coleman, Donald McRaild and Rory Sweetman.
47 Fraser, *To Tara via Holyhead*, p. 57; Fraser, 'No one but black strangers to spake to god help me': Irish women's migration to the West Coast, 1864–1915', in Fraser & Pickles (eds), *Shifting Centres*, p. 59.
48 Fraser, *To Tara via Holyhead*, p. 108.
49 Seán Brosnahan, 'Shaming the "Shoneens": the *Green Ray* and the Maoriland Irish society in Dunedin, 1916–22', in Fraser (ed.), *A Distant Shore*, pp. 117–34.
50 Phillips, *A Man's Country?*, p. 305.
51 William Pember Reeves, *State Experiments in Australia and New Zealand*, vol. 1, pp. 31–2; Pember Reeves, *The Long White Cloud*, pp. 399–400.
52 Dorris Taylor, 'From Cornwall and Ireland to Canterbury, New Zealand', MS-Papers-4280-094, ATL.
53 Margaret Gray, *Abbott's-Ford*, pp. 155, 165–7.
54 Alan Mulgan, *Home: A Colonial's Adventure*, p. 6.
55 H. R. Jackson, *Churches and People in Australia and New Zealand 1860–1930*, pp. 116–24. See also John Stenhouse, 'God's own silence: secular nationalism, Christianity and the writing of New Zealand history', *NZJH*, vol. 38, no. 1, 2004, pp. 52–71.
56 *NZPD*, vol. XII, 1872, pp. 216–17; vol. XX, 1876, p. 546.
57 J. Malton Murray & the Rev. J. Cocker, *Temperance and Prohibition in New Zealand*, p. 156.
58 Francis Bennett, *A Canterbury Tale*, p. 66.
59 Rory Sweetman, *Bishop in the dock: the sedition trial of James Liston*.
60 Thomson, *A World without Welfare*.
61 Michael Bassett, *The State in New Zealand, 1840–1984*.
62 See especially Miles Fairburn, 'The rural myth and the new urban frontier, 1870–1940', *NZJH*, vol. 9, no. 1, 1975, pp. 3–21.
63 Reay, *Rural Englands*, p. 56.
64 See especially Eve Ebbett, *Victoria's Daughters*.
65 Angela McCarthy, *Irish Migrants in New Zealand, 1840–1937*, p. 132.

APPENDIX

1 Ruth Alexander, *The Royal New Zealand Fencibles 1847–52*.
2 Hugh and Lyn Hughes, *Discharged in New Zealand*.
3 Kay Guthrie, *Patrick Henderson Shipping Company*.
4 *Appendix to the Journals of the House of Representatives*.

Select Bibliography

MANUSCRIPTS AND ARCHIVES

Alexander Turnbull Library, Wellington (ATL)
Beer, Elizabeth Jessie, 'George Beer: The Saga of His Family', MS-Papers-4280-097.
Dickinson, Coral, 'The Dickinson Brothers', MS-Papers-4280-060.
Fissenden, Vicki Joy, 'Success or Defeat: An Immigrant's Account', MS-Papers-4280-052.
Innes, Dulcie, 'Scant Rest in the Gloaming', MS-Papers-4280-072.
Kenney, Dorothea, 'Of British Descent', MS-Papers-4280-020.
Lander, Sarah Jane, 'The Salt of the Earth That Simply Endured', MS-Papers-4280-065.
Little, Christine, 'The Donovan Story', MS-Papers-4280-079.
Malcolm, Madge, 'Girls All the Way', MS-Papers-4280-011.
Petrie, Hazel, 'Mixed Origins', MS-Papers-4280-030.
Richards, Lynne, 'A Colonising Achievement', MS-Papers-4280-078.
Taylor, Doris, 'From Cornwall and Ireland to Canterbury, New Zealand', MS-Papers-4280-094.
Wood, Val, 'Recording My Murphy Family', MS-Papers-4280-041.
Public Record Office (Kew), (PRO)
Register of Emigrant Labourers Applying for Free Passage to New Zealand, Colonial Office (CO) 208/273

OFFICIAL PUBLICATIONS

Appendix to the Journals of the House of Representatives (*AJHR*)
Busby, J., *Despatches of the British Resident in New Zealand, 1833–1840*
Census of New Zealand, 1871
New Zealand Parliamentary Debates (NZPD)

NEWSPAPERS AND PERIODICALS

Paisley Advertiser
Sydney Herald

BOOKS AND CHAPTERS

Adams, Peter, *Fatal Necessity: British Intervention in New Zealand 1830–1847*, Auckland University Press, Auckland, 1977.
Akenson, Donald, *Half the World from Home: Perspectives on the Irish in New Zealand, 1860–1950*, Victoria University Press, Wellington, 1990.
Alexander, Ruth, *The Royal New Zealand Fencibles 1847–52*, New Zealand Fencible Society, Auckland, 1997.
Armstrong, Alan, *Farmworkers in England and Wales: A Social and Economic History 1770–1980*, Iowa State University Press, Ames, Iowa, 1988.
Armstrong, W. A., 'The Countryside', in F. M. L. Thompson (ed.), *The Cambridge Social History of Britain, 1750–1950*, Cambridge University Press, Cambridge, 1990.
Arnold, Rollo, *The Farthest Promised Land: English Villagers, New Zealand Immigrants of the 1870s*, Victoria University Press, Wellington, 1981.
Bade, James N. (ed.), *The German Connection: New Zealand and German-speaking Europe in the Nineteenth Century*, Oxford University Press, Auckland, 1993.
Bailey, Ray, with Mary Earle, *Home Cooking to Takeaways: Changes in Food Consumption in New Zealand during 1880–1990*, Massey University, Palmerston North, 1999.
Baines, Dudley, *Migration in a Mature Economy: Emigration and Internal Migration in England and Wales, 1861–1900*, Cambridge University Press, Cambridge, 1985.

Bassett, Michael, *The State in New Zealand, 1840–1984: Socialism Without Doctrines?*, Auckland University Press, Auckland, 1998.

Bathgate, Alexander, *Waitaruna: A Story of New Zealand Life*, Sampson Low, Marston, Searle & Rivington, London, 1881.

Belich, James, *Making Peoples: A History of the New Zealanders: From Polynesian Settlement to the End of the Nineteenth Century*, Allen Lane, Auckland, 1996.

Bennett, Carol, *In Search of the Red Dragon: The Welsh in Canada*, Juniper Books, Ontario, 1985.

Bennett, Francis, *A Canterbury Tale: The Autobiography of Dr Francis Bennett*, Oxford University Press, Wellington, 1980.

Bentley, Trevor, *Pākehā Māori: The Extraordinary Story of the Europeans Who Lived as Māori in Early New Zealand*, Penguin, Auckland, 1999.

Bohan, Edmund, *Edward Stafford: New Zealand's First Statesman*, Hazard Press, Christchurch, 1994.

Brett, Henry, *White Wings, Volume 1: Fifty Years of Sail in the New Zealand Trade, 1850–1900*, Brett Printing Company, Auckland, 1924.

Brett, Sir Henry, and Henry Hook, *The Albertlanders: Brave Pioneers of the 'Sixties*, Capper Press, Christchurch, 1979.

Brooking, Tom, *Lands for the People? The Highland Clearances and the Colonisation of New Zealand: A Biography of John McKenzie*, University of Otago Press, Dunedin, 1996.

Brooking, Tom, and Jennie Coleman (eds), *The Heather and the Fern: Scottish Migration and New Zealand Settlement*, University of Otago Press, Dunedin, 2003.

Brosnahan, Seán G., *The Kerrytown Brosnahans*, R. J. & H. P. Brosnahan, Timaru, 1992.

Butterworth, Susan, with Graham Butterworth, *Chips Off the Auld Rock: Shetlanders in New Zealand*, Shetland Society of Wellington, Wellington, 1997.

Carrier, N. H., and J. R. Jeffery, *External Migration: A Study of Available Statistics, 1815–1950*, HMSO, London, 1953.

Chamier, George, *Philosopher Dick: Adventures and Contemplations of a New Zealand Shepherd*, T. Fisher Unwin, London, 1891.

Chartres, J. A., and G. L. Turnbull, 'Country Craftsmen,' in G. E. Mingay (ed.), *The Victorian Countryside, Volume 1*, Routledge & Kegan Paul, London, 1981.

Clark, Charles R., *Women and Children Last: The Burning of the Emigrant Ship Cospatrick*, University of Otago Press, Dunedin, 2006.

Clarke, Alison, *Holiday Seasons: Christmas, New Year and Easter in Nineteenth-Century New Zealand*, Auckland University Press, Auckland, 2007.

Collins, E. J. T. (ed.), *The Agrarian History of England and Wales, Volume VII, 1850–1914 (Part I)*, Cambridge University Press, Cambridge, 2000.

Constantine, Stephen, 'Immigration and the Making of New Zealand', in S. Constantine (ed.), *Emigrants and Empire: British Settlement in the Dominions Between the Wars*, Manchester University Press, Manchester, 1990.

Crawford, Sheila S., *Sheep and Sheepmen of Canterbury, 1850–1914*, Simpson & Williams, Christchurch, 1949.

Davis, Richard P., *Irish Issues in New Zealand Politics, 1868–1922*, University of Otago Press, Dunedin, 1974.

Devine, T. M. (ed.), *Scottish Emigration and Scottish Society: Proceedings of the Scottish Historical Studies Seminar, University of Strathclyde, 1990–91*, John Donald, Edinburgh, 1992.

Dieffenbach, Ernest, *Travels in New Zealand: With Contributions to the Geography, Geology, Botany and Natural History of That Country*, J. Murray, London, 1843.

Ebbett, Eve, *Victoria's Daughters: New Zealand Women of the Thirties*, Reed, Wellington, 1981.

Erikson, Charlotte, 'Who Were the English and Scots Emigrants to the United States in the Later Nineteenth Century?', in D. V. Glass and R. Revelle (eds), *Population and Social Change*, Crane, Russak, New York, 1972.

Evans, Rex, and Adriene Evans (comp.), *The Descendants of John and Ann Howell*, Evagean Publishing, Auckland, 1997.

Fairburn, Miles, *The Ideal Society and its Enemies: The Foundations of Modern New Zealand Society, 1850–1900*, Auckland University Press, Auckland, 1989.

Faull, Jim, *The Cornish in Australia*, Australasian Educational Press, Melbourne, 1983.

Ferenczi, Imre, and Walter F. Willcox (eds), *International Migrations*, 2 vols, National Bureau of Economic Research, New York, 1929, 1931.

Fitzgerald, Caroline (ed.), *Letters from the Bay of Islands: The Story of Marianne Williams*, Penguin, Auckland, 2006.

Fraser, Lyndon, *To Tara via Holyhead: Irish Catholic Immigrants in Nineteenth-Century*

Christchurch, Auckland University Press, Auckland, 1997.

——, *Castles of Gold: A History of New Zealand's West Coast Irish*, Otago University Press, Dunedin, 2007.

Fraser, Lyndon (ed.), *A Distant Shore: Irish Migration and New Zealand Settlement*, University of Otago Press, Dunedin, 2000.

Fraser, Lyndon, and Katie Pickles (eds), *Shifting Centres: Women and Migration in New Zealand History*, University of Otago Press, Dunedin, 2002.

Gardner, W. J., *The Amuri: A County History*, Amuri County Council, Culverden, 1983.

Gash, Norman, *Aristocracy and People: Britain 1815–1865*, Edward Arnold, London, 1979.

Gayer, Arthur D., W. W. Rostow and Anna Jacobson Schwarz, *The Growth and Fluctuation of the British Economy, 1790–1850: An Historical, Statistical, and Theoretical Study of Britain's Economic Development*, Clarendon Press, Oxford, 1952.

Goodall, V. C., *'Flockhouse': A History of the New Zealand Sheepowners' Acknowledgement of Debt to British Seamen Fund*, Keeling & Mundy, Palmerston North, 1962.

Gordon, Elizabeth, Lyle Campbell, Jennifer Hay, Margaret Maclagan, Andrea Sudbury and Peter Trudgill, *New Zealand English: Its Origins and Evolution*, Cambridge University Press, Cambridge, 2004.

Grady, Don, *Guards of the Sea*, Whitcoulls, Christchurch, 1978.

Gray, Margaret, *Abbott's-Ford: A History of Waipawa*, Waipawa Village Committee, Waipawa, 1989.

Guthrie, Kay, *Patrick Henderson Shipping Company: Paying Passengers to New Zealand Ports, 1871–1880*, New Zealand Society of Genealogists, Auckland, 1993.

Hall-Jones, F. G., *Kelly of Inverkelly: The Story of Settlement in Southland 1824–1860*, Southland Historical Committee, Invercargill, 1944.

Harper, Marjory, *Emigration from Scotland Between the Wars: Opportunity or Exile?*, Manchester University Press, Manchester, 1998.

Hastings, David, *Over the Mountains of the Sea: Life on the Migrant Ships 1870–1885*, Auckland University Press, Auckland, 2006.

Hellier, Donna, '"The Humblies": Scottish Highland Migration into Nineteenth-Century Victoria', in Patricia Grimshaw, Chris McConville and Ellen McEwen (eds), *Families in Colonial Australia*, George Allen & Unwin, Sydney, 1985.

Hughes, Hugh, and Lyn Hughes, *Discharged in New Zealand: Soldiers of the Imperial Foot Regiments Who Took Their Discharge in New Zealand 1840–1870*, New Zealand Society of Genealogists, Auckland, 1988.

Ip, Manying (ed.), *Unfolding History, Evolving Identity: The Chinese in New Zealand*, Auckland University Press, Auckland, 2003.

Jackson, H. R., *Churches and People in Australia and New Zealand, 1860–1930*, Allen & Unwin/ Port Nicholson Press, Wellington, 1987.

Jones, William D., *Wales in America: Scranton and the Welsh, 1860–1920*, University of Scranton Press, Scranton, 1996.

Jupp, James (ed.), *The Australian People: An Encyclopedia of the Nation, Its People and Their Origins*, 2nd edn, Cambridge University Press, Cambridge, 2001.

Kennedy, Liam J., 'The Rural Economy', in Liam Kennedy and Philip Ollerenshaw (eds), *An Economic History of Ulster, 1820–1940*, Manchester University Press, Manchester, 1985.

King, Michael, *Being Pākehā Now: Reflections and Recollections of a White Native*, Penguin, Auckland, 2004.

Kirkby, Gaynor (comp.), *Passenger Lists, Victoria, Australia Outwards to New Zealand 1852 Onwards*, New Zealand Society of Genealogists, Auckland, 1996–2003.

Lee, Jack, *'I have named it the Bay of Islands…'*, Hodder & Stoughton, Auckland, 1983.

McCarthy, Angela, *Irish Migrants in New Zealand, 1840–1937: 'The Desired Haven'*, Boydell Press, Rochester, New York, 2005.

Macdonald, Charlotte, *A Woman of Good Character: Single Women as Immigrant Settlers in Nineteenth-Century New Zealand*, Allen & Unwin/Historical Branch, Wellington, 1990.

——, 'Too Many Men and Too Few Women: Gender's Fatal Impact in Nineteenth-Century Colonies', in Caroline Daley and Deborah Montgomerie (eds), *The Gendered Kiwi*, Auckland University Press, Auckland, 1999.

McIvor, Timothy L., *The Rainmaker: A Biography of John Ballance, Journalist and Politician, 1839–1893*, Heinemann Reed, Auckland, 1989.

McKenzie, N. R., *The Gael Fares Forth: The Romantic Story of Waipu and Sister Settlements*, Whitcombe & Tombs, Auckland, 1935.

McKinnon, Malcolm (ed.), with Barry Bradley and Russell Kirkpatrick, *Bateman New Zealand*

Historical Atlas: Ko Papatuanuku e Takoto Nei, David Bateman/Historical Branch, Department of Internal Affairs, Auckland, 1997.

McNab, Robert, *Murihiku and the Southern Islands: A History of the West Coast Sounds, Foveaux Strait, Stewart Island, the Snares, Bounty, Antipodes, Auckland, Campbell and Macquarie Islands, from 1770 to 1829*, William Smith, Invercargill, 1907.

Main, Colleen P. (ed.), *Our Lesser Stars: Twelve New Zealand Family Biographies*, New Zealand Society of Genealogists, Auckland, 1990.

Marjoribanks, Alexander, *Travels in New Zealand: With a Map of the Country*, Smith, Elder, London, 1846.

Miller, Kerby A., *Emigrants and Exiles: Ireland and the Irish Exodus to North America*, Oxford University Press, Oxford, 1985.

Mingay, G. E. (ed.), *The Vanishing Countryman*, Routledge, Kegan Paul, London, 1989.

——, *The Agrarian History of England and Wales, Volume VI, 1750–1850*, Cambridge University Press, Cambridge, 1989.

Molloy, Maureen Anne, *Those Who Speak to the Heart: The Nova Scotian Scots at Waipu, 1854–1920*, Dunmore Press, Palmerston North, 1991.

Mulgan, Alan, *Home: A Colonial's Adventure*, Longmans Green, London, 1927.

Murray, J. Malton, and the Rev. J. Cocker (eds), *Temperance and Prohibition in New Zealand*, Epworth Press, London, 1930.

Ng, J., *Windows on a Chinese Past*, 4 vols, Otago Heritage Books, Dunedin, 1993–1999.

Nicholson, Heather, *The Loving Stitch: A History of Knitting and Spinning in New Zealand*, Auckland University Press, Auckland, 1998.

Nolan, Melanie, *Kin: A Collective Biography of a Working-Class New Zealand Family*, Canterbury University Press, Christchurch, 2005.

O'Farrell, Patrick, *Vanished Kingdoms: Irish in Australia and New Zealand: A Personal Excursion*, New South Wales University Press, Kensington, NSW, 1990.

——, 'How Irish Was New Zealand?' in Sarah Briggs, Paul Hyland and Neil Sammells (eds), *Reviewing Ireland: Essays and Interviews from Irish Studies Review*, Sulis Press, Bath, 1998.

Oliver, W. H., *The Story of New Zealand*, Faber & Faber, London, 1960.

——, *Looking for the Phoenix: A Memoir*, Bridget Williams Books, Wellington, 2002.

Orsman, H. W. (ed.), *The Dictionary of New Zealand English: A Dictionary of New Zealandisms on Historical Principles*, Oxford University Press, Auckland, 1997.

Owens, J. M. R., 'New Zealand Before Annexation', in W. H. Oliver (ed.), with B. R. Williams, *The Oxford History of New Zealand*, Oxford University Press, Wellington, 1981.

Patterson, Brad (ed.), *The Irish in New Zealand: Historical Contexts and Perspectives*, Stout Research Centre, Wellington, 2002.

——, *Ulster–New Zealand Migration and Cultural Transfers*, Four Courts Press, Dublin, 2006.

Payton, P. J., *The Cornish Miner in Australia (Cousin Jack Down Under)*, Dyllansow Truran, Trewolsta, Cornwall, 1984.

Pearce, G. L., *The Scots of New Zealand*, Collins, Auckland, 1976.

Pember Reeves, William, *The Long White Cloud: Ao Tea Roa*, Horace Marshall, London, 1898.

——, *State Experiments in Australia and New Zealand*, vol. 1, Allen & Unwin, London, 1902.

Phillips, Jock, *A Man's Country? The Image of the Pakeha Male, A History*, Penguin, Auckland, rev. edn, 1995.

Pool, Ian, Arunachalam Dharmalingam and Janet Sceats, *The New Zealand Family from 1840: A Demographic History*, Auckland University Press, Auckland, 2007.

Reay, Barry, *Rural Englands: Labouring Lives in the Nineteenth Century*, Palgrave Macmillan, Basingstoke, 2004.

Richards, Eric, *Britannia's Children: Emigration from England, Scotland, Wales and Ireland Since 1600*, Hambledon & London, London and New York, 2004.

Richardson, Len, *Coal, Class & Community: The United Mineworkers of New Zealand, 1880–1960*, Auckland University Press, Auckland, 1995.

Robson, L. L., *The Convict Settlers of Australia: An Inquiry into the Origin and Character of the Convicts Transported to New South Wales and Van Dieman's Land 1787–1852*, Melbourne University Press, Melbourne, 1965.

Samuel, Raphael, *Island Stories: Unravelling Britain*, Verso, London, 1997.

Saville, John, *Rural De-population in England and Wales, 1851–1951*, Routledge & Kegan Paul, London, 1957.

Schofield, Roger, 'British Population Change, 1700–1871', in Roderick Floud and Donald McCloskey (eds), *The Economic History of Britain since 1700, Volume 1: 1700–1860*, Cambridge University Press, Cambridge, 1981.

Scholefield, Guy H., *New Zealand in Evolution: Industrial, Economic and Political*, Fisher Unwin, London, 1909.

Schouten, Hank, *Tasman's Legacy: The New Zealand–Dutch Connection*, New Zealand–Netherlands Foundation, Wellington, 1992.

Shortland, Edward, *The Southern Districts of New Zealand: A Journal, with Passing Notices of the Customs of the Aborigines*, Longman, Brown, Green & Longmans, London, 1851.

Shrimpton, A. W., and Alan E. Mulgan, *Maori & Pakeha: A History of New Zealand*, Whitcombe & Tombs, Auckland, 1922.

Simpson, Tony, *The Immigrants: The Great Migration from Britain to New Zealand, 1830–1890*, Godwit, Auckland, 1997.

——, *A Distant Feast: The Origins of New Zealand's Cuisine*, Godwit, Auckland, 1999.

Sinclair, Keith, *A History of New Zealand*, Penguin Books, London, 1959.

Sweetman, Rory, *Bishop in the Dock: The Sedition Trial of James Liston*, Auckland University Press, Auckland, 1997.

Taylor, Nancy M. (ed.), *Early Travellers in New Zealand*, Clarendon Press, Oxford, 1959.

Te Ara: The Encyclopedia of New Zealand: *Settler and Migrant Peoples of New Zealand*, Bateman/Ministry for Culture and Heritage, Auckland/Wellington, 2006.

Thomson, David, *A World Without Welfare: New Zealand's Colonial Experiment*, Auckland University Press with Bridget Williams Books, Auckland, 1998.

——, 'Marriage and the Family on the Colonial Frontier', in Tony Ballantyne and Brian Moloughney (eds), *Disputed Histories: Imagining New Zealand's Pasts*, Otago University Press, Dunedin, 2006.

Tiwari, Kapil N. (ed.), *Indians in New Zealand: Studies in a Sub Culture*, Price Milburn, Wellington, 1980.

Trevor-Roper, Hugh, 'The Invention of Tradition: The Highland Tradition of Scotland', in Eric Hobsbawm and Terence Ranger (eds), *The Invention of Tradition*, Cambridge University Press, Cambridge, 1992.

Trlin, Andrew, *Now Respected, Once Despised: Yugoslavs in New Zealand*, Dunmore Press, Palmerston North, 1979.

Ward, Louis E. (comp.), *Early Wellington*, Whitcombe & Tombs, Auckland, 1928.

Wilson, John, *Waikakahi: Fulfilling the Promise*, Waikakahi Centennial 1999 Inc. Soc., Waimate, 1999.

Wood, Val, *War Brides: They Followed Their Hearts to New Zealand*, Random Century, Auckland, 1991.

Wright, Harrison M., *New Zealand, 1769–1840: Early Years of Western Contact*, Harvard University Press, Cambridge, Mass., 1959.

Wrigley, E. A., 'Men on the Land and Men in the Countryside: Employment in Agriculture in Early Nineteenth-Century England', in Lloyd Bonfield, Richard Smith and Keith Wrightson (eds), *The World We Have Gained: Histories of Population and Social Structure*, Blackwell, Oxford, 1986, pp. 295–336.

JOURNAL ARTICLES

Akenson, Donald, 'The Irish in New Zealand', *Familia: Ulster Genealogical Review*, vol. 2, no. 5, 1989, pp. 7–12.

Arnold, Rollo, 'Some Australasian Aspects of New Zealand Life', *New Zealand Journal of History*, vol. 4, no. 1, 1970, pp. 54–76.

Beaglehole, J. C., 'New Zealand Since the War, 4: Politics and Culture', *Landfall*, vol. XV, no. 2, 1961, pp. 138–52.

Brosnahan, Seán, 'The "Battle of the Borough" and the "Saige O Timaru": Sectarian Riot in Colonial Canterbury', *New Zealand Journal of History*, vol. 28, no. 1, 1994, pp. 41–59.

Chapman, R. M., 'Fiction and the Social Pattern', *Landfall*, vol. VII, no. 1, 1953, pp. 26–58.

Crafts, N. F. R., 'Average Age at First Marriage for Women in Mid-Nineteenth Century England and Wales: A Cross-section Study', *Population Studies*, no. 32, 1978, pp. 21–5.

Dalziel, Raewyn, 'Popular Protest in Early New Plymouth: Why Did It Occur?', *New Zealand Journal of History*, vol. 20, no. 1, 1986, pp. 3–26.

——, 'Emigration and Kinship: Migrants to New Plymouth 1840–1843', *New Zealand Journal of History*, vol. 25, no. 2, 1991, pp. 112–28.

Eversley, Lord, 'The Decline in the Number of Agricultural Labourers in Great Britain', *Journal of the Royal Statistical Society*, June 1907, pp. 267–319.

Fairburn, Miles, 'The Rural Myth and the New Urban Frontier, 1870–1940', *New Zealand Journal of History*, vol. 9, no. 1, 1975, pp. 3–21.
Galt, Margaret, 'Who Came to New Zealand? New Light on the Origins of British Settlers, 1840–1889', *New Zealand Population Review*, vol. 21, nos 1& 2, May/Nov. 1995, pp. 50–71.
Haines, Robin, and Ralph Shlomowitz, 'Immigration from the United Kingdom to Colonial Australia: A Statistical Analysis', *Journal of Australian Studies*, no. 34, 1992, pp. 43–52.
McDonald, John, and Eric Richards, 'The Great Migration of 1841: Recruitment for New South Wales in British Emigration Fields', *Population Studies*, no. 51, 1997, p. 337–55.
Olssen, Erik, 'Where To From Here? Reflections on the Twentieth-Century Historiography of Nineteenth-Century New Zealand, *New Zealand Journal of History*, vol. 26, no. 1, 1992, pp. 54–77.
Phillips, J. O. C., 'Musings in Maoriland: Or Was There a *Bulletin* School in New Zealand?', *Historical Studies*, vol. 20, no. 81, 1983, pp. 520–35.
Phillips, Jock, 'Of Verandahs and Fish and Chips and Footie on Saturday Afternoon', *New Zealand Journal of History*, vol. 24, no. 2, 1990, pp. 107–23.
Pickens, Keith, 'The Writing of New Zealand History: A Kuhnian Perspective', *Historical Studies: Australia and New Zealand*, vol. 17, no. 68, 1977, pp. 384–98.
Pocock, J. G. A., 'British History: A Plea for a New Subject', *New Zealand Journal of History*, vol. 8, no. 1, 1974, pp. 3–21.
Stenhouse, John, 'God's Own Silence: Secular Nationalism, Christianity and the Writing of New Zealand History', *New Zealand Journal of History*, vol. 38, no. 1, 2004, pp. 52–71.

THESES AND RESEARCH ESSAYS

Bueltmann, Tanja, 'Keeping Up the Name of Scotland', unpublished paper, Jun. 2007.
Galbreath, Alasdair, 'New Zealand's "Invisible Irish": Irish Protestants in the North Island of New Zealand, 1840–1900', MA thesis, University of Auckland, 1998.
Gordon, L. G., 'Immigration into Hawkes Bay, 1858–1876', MA thesis, Victoria University of Wellington, 1965.
Hudson, Paul, 'English Emigration to New Zealand, 1839–1850: An Analysis of the Work of the New Zealand Company', PhD thesis, University of Lancaster, 1996.
Khan, L., 'Immigration into Wellington Province, 1853–1876', PhD thesis, Victoria University of Wellington, 1968.
McClean, R., 'Scottish Emigration to New Zealand, 1840–1880: Motives, Means and Background', PhD thesis, University of Edinburgh, 1991.
Morris, John, 'The Assisted Immigrants to New Zealand, 1871–79: A Statistical Study', MA thesis, University of Auckland, 1973.
Northover, N. J., 'The Control of Immigration into Canterbury, 1850–1853', MA thesis, University of Canterbury, 1951.
O'Regan, P. M., 'The Control of Immigration into Canterbury, 1854–1870', MA thesis, University of Canterbury, 1953.
Payton, Philip, 'The Cornish and the Dominions: A Case-Study in Sub-National Imperial Contact', unpublished paper, Jul. 1998.
Powell, Debra, 'It was hard to die frae hame': Death, Grief and Mourning Among Scottish Migrants to New Zealand, 1840–1890', MA thesis, University of Waikato, 2007.
Silcock, R. H., 'Immigration into Canterbury under the Provincial Government', MA thesis, University of Canterbury, 1963.
Ward, Violet, 'Immigrants and Immigration in the Auckland Province, 1792–1876', MA thesis, University of Auckland, 1943.
Wigglesworth, R. P., 'The New Zealand Timber and Flax Trade 1769–1840', PhD thesis, Massey University, 1981.

ELECTRONIC SOURCES

Dictionary of New Zealand Biography (DNZB): http://www.dnzb.govt.nz/
Angus, Janet C., 'Cuddie, Mary 1823–1889', updated 22 Jun. 2007
Arnold, Rollo, 'Clayden, Arthur 1829–1899', updated 22 Jun. 2007
Atkinson, Neill, 'Garrard, William George 1832-1835?–1906', updated 7 Apr. 2006
——, 'Young, Frederick George 1888–1962, updated 7 Apr. 2006

Beaglehole, Diana, 'Tricker, Walter Pettit 1823?–1907', updated 22 Jun. 2007
Bush, Graham W. A., 'Allum, John Andrew Charles 1889–1972', updated 22 Jun. 2007
Byrnes, Giselle M., 'Smith, Stephenson Percy 1840–1922', updated 7 Apr. 2006
Chalklen, Mollie, 'Crewes, John 1847–1925', updated 22 Jun. 2007
Church, Ian, 'Parris, Robert Reid 1816?–1904', updated 7 Apr. 2006
Coleridge, Kathleen A., 'Carpenter, Robert Holt 1819/1820?–1891', updated 22 Jun. 2007
——, 'Revans, Samuel 1807/1808?–1888', updated 7 Apr. 2006
Cooper, Barbara, and Brian O'Brien, 'Lofley, Edward 1838-1840–1889', updated 22 Jun. 2007
Crawford, J. A. B., 'Porter, Thomas William 1843–1920', updated 7 Apr. 2006
Crawford, Noel, 'Grant, William 1843–1910', updated 22 Jun. 2007
Easton, Brian, 'Sutch, William Ball 1907–1975', updated 22 Jun. 2007
Ellis, Ellen, 'Chemis, Annie 1862–1939', updated 7 Apr. 2006
Fleming, J. F., 'Fleming, Thomas 1848–1930', updated 7 Apr. 2006
Fogarty, Philippa, 'Wells, Ada 1863–1933', updated 22 Jun. 2007
Francis, Margaret, 'Alabaster, Ann O'Connor 1842–1915', updated 7 Apr. 2006
Graham, Philippa, 'Poingdestre, Henry 1832?–1885', updated 22 Jun. 2007
Grant, S. W., 'Russell, William Russell 1838?–1913', updated 7 Apr. 2006
Hanline, Judy, 'Hood, Mary 1822?–1902', updated 7 Apr. 2006
Hearn, T. J., 'Ewing, John 1844–1922', updated 7 Apr. 2006
——, 'McQueen, Charles 1836–1906', updated 7 Apr. 2006
Hudson, Switzer, 'Anderton, William Theophilus 1891–1966', updated 7 Apr. 2006
Hutchison, Anne, 'Weldon, Barbara 1829-1837?–1882', updated 7 Apr. 2006
Laracy, Hugh, 'Dignan, Patrick 1813/1814?–1894', updated 7 Apr. 2006
——, 'Kennedy, Martin 1839/1840?–1916', updated 7 Apr. 2006
Lawn, R. G., 'Lawn, John 1840–1905', updated 22 Jun. 2007
Locke, Elsie, 'Small, Mary Elizabeth 1812/1813?–1908', updated 7 Apr. 2006
——, 'Thorn, Margaret 1897–1969', updated 22 Jun. 2007
Long, Moira M., 'Harris, Emily Cumming 1836/1837?–1925', updated 7 Apr. 2006
Lowe, Peter, 'Anderson, John 1820–1897', updated 7 Apr. 2006
Macdonald, Charlotte, 'Crowe, Ellen 1845-1847?–1930', updated 7 Apr. 2006
——, 'Howard, Caroline Cadette 1821–?', updated 7 Apr. 2006
McDonald, Kathleen C., 'O'Donnell, Ann 1857-1860?–1934', updated 7 Apr. 2006
McDonnell, Hilda, 'Meech, Matilda 1825?–1907', updated 22 Jun. 2007
McKenna, Neva Clarke, 'Ball, Thomas 1809–1897', updated 22 Jun. 2007
Mairs, Elspeth, 'Wallis, Mary Ann Lake 1821–1910', updated 7 Apr. 2006
Malone, C. B., 'Anstice, Sophia 1849–1926', updated 22 Jun. 2007
Matthews, Kay Morris, 'Bates, Sophia Ann 1817–1899', updated 22 Jun. 2007
Minehan, Francis, 'Cassidy, Hugh 1840–1922', updated 7 Apr. 2006
Mogford, Janice C., 'Whisker, Alexander 1819–1907', updated 7 Apr. 2006
Nicholls, Roberta, 'Stewart, Catherine Campbell 1881–1957', updated 7 Apr. 2006
Ogilvie, Gordon, 'Wigram, Henry Francis 1857–1934', updated 22 Jun. 2007
Olssen, Erik, 'Allen, Ernest John Bartlett 1884–1945', updated 7 Apr. 2006
——, 'Arnold, James Frederick 1859–1929', updated 22 Jun. 2007
Peacocke, Kathryn, 'Ranstead, William 1859–1944', updated 7 Apr. 2006
Renwick, William, 'Pope, James Henry 1837–1913', updated 22 Jun. 2007
Roberts, Heather, 'Mackay, Jessie 1864–1938', updated 22 Jun. 2007
Roth, Herbert, 'Griffin, William 1810/1811?–1870', updated 7 Apr. 2006
——, 'Rae, Charles Joseph 1819-1821?–1894', updated 7 Apr. 2006
Smith, Jo-Anne, 'Gibb, Helen 1838–1914', updated 7 Apr. 2006
Starky, Suzanne, 'Garmson, Aileen Anna Maria 1861-1863?–1951', updated 7 Apr. 2006
——, 'Little, James 1834–1921', updated 7 Apr. 2006
Sutherland, G. H., 'Carter, Charles Rooking 1822–1896', updated 22 Jun. 2007
Winton, Pat Irene, 'Hewlett, Hilda Beatrice 1864–1943', updated 22 Jun. 2007

OTHER ELECTRONIC SOURCES

Blainey, Geoffrey, 'Hannan, Patrick (1840–1925)', *Australian Dictionary of Biography*, http://www.adb.online.anu.edu.au/biogs/A090184b.htm
Immigrant Ships to New Zealand from the United Kingdom & Ireland 1835–1910, http://freepages.genealogy.rootsweb.com/~shipstonz/ships_uk&i.html

Index

Place names in England, Ireland and Scotland are listed under those country names.
All other place names are listed individually.
Page numbers for photographic entries are italicised.